HIDDEN®

Baja

HIDDEN®
Baja

Richard Harris

Ulysses Press®
BERKELEY, CALIFORNIA

Published by:
ULYSSES PRESS
P.O. Box 3440
Berkeley, CA 94703-3440

Library of Congress Catalog Card Number 97-60634
ISBN 1-56975-124-2

Printed in Canada by Transcontinental Printing

10 9 8 7 6 5 4 3 2 1

MANAGING EDITOR: Claire Chun
COPY EDITOR: James Donnelly
EDITORIAL ASSOCIATES: Aaron Newey, Lily Chou,
    Patricia Wakida
TYPESETTER: David Wells
CARTOGRAPHY: XNR Productions
HIDDEN BOOKS DESIGN: Sarah Levin
COVER DESIGN: Leslie Henriques
INDEXER: Sayre Van Young
COVER PHOTOGRAPHY: Front and back: Robert Holmes
    Circle and back: Kerrick James
ILLUSTRATOR: Doug McCarthy

Distributed in the United States by Publishers
Group West, in Canada by Raincoast Books,
and in Great Britain and Europe by World
Leisure Marketing

Write to us!

If in your travels you discover a spot that captures the spirit of Baja, or if you live in the region and have a favorite place to share, or if you just feel like expressing your views, write to us and we'll pass your note along to the author.

We can't guarantee that the author will add your personal find to the next edition, but if the writer does use the suggestion, we'll acknowledge you in the credits and send you a free autographed copy of the new edition.

ULYSSES PRESS

P.O. Box 3440

Berkeley, CA 94703-3440

E-mail: readermail@ulyssespress.com

What's Hidden?

At different points throughout this book, you'll find special listings marked with a hidden symbol:

◀ *HIDDEN*

This means that you have come upon a place off the beaten tourist track, a spot that will carry you a step closer to the local people and natural environment of Baja.

The goal of this guide is to lead you beyond the realm of everyday tourist facilities. While we include traditional sightseeing listings and popular attractions, we also offer alternative sights and adventure activities. Instead of filling this guide with reviews of standard hotels and chain restaurants, we concentrate on one-of-a-kind places and locally owned establishments.

Our authors seek out locales that are popular with residents but usually overlooked by visitors. Some are more hidden than others (and are marked accordingly), but all the listings in this book are intended to help you discover the true nature of Baja and put you on the path of adventure.

Contents

Maps

OUTDOOR ADVENTURE SYMBOLS

The following symbols accompany national, state and regional park listings, as well as beach descriptions throughout the text.

▲	Camping	🏄	Surfing
🚶	Hiking	🏄	Windsurfing
🚲	Biking	🛶	Canoeing or Kayaking
🏇	Horseback Riding	🚤	Boating
🏊	Swimming	🚣	Boat Ramps
🤿	Snorkeling or Scuba Diving	🐟	Fishing

ONE

The Other California

Sitting in the shade of a 30-foot-tall cardón cactus on a rocky hilltop, you can look out across a turquoise-blue bay so clear that golden tropical fish can be seen dancing beneath the surface. Vultures drift in lazy circles overhead, pelicans skim the water, and cormorants dive for fish from high in the sky. A pod of dolphins leaps along the surface of the bay in joyful abandon, and far off in the distance a whale spouts, looking like a geyser on a drifting desert island. Palms line the gracefully curving beach of sugary sand and thatch-roofed shelter where you've made camp for the night—and maybe the next week or so. A Oaxacan vendor comes by, selling drinking water, fresh fruit and colorful handwoven blankets. It's the way you imagine a South Pacific tropical paradise would be—except for one thing. You can drive there. You don't even need a passport.

This is one aspect of the Baja peninsula, a scantily populated wilderness that is startling in its immensity. Much of the wild interior has been set aside as national parks, biosphere reserves and other protected areas. Here you will discover majestic mountain peaks, cool forests, and some of the most dramatic desert scenery on earth, studded with volcanoes and alive with giant cactuses and strange species—elephant trees, incense trees, boojum trees—found nowhere else on earth. You'll visit exotic port cities and graceful old colonial towns built around centuries-old mission churches. You may linger in laid-back fishing villages or bask on the beaches at world-class resort areas.

A road trip from the U.S. border to Los Cabos and back—just over 2000 miles—has all the elements of a once-in-a-lifetime adventure. But the fact is, once bitten by the Baja bug, most people return year after year. There are seemingly endless "hidden" places to explore, and with the gradual improvement of many secondary roads, more such places become accessible to motorists each year. Read on and start planning your own journey of discovery in Baja.

▼▼▼▼▼▼▼▼▼▼
Where to Go

Only one main highway runs the length of the Baja peninsula, so you'd think trip planning would be a snap. But as you'll discover in later chapters of this book, the best Baja adventures can be found on side trips from the main highway by back road or boat. Where you decide to spend most of your time will depend on the season, the duration of your trip and the outdoor activities you enjoy most.

Most travelers from the West Coast cross the U.S.–Mexican border at one of two ports of entry in Tijuana, a large city that also attracts many daytrippers with its duty-free shopping, raunchy nightlife and bullfights. Some travelers avoid Tijuana traffic by crossing at the industrial border town of Tecate, though it's questionable whether this plan is either faster or simpler. Mexicali, the capital city of Baja California, is a convenient border crossing for travelers from Arizona and points east, as well as for anybody headed for San Felipe. The truly "hidden" border crossing for Baja is Algodones, near the California/Arizona line.

Northern Baja is a study in contrasts. An hour's drive south of Tijuana on the Baja Highway, Ensenada offers shopping and sightseeing possibilities along with plenty of traditional Mexican seaport charm. The coastline and mild, sometimes misty climate resemble San Diego's. At the opposite extreme, San Felipe on the Sea of Cortez, a fishing village turned RVers' paradise, is surrounded by the driest desert in Baja. San Quintín, south of Ensenada, hardly looks like it belongs in Baja: Irrigation has transformed the coastal plain into a rich agricultural zone. Some of the best Pacific beaches lie south of San Quintín, but the area's most spectacular attraction is Parque Nacional Sierra de San Pedro Mártir, with its cool alpine forests and Baja's highest mountain peaks.

As you enter central Baja, you suddenly find yourself in the vast, mainly uninhabited Desierto Central. The Baja Highway takes you through the surreal heart of the Cataviña boulder field —all huge cactuses, bizarre trees and rocks the size of houses. Rocky side roads lead to old mission ruins and far older cave paintings. Toward the south end of the desert, a paved side road takes you to Bahía de los Angeles on the Sea of Cortez. This quintessential gringo enclave has great fishing and sea kayaking, but no telephones.

If you decline to take this turnoff and continue south on the main highway, you'll reach the Pacific Coast at Guerrero Negro soon after crossing into Baja California Sur. This rather bleak company town (nearly everybody works at the nearby salt mines) has emerged as a major ecotourism center thanks to the gray whales that return to nearby Scammon's Lagoon each winter to calve and breed. Beyond Guerrero Negro, the vast Desierto Vizcaíno sprawls across the widest part of the peninsula. A long backroad

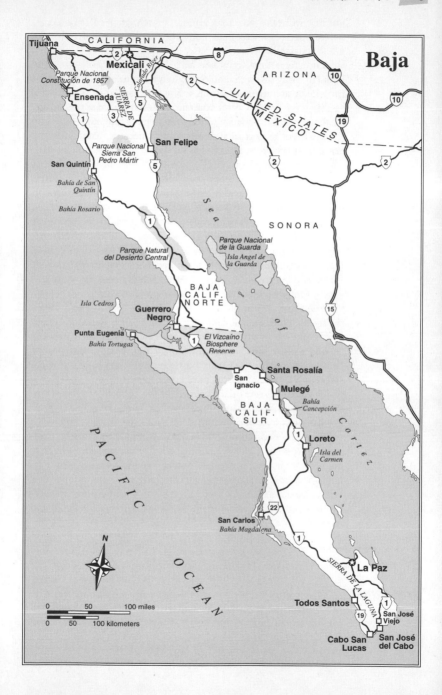

journey will take you to a remote stretch of the Pacific coast, where huge colonies of sea lions and elephant seals inhabit the offshore islands.

Palm trees appear as **southern Baja** begins. Following the Baja Highway through landlocked San Ignacio, the starting point for whalewatching expeditions to the pristine Bahía San Ignacio, you'll hit the Sea of Cortez coast at Santa Rosalía, a strangely un-Mexican town founded by European copper miners.

My favorite part of Baja lies south of Santa Rosalía, on the Sea of Cortez, near the hidden refuges of Mulegé and Loreto. Along the highway between the two towns, the beaches of Bahía Concepción have palm trees, sea shells, tropical fish, big cactuses, crystalline turquoise water and creamy sand that slides through your fingers like sugar. Snorkeling the bay or gliding across it in a kayak, you could easily decide never to return to civilization at all (though you'd change your mind when summer arrived). Beyond Loreto, the Baja Highway begins another long desert crossing, which you can break into manageable segments by taking a side excursion to San Carlos on Bahía Magdalena, the southernmost of Baja's famous gray-whale calving bays.

The **Cape region** of Baja California Sur begins with La Paz, the state capital, a small, laid-back city on a lovely harbor. Though sightseeing attractions are few, you won't notice their absence as you explore the cheerful city streets and the exquisite nearby beaches. From there, it's on to bustling Los Cabos, as San José del Cabo and Cabo San Lucas have come to be known. This mega-resort vacation zone on the very tip of the peninsula is Baja's epi-center of mainstream tourism, where beaching, boating and deep-sea fishing attract more visitors than all other Baja destinations south of Ensenada combined. Being surrounded by the industrial-strength tourism of Los Cabos can quickly become a lot like having bees live in your head, but "hidden" getaways are nearby. Perhaps the best is Todos Santos, an emerging artist community that boasts legendary surfing beaches. It's one starting point for hiking and horseback trips into the Sierra la Laguna, an isolated and unique natural area.

▼▼▼▼▼▼▼▼▼▼
When to Go

SEASONS

There is no wrong time to go to Baja. Peak tourist seasons are May through September on the Pacific coast and Christmas week through early April on the Sea of Cortez. As the growing hordes of snowbirds and whalewatchers who head down the peninsula in January, February and March will not hesitate to caution you, some winter days can make you wish you'd brought your parka, especially along the windblasted Pacific coast. More often than not, however, the winter climate is mild, with temperatures in Ensenada running about the same as in San Diego and those in Los Cabos about 15 degrees warmer. Deep snow can render the high sierra inaccessible.

Spring offers an ideal climate for travel on the Baja Highway. It's not too hot for desert hiking, and after a wet winter, you'll see incomparable displays of desert wildflowers. Off-season rates prevail everywhere. The only downside to a spring trip is that the water off both coasts is still too cool for comfortable swimming or snorkeling.

Summer is relentlessly humid and hot on the Sea of Cortez; the Pacific coast can be more inviting. Desert areas are unbearable by day but may cool down by 40 degrees at night; on the Sea of Cortez, temperatures typically reach well above 100 degrees and stay there, day and night, for weeks on end. Water temperatures in the Sea of Cortez are nearly as high as air temperatures. Tropical storms called *chubascos* can pummel the coast without warning. The summer climate is extremely humid, and this is the only time of year when you'll encounter mosquitoes. On the plus side, the warm seas attract marlin, sailfish and other big game fish in large numbers—summer is prime time for sportfishing.

Autumn means warm water, moderate temperatures, low room rates and—in September and October—unpredictable weather patterns. Many sporting events, from huge bicycle races with thousands of contestants to the legendary Baja 1000 car and motorcycle races, take place at this time of year. Early December marks the beginning of snowbird season, when RV campers begin arriving in droves.

CALENDAR OF EVENTS

Early January   Not many events take place in January, though the snowbird season is at its peak. **El Día de los Santos Reyes,** January 6, marks the end of the Christmas holiday season. It is on this day, not Christmas Day, that Mexicans feast and exchange gifts.

JANUARY

During February   In Ensenada, San Felipe and La Paz, **Carnaval** (the Latin Mardi Gras) is celebrated with five days of parades, fireworks, costumes and dancing in the streets.

FEBRUARY

Late February   Sports car racers compete in the **Mexicali Grand Prix.** San Felipe hosts the **Mid-Winter West Hobie Regatta,** a three-day sailing event for Hobie Catamarans.

Early March   The desert around San Felipe provides the course for extreme off-road racing in the **Score San Felipe 250,** a scaled-down version of the famous Baja 1000.

MARCH

Late March   Over **Spring Break,** traditionally the third and fourth weeks of March, college students from all over the western United States descend on Baja. The San Felipe area is hit hardest; Rosarito, Ensenada and Los Cabos are also packed with student bodies. The **Fiesta de San José**, honoring San José del Cabo's patron saint, falls right in the middle of Spring Break.

APRIL

During April   Holy Week (**Semana Santa**), the week leading up to Easter, is not as crowded in Baja as elsewhere in Mexico. But many people visit relatives on the "mainland," and many businesses shut down from Wednesday through Sunday. San Felipe hosts a series of beach-style sporting events through the month, including the **Posada del Mar Aerobics Meet**, the **San Felipe Triathlon**, and the **Beach Volleyball Slam Festival**. Around the same time, 10,000 cyclists participate in the semiannual **Rosarito to Ensenada Bicycle Race**, and the **Newport-Ensenada Yacht Race** draws so many boaters that it claims to be the world's largest regatta.

Late April   What better place to recover from the month's fitness events than at the **Tijuana Pizza Festival**?

MAY

Early May   The streets of Cabo San Lucas are the scene of the annual **Fireman's Chili Cookoff Festival**, which also features dancing, entertainment and a pie-eating contest.

Late May   Vaqueros (Mexican cowboys) come from all over Baja and northern Mexico to compete for prizes in the **Tecate Rodeo**.

JUNE

Early June   The biggest happening of the month is **Día de la Armada** (Navy Day), when Mexican naval bases stage military boat processions for the people of nearby coastal towns.

JULY

During July   July 11 marks the **Anniversary of Tijuana**, founded in 1899. The fiesta lasts all month; it's sure to be especially crazy in 1999. Baja's economic development, from factories to farming cooperatives, is the focus of **Expo Ensenada**.

AUGUST

During August   Tecate's **La Pamplonada** is patterned after the Running of the Bulls in Pamplona, Spain, and every bit as dangerous. The event is followed by the **Guadalupe Valley Wine Festival** in the vineyard country around Tecate. The **Feria de Tijuana** features entertainment, carnival rides and livestock shows at Agua Caliente racetrack from mid-August through mid-September.

SEPTEMBER

Early September   The **Fiesta de Santa Rosalía** is colorfully celebrated in both Santa Rosalía and Mulegé. A few days later, Loreto's **Día de la Virgen de Loreto** climaxes with a spectacular street procession.

Mid-September   Many Baja towns celebrate Mexico's **Independence Day**, September 16, with fireworks and festivities. In Mexicali and La Paz, the observance lasts for two days and includes an array of cultural events.

During October   El Día de la Raza (The Day of the Race, re-
ferring to mestizos) is celebrated in place of Columbus Day.
Late October   The **Mexicali-San Felipe Sports Weekend** features a Mexicali-San Felipe Bicycle Ride (55 miles or 125 miles), a San Felipe Mountain Bike Ride (10 miles or 20 miles) and a Mexicali-San Felipe Five-Person Running Relay. Around the same time, the 50-mile **Rosarito-Ensenada Bicycle Race** draws even more participants than the same race held in the springtime; cyclists have numbered around 16,000 in recent years.

Early November   El Día de los Muertos, or Day of the Dead—
actually two days, November 1 and 2—is generally a quiet, stay-at-home time in Baja; most businesses close. Soon afterward, San Felipe's biggest party of the year, the **Shrimp Festival**, fills three days with music, dancing, seafood and beach fun.
Mid-November   Granddaddy of backroad Baja races, the **Baja 1000** follows different routes in different years, alternating between the traditional 1000-mile Ensenada-La Paz race (a Baja institution long before the highway was paved) and a 1000-kilometer circuit of Baja California Norte. The race has four divisions—motorcycles, dune buggies, stock cars and four-wheel-drive trucks.

Early December   San Felipe stages a **Snowbird Welcome Fiesta**
in observance of the annual mass migration of RVers to its beaches.

The **Secretaría de Turismo de México** (SECTUR) main-   ▼▼▼▼▼▼▼▼▼▼▼▼
tains tourism offices in Baja's two state capitals, Mexicali (Centro Comercial Baja California #4-C, Calzada
Independencia at Calle Calafia; 556-1172, fax 556-1282) and La
Paz (Km. 5.5 Carretera Transpeninsular; 822-7975). SECTUR operates tourist information offices in Ensenada, San Felipe, Tecate, Tijuana and San José del Cabo; their locations and phone numbers are listed in the "Addresses & Phone Numbers" sections at the end of each chapter of this book, beginning with Chapter Four. For many travelers, the easiest SECTUR tourist office to visit is the one north of the border. ~ 7860 Mission Center Court, Suite 202, San Diego, CA 92108; 619-298-4105, 800-522-1516.

Some Baja cities and towns have tourist offices operated by a municipal **Comite de Turismo y Convenciones** (COTUCO). They also appear in the "Addresses & Phone Numbers" sections.

Among the most valuable travel information sources are two English-language monthlies sold at newsstands and campgrounds all over the peninsula. The **Baja Sun** newspaper has a calendar of events and a mix of travel, financial and other coverage of in-

terest to expatriates and travelers. ~ Editorial El Sol de Baja, Avenida Pedro Loyola 295, Las Palmas at Fraccionmento Acapulco,
Ensenada; 76-91-92; www.bajasun.com. **Baja Life**, a slick, colorful magazine, covers topics from fishing and wildlife watching
to new resort hotels and Mexican property taxes. ~ Baja Com-
munications Group, P.O. Box 4917, Laguna Beach, CA 92652;
949-376-2252, fax 949-376-7575; www.bajalife.com.

Several California-based travel clubs rank among the best
sources of up-to-date information on road conditions, weather,
fuel availability, fishing and such. They also offer discount rates
for hotels, restaurants, RV parks, kayaking and sportfishing trips,
books and maps; member discounts on Mexican car and boat insurance can save you more than the price of membership (in the
$30- to $40-a-year range). Leading travel clubs include **Vagabundos del Mar Boat and Travel** (190 Main Street, Rio Vista,
CA 94571; 707-374-5511, 800-474-2252, fax 707-374-6843),
Mex Club (660 Bay Boulevard, Suite 214, Chula Vista, CA 91910;
619-585-3033, fax 619-420-8133), and **Discover Baja Travel
Club** (3089 Clairemont Drive, Suite A-2, San Diego, CA 92117;
619-275-4225, 800-727-2252, fax 619-275-1836).

PACKING   Flying to Los Cabos? Keep your packing simple. A camera plus
whatever else you can fit in your daypack or weekender will be
fine, as long as it includes a wad of cash or a major credit card.
Bring a bathing suit or buy one there. A T-shirt, shorts, athletic
shoes and a shady hat, along with a pair of long pants or a skirt
for café evenings in San José, are sufficient. Dressing up is unheard
of even in the best restaurants. More than one change of clothes
may be superfluous, since many hotels in all price ranges offer
overnight laundry service. If you're going in the winter, take a
sweater or light jacket. You can rent sports equipment when you
get there. If you plan to explore the desert and sierra, at minimum
you'll need hiking boots, a canteen and a bandanna that you can
wet down to keep cool.

If you're driving, the situation is different. No matter how
small your vehicle, you should be equipped to camp at least part
of the time. In many areas, the camping beaches are more appealing than the hotels. In a passenger car, a tent, sleeping bags and
other basic gear may take up a lot of trunk space, making it wise
to limit your material possessions almost as much as if you were
flying. Cooking gear is good to have along. More important for
motorists who plan to explore beyond the paved main highways
is safety and repair gear. This should include a first-aid kit, a
flashlight, motor oil, transmission fluid and brake fluid, tire inflation cans, replacement V-belts, hoses and fuel line. And be sure
to bring a toolkit that's adequate to replace these bits and pieces.

As your packing list grows, keep in mind that if you pack a car too tight, it will "explode." After a couple of days' beach camping, the prospect of fitting all that stuff back into the car may look so daunting that you may be forced to remain at the beach for the rest of the winter.

Obviously, with a large motor home the situation is different. One of the biggest joys of RV travel is the materialistic satisfaction of taking along every possession you could conceivably want. Before your trip, you can spend weeks thinking up hypotheticals like, "Okay, suppose we're on this idyllic tropical beach and there are all these coconuts around that would be perfect for making a Thai fish curry. Better take the electric wok, huh?"

LODGING

There are only a few places in Baja where hotel and motel rooms outnumber campsites. The 120-kilometer stretch of road between Rosarito and Ensenada, all within an hour's drive of the U.S. border, boasts an abundance of stylish beach resort hotels, as well as motels with more moderate rates across the highway from the beach.

From there all the way to La Paz, a distance of 1400 kilometers, lodgings of any description are few and far between. Most towns along the way have just one or two motels. As the state capital of Baja California Sur and a main port for travelers arriving from the Mexican mainland, La Paz hosts more business travelers and politicians than tourists. There are plenty of good hotels across the street from the beach and waterfront promenade that run along the Bahía de La Paz, and rates are among the lowest in Baja.

Los Cabos—the towns of Cabo San Lucas and San José del Cabo and the luxury resort developments that line the 30-kilometer stretch of divided highway between the two towns—has

FLOATING ROOM RATES

Room rate categories are necessarily very approximate because of fluctuating currency exchange rates. International resort hotels that merit four or five stars in the Mexican government's hotel rating system are allowed to set their rates in U.S. dollars as protection against possible peso devaluations. Lesser hotels—generally, those that fall into the budget and moderate categories—set their rates in pesos and are subject to federal price controls, so during Mexico's recurring periods of economic instability, lower-priced lodgings tend to become absurdly cheap in dollars, while the expensive places cost as much as ever.

the most plentiful and most expensive accommodations in Baja. Even there, however, rooms are available at lower rates if you know where to look.

Budget-minded travelers can save by visiting during the off-season, which is different in various regions of Baja. Ensenada's off-season runs from October through April; rates drop by about 20 percent during these months. Hotels in the area are packed to capacity on weekends but empty out during the week, so there is often a discount on Sunday through Thursday nights. In Los Cabos, rates are highest from Christmas week through early April, and lowest from September through early December. Less dependent on tourism, La Paz hotels have no high or low season. In all beach resort areas, rooms that face away from the water cost less than those with sea views, and motels across the highway cost less than those with beachfront locations. Another way to economize is by reserving a room with a kitchen.

To help you decide on a place to stay, I've described the accommodations not only by area and amenities, but also according to price. Rate categories listed are for two adults during the high season. *Budget* hotels are generally less than $35 a night for two people. The rooms will be clean and basic, lacking such luxuries as air conditioning and in-room telephones. All hotels listed in this book do have private baths. *Moderate*-priced hotels, at $35 to $70 a night, provide larger rooms and plusher furnishings. They generally have air conditioning and satellite TV and may have phones. At a *deluxe* accommodation you can expect to spend $70 to $105 for a double. These places are generally large beach resorts with spacious rooms, balconies overlooking the sea, and guest amenities that include swimming pools. With rare exceptions, only in Los Cabos will you encounter *ultra-deluxe* hotels where rooms begin at $105 a night for double occupancy. These world-class resorts have spectacular locations and every imaginable amenity, including tennis courts, landscaped grounds and sometimes golf courses. Guest accommodations, whether spacious, semi-divided rooms or full suites, will be stylishly decorated and enjoy exceptional sea views.

DINING   Within a particular chapter, the restaurants are categorized geographically. Restaurants listed offer lunch and dinner unless otherwise noted. Each restaurant entry describes the establishment's cuisine and ambience along with a price category—budget, moderate, deluxe or ultra-deluxe. *Budget* eateries usually cost $5 or less for dinner entrées; *moderate* restaurants range from $5 to $10 at dinner and offer pleasant decor and a broader menu than budget restaurants; *deluxe* establishments tab their entrées between $10 and $18 and feature sophisticated cuisines and personalized service; and *ultra-deluxe* restaurants are generally priced above $18. Restaurants add a 15 percent IVA (sales tax), and some resorts add a 15 percent service charge on top of that. Prices given are necessarily very approximate because of fluctuating currency exchange rates.

Besides modest indoor restaurants, the budget category includes roadside stands that sell tamales, fish tacos and whole fried fish to motorists on the go, as well as *comedores,* open-air fast-food places where the cook prepares your food while you watch, and you eat it at a nearby picnic table. The food is good at these places, and the prices are great.

Some travelers shun food stands and *comedores* for fear of contracting "Montezuma's revenge." Mexicans, too, believe that gringos will get sick if they eat local food because their digestive systems are not accustomed to it. The truth is, travelers in Baja today rarely get the dread distress in the lower tract. As in the United States, food sellers are licensed and subject to government inspection, and health regulations are strictly enforced in areas that depend on tourism.

> Travelers with preteen youngsters would do well to try a test excursion to San Felipe to learn how your kids cope with long hours on the road and few diversions, before committing to drive the length of the Baja.

As for restaurants, you don't have to be in Ensenada or Los Cabos to find great food. RVers spread the word quickly, and memorable meals tend to wait at the end of long desert crossings. Some of the finest dining in Baja is found in unexpected places like San Quintín, Guerrero Negro and Santa Rosalía.

TRAVELING WITH CHILDREN

Baja is an ideal vacation destination for family camping adventures. It lets kids and parents experience a vast, strange desert wilderness between idyllic beaches, and it provides a low-stress introduction to foreign travel. Virtually all restaurants, hotels and campgrounds are comfortable with kids. Campgrounds often provide opportunities for "gringitos" to meet Mexican kids their own age.

Planning the trip with your kids stimulates their imagination. Books about travel, beaches, whales and deserts help prepare even a two-year-old for an adventure. So do cassette tapes designed to introduce young children to Spanish.

The biggest drawback to traveling with kids in Baja is the long-distance driving. In a land where you can drive through desert for many hours without passing a single house, there may be no acceptable answer to "When are we gonna get there?" Some kids also have problems with the lack of roadside restrooms. Which leads us to another drawback: Parenthood can be nervewracking in a land where the common wildlife includes scorpions, tarantulas, rattlesnakes, stingrays, jellyfish and sharks, and where almost every plant has sharp thorns. Obviously, it's important to educate the kids about these hazards and how to avoid them. While you're at it, why not commit yourself to practicing the delicate art of not worrying. This is, after all, an adventure. Oh, yes . . . and pack a complete first-aid kit just in case. Full-service hospital facilities in Baja are: in Mexicali, **Hospital Civil** on Calle del Hospital ~ 57-37-00; in Ensenada, **Hospital General** on Carretera Transpeninsular, Km. 111 ~ 76-76-00 and **Hospital Las Américas** on Avenida Las Dunas 130 ~ 76-03-01; in La Paz, **Hospital Salvatierra** on Calle Bravo at Ortiz de Domínguez ~ 2-14-96 or 2-15-96; and in San José del Cabo, **Hospital Municipal** on Calle Doblado at Avenida Márquez de León; 2-03-16.

TRAVELING WITH PETS

Technically, if you want to bring a pet with you to Mexico, you need an International Health Certificate for Dogs and Cats (Form 77-043) signed by a U.S. veterinarian verifying that the animal is in good health, as well as a separate certificate stating that the animal has been immunized against distemper and rabies within the last six months. Both are supposedly required by U.S. Customs when you re-enter the United States. Mexico theoretically requires a visa for animals, which must be obtained in advance at a Mexican consulate in the region of the United States where you live. You need to show the International Health Certificate and pay a small fee.

In practice, so many RVers and campers travel with dogs that authorities on both sides of the border pay no attention to them. In extensive travels throughout Baja with my dog, Oso, who is big enough so that it's hard not to notice him, I have never once been asked to produce his paperwork. Of course, a current rabies vaccination is especially important in Baja, where a combination of infected rodents and stray dogs makes the disease more prevalent than in the United States.

Mexican law prohibits domestic animals, including dogs, in hotel and motel rooms. Mexican dogs, like pigs and turkeys, are allowed to roam loose—but only outdoors. Beaches and campgrounds, however, have no leash laws. Local dogs often form a welcoming committee to give campers' dogs a guided tour of the neighborhood.

WOMEN TRAVELING ALONE

Although sexual assaults and other crimes of violence by local residents against women tourists are rare in Baja, unwanted sexual advances can be a nuisance for some gringas. Torn between the rising tide of feminism in Latin America and the old code of machismo, Mexican men often behave unpredictably toward North American and European women. There is a widespread belief, born of countless Hollywood sex-and-violence flicks, that many gringa women are wildly promiscuous. Anything a gringa does that a Mexican woman would not do may be seen by some men as provocative. This includes hitchhiking, drinking alone in a cantina, and, to a certain extent, simply traveling alone. Mexican women often travel on trains and buses without a male companion, but they bring their children. Perhaps as a consequence of this strange attitude, many Mexican men turn into strutting, drooling idiots in the presence of a woman with blonde hair.

I have made a point over the years of interviewing women who are seasoned Mexico travelers about this subject. One gringa in her thirties, who has dark hair and speaks fluent Spanish, says she finds Mexico a comfortable place for women traveling alone: "To avoid problems, dress modestly," she suggests. "Flirting—or forwardness that may be mistaken for flirting—can attract more attention than you expect. But Mexican people are very friendly and like to flirt in a joking way that's not intended to be taken seriously. A light attitude goes a long way. Women travelers in small towns and villages are in a better position to meet local women, who may not speak to foreign men at all but will often invite a gringa to meet their children or see their kitchens."

The best way to obviate harassment is to travel with companions. Two or more women, or a woman traveling with children, will almost never be harassed. Many North American and European women (as well as many Mexican women) travel independently by temporarily joining up with other women travelers.

GAY & LESBIAN TRAVELERS

Mexico's Catholic, family-oriented society is far behind the United States and Canada in coming to terms with its own gay and lesbian community. This is not to suggest that homosexuality is any less common in Mexico than anywhere else, just that the closet door is still closed, though the knob may be turning.

Puerto Vallarta, on the Mexican mainland 250 miles down the coast from Los Cabos, has emerged as a major international gay zone in the past few years, and there is no apparent reason that the same could not happen in Los Cabos or some more secluded spot like Todos Santos or Loreto. So far, though, it has not.

Today, Baja has just a few gay nightclubs—in Tijuana, Ensenada and La Paz. If there is a gay beach resort anywhere on the peninsula, it is remarkably well hidden.

The good news is that Baja residents have long since given up being shocked by anything gringo tourists do, creating at least a grudging tolerance. Public displays of affection are okay on out-of-town beaches but not in hotel lobbies. You are likely to encounter gay and lesbian couples and groups camping on many beaches, especially in the Bahía Concepción and Todos Santos areas.

Information on organized gay and lesbian tours worldwide is available at **Now Voyager**. ~ 4406 18th Street, San Francisco, CA 94114; 415-626-1169, 800-255-6951. In addition to organized Baja tours, **Compass Rose Travel** arranges cruises. ~ 6585-C Commerce Boulevard, Rohnert Park, CA 94929; 800-266-5351, fax 707-584-1117; www.cruising-america.com/comrose.

SENIOR TRAVELERS   Look behind the steering wheel of any monster motor home, travel-trailer-hauling truck, fishing boat or Baja bug and chances are better than even that you'll find a senior citizen. Many retired Americans and Canadians make their homes in Baja (though only the most diehard fishing fanatics stay during the sweltering summer), and many others migrate down the snowbird trail in motor homes for the winter season. Active seniors will find opportunities to meet like-minded new friends daily, and the English-language periodicals feature articles of special interest to retirees.

The only real drawback to Baja travel for seniors is the absence of medical facilities in many areas. Full-service hospital facilities in Baja are: in Mexicali, **Hospital Civil** on Calle del Hospital ~ 57-37-00; in Ensenada, **Hospital General** on Carretera Transpeninsular, Km. 111 ~ 76-76-00 and **Hospital Las Américas** on Avenida Las Dunas 130 ~ 76-03-01; in La Paz, **Hospital Salvatierra** on Calle Bravo at Ortiz de Domínguez ~ 2-14-96 or 2-15-96; and in San José del Cabo, **Hospital Municipal** on Calle Doblado at Avenida Márquez de León ~ 2-03-16. Other towns have public health clinics staffed by nurses, and major tourist towns have English-speaking doctors in private practice. Most areas have local *Cruz Roja* (Mexican Red Cross) contacts who can quickly arrange helicopter ambulance service for serious medical emergencies.

Make sure that your health insurance policy provides coverage outside the U.S. Most do; Medicaid does not. Hospital Las Américas in Ensenada is set up to bill most U.S. health insurance companies directly; in all other hospitals, you must pay at the time of treatment and seek insurance reimbursement later. If you require medication, you'll want to bring a sufficient supply for your whole stay in Mexico, since not all prescription drugs are readily available south of the border. Don't throw away your empty prescription vials, though. Many popular pharmaceuticals are sold over the counter at *much* lower prices in Mexican *farmacias,* but you can only take them back to the United States legally if you have a valid prescription.

DISABLED TRAVELERS   Mexican society has traditionally been insensitive to the needs of physically challenged people; they are viewed as burdens imposed on their families as divine punishment and are often reduced to begging. So far, this attitude has shown few if any signs of changing. Mexico has no regulations equivalent to the Americans with Disabilities Act. Newer resort hotels, found mostly in Los Cabos, are designed to accommodate disabled visitors. In most other areas, the physically challenged are likely to encounter more challenges than they might wish.

U.S. and Canadian citizens become foreigners the minute they set foot on Mexican soil. Although the United States is an overwhelming influence in Baja, local people go out of their way to extend the same courtesy to all foreigners, including the growing number of visitors from Asia and the Pacific Rim.

FOREIGN TRAVELERS

Passports and Visas   U.S. and Canadian citizens do not need a visa or tourist card to travel in Baja by car or boat. It is important to carry a passport or birth certificate in case you have to prove your citizenship to the Mexican authorities for any reason. If you use your birth certificate as proof, you should also carry a picture ID such as a driver's license. U.S. Immigration and Naturalization officers may want to see it when you reenter the United States, since Tijuana is awash in fraudulent birth certificates these days. Persons arriving in Baja by plane still have to fill out a tourist card and have it stamped when they land. The cards are provided by airline clerks when you check in for a flight to Mexico; proof of citizenship is required. Travelers from countries other than the United States or Canada must have valid passports.

Customs Requirements   Baja California is a free-trade zone, exempt from the high protective tariffs that Mexico imposes on imports in the rest of the country. Mexicans go through customs when they travel from Baja to the "mainland." Travelers, whether Mexican or gringo, rarely even have occasion to talk to a customs agent when they cross the border from the United States into Baja. Once in Baja, however, motorists don't get far without experiencing the first of the guns-and-drugs roadblocks that symbolize the mounting border tension between Mexico and the United States.

Most marijuana, cocaine and heroin imported into the United States today comes across the border from Mexico. The U.S. government considered this a major international relations problem even before March 1997, when the chief of Mexican drug enforcement was exposed for accepting drug cartel bribes. The United States Congress threatened to cut off economic aid to Mexico, and to demonstrate that his country was doing its part to stem the flow of drugs, Mexican president Ernesto Zedillo shifted the responsibility for narcotics interdiction to the army. Today, there is an army checkpoint at every main road junction in Baja California Norte. (They are rare in Baja California Sur.) They briefly search every vehicle that passes, especially those with U.S. license plates.

Hand-lettered signs explain in Spanish that the checkpoints are "for the safety of your entire family." The soldiers, most of them 18 or 19 years old, are courteous, usually bored, and often curious about what gringos carry along on vacation. Their mission is to create the appearance of cooperation in the War on Drugs, not to cause tourists any real problems. They do not solicit or accept bribes. They do not use dope-sniffing dogs. One word of warning, though: never drive through an army checkpoint without stopping, or you'll have a jeepload of irate soldiers with assault weapons in hot pursuit.

Mexicans, by and large, do not accept the slightest blame for drug abuse in the United States. They sing ballads about the bold exploits of drug smugglers. They see narcotics use in their own country as a public health problem and narcotrafficking as a risky route to riches.

The real problem, from the Mexican point of view, is guns. With a few minor exceptions, firearms and ammunition are as illegal in Mexico as heroin is in the United States. This has been the law since soon after the Mexican Revolution, when disarming the populace was an essential step toward a stable government, and for generations it has kept the rate of violent crime much lower than in the United States. But in the past few years, under the influence of the drug trade and American action movies, guns have been flooding from Southern California through Tijuana, most of them bound for the Mexican mainland. Political unrest in states such as Chiapas and Guerrero has heightened government concern about gunrunning to a fever pitch. Officials complain that the United States is not doing enough to halt the flow of guns across the border. Most Mexicans believe that guns —not drugs—threaten to destroy the fabric of their society. Don't even consider traveling in Mexico with a gun in your possession. The risk is high, and penalties are extreme.

Returning to the United States, customs is a different story. The uniformed agent who checks you out as you cross the California border is trained to prevent illegal drugs, not to mention switchblade knives, Cuban cigars and firecrackers, from entering the United States. The problem is, border crossings between Southern California and Baja California Norte are among the busiest in the world. Customs agents are under pressure to keep traffic moving. While almost all gringos in vehicles bearing U.S. plates are waved through with a few cursory questions, occasionally— perhaps once in 200 cars—one is diverted into a "secondary inspection area," where agents thoroughly search the vehicle and sometimes the driver and passengers. Drug-sniffing dogs are often used. Customs agents say that the driver's attitude and demeanor, not appearance, are the main factors determining who gets searched. Though they say they do not watch for people fitting any predetermined smuggler "profile," agents admit that they are more likely to search carloads of teens or college students.

Driving   A valid U.S., Canadian or international driver's license is required to operate a vehicle in Baja. Some car rental companies require that visitors from places other than the U.S. or Canada present both a driver's license from their own country and an international license.

Currency The official currency of Baja is the Mexican peso. In Baja California and in all major towns of Baja California Sur, however, almost every business accepts United States currency as readily as pesos. Plagued by runaway inflation in the aftermath of the 1994 peso devaluation, many Mexican entrepreneurs believe a horde of dollars at home is safer than pesos in a bank, and taking payment in U.S. currency makes it simple.

The exchange rate restaurants and stores use when translating their prices into dollars is rounded down to the next lowest half-peso. For instance, if the official exchange rate is 8.85 pesos to the dollar, most places figure it based on 8.50 and make an extra profit of about four-and-a-half cents on each dollar you spend. It's a small price to pay to avoid standing in a long, slow line at the bank or searching for a *casa de cambio*.

Businesses customarily make change for U.S. dollars in U.S. bills and coins, and for pesos in pesos. When you pay in dollars, be sure to ask for change in pesos; that way you can pay in pesos next time. The cash savings from spending pesos instead of dollars is minor, but the first time you ask, *"¿Y en pesos, cuánto vale?"*—"And in pesos, what's it worth?"—you'll instantly feel less like a tourist and more like a traveler.

While Mexican currency is easy to figure out, coins are another matter. There are nine different denominations, and sorting them out can be tricky. It pays to sit down one evening and study the various coins. Those worth less than a peso are made from aluminum and range from the tiny silver-colored centavo to the large, gold-hued 50-centavo piece. Coins worth from one to five pesos are heavier and two-toned, with nickel around the outside and a brass plug in the center. They are not very different in size. The largest-denomination coins—10 and 20 pesos—are slightly larger than the others, with brass around a nickel plug. Don't judge coins by their size alone. A 5-peso coin is smaller (though heavier) than a 50-centavo coin worth one-tenth as much. Take care not to minimize coins when leaving a tip or giving alms. A 20-peso coin may be only the size of a U.S. quarter, but it's worth more than $2.

The peso sign is identical to the dollar sign except that it has one vertical line through it instead of two. Prices in pesos are usually followed by a dash ("$10—" means ten pesos) instead of decimals ("$1.25" means a dollar and a quarter). Many places mark their prices in dollars; when in doubt, ask.

MasterCard, Visa and some other major credit cards are as widely accepted in most parts of Baja as they are in the United States. They do not work in remote places like Bahía de los Angeles, where there are no telephones. Credit card transactions often take longer in small towns, where it is common practice for merchants to call their bank, which in turn calls the credit card company for authorization. A bank charge of 7 percent is assessed on credit card transactions, and some hotels assess additional charges.

If you need a financial transfusion while on the road, transfers can be made via Western Union (*usually* taking one day) or via any big bank at home through one of its Mexican affiliates (which can take up to five working days). Check before you leave home to see whether your bank offers this service.

Electricity and Electronics   Electric outlets use currents of 110 volts, 60 cycles, the same as in the United States and Canada. To use appliances made for other electrical systems, you need a transformer or adapter.

Weights and Measurements   Baja is officially on the metric system, like all of Mexico, but the same bicultural attitude that applies to currency and language goes for weights and measures as well. You're equally likely to find measurements expressed in kilometers or miles, meters or feet, pounds or kilograms, liters or gallons. Throughout this book I use kilometers for all road distances because the highways are marked with kilometer signs. Trail mileages and other geographic distances that don't refer to roads are given in miles because they are easier for most gringos to visualize.

Temperatures are always given in Celsius. To convert from Celsius to Fahrenheit, multiply times 9, divide by 5 and add 32. For example, 18°C—the average temperature in Loreto in January —equals [(18 x 9)/5] + 32, or (162/5) + 32, or 32.4 + 32, or about 64°F. If you don't have a pocket calculator along (you should), just remember that 0°C is 32°F and that each Celsius degree is roughly two fahrenheit degrees. Here are some other useful conversion equations:

- 1 mile (*milla*) = 1.6 kilometers (*kilometros*). 1 kilometer = $^3/_5$ mile.
- 1 foot (*pie*) = .03 meter (*metro*). 1 meter = $3^1/_3$ feet
- 1 pound (*libra*) = 0.45 kilogram (kilo). 1 kilo = $2^1/_5$ pounds.
- 1 gallon (*galón*) = 3.8 liters (*litros*). 1 liter = about one quart.

MAIL   Mail from Baja to the United States is quite reliable and generally takes less than two weeks to reach its destination. If you want to mail goods to the United States, you may send items of less than $50 value duty-free to a given address (but not your own) as often as every 24 hours. Mark the parcel "Unsolicited Gift— Value under $50" and enclose a sales receipt to prove it.

While on the road, you can receive mail at the main post office of any city via *Lista de Correos* (similar to General Delivery in the United States). Use this address format: [Your Name], Lista de Correos, [City Name], [State—"BC" or "BCS"], Mexico. The post office holds Lista de Correos mail for only ten days, then returns it to the sender. The post office will charge you a small fee, and you will need identification to pick up your mail.

Some gringo communities and campgrounds in Baja have their own "U.S. Mail" drops. Whoever is heading back to the United States for any reason takes responsibility for carrying accumulated mail north and dropping it in the first mailbox they come to after crossing the border. Most of the time, this method gets letters to U.S. destinations faster than the Mexican post office does, even though they may sit for days before somebody comes along to carry it north. (Actually, the same is true of letters mailed in a Mexican post office, where a certain quantity of international mail must accumulate before it can be processed, which accounts for much of the slowness.)

PHONES

Calling into Mexico can be a frustrating experience, but recent changes have made the process somewhat easier. To call a number in Mexico, dial 011 (international code), 52 (country code), then the two- or three-digit city code, followed by the local number. Contact the international operator for city codes.

Mexico deregulated its telephone system in the early 1990s, allowing private corporations to go into competition with Telmex, the national phone company, and share the cost of new microwave transmitters and fiberoptic telephone cables. For many small towns in Baja, this has meant getting telephone service for the first time. For city dwellers, it has meant reduced rates and shorter waiting lists for installation. For travelers, however, it means an array of options for phoning home—with widely varying costs.

> The more away-from-it-all towns in Baja, including the "gringo villages" of Puertecitos and Bahía de los Angeles, have no telephone service.

By far the most common are the ones with no dial or number, just a big sign that reads, "Call the USA—credit card or collect." They are located at almost every campground, hotel lobby, restaurant, grocery store and gas station on the peninsula. Such convenience costs a lot, though—more than $8 a minute!

Many hotels that have telephones in the rooms add a surcharge to your bill for each long-distance call you make, including calling-card, collect and toll-free calls. This practice is especially common at big resort hotels, where the surcharge is often several dollars a call.

Casetas de larga distancia, which were the main means of calling the United States until a few years ago, are few and far between in Baja today. Most major towns have someplace—a photocopy and fax service, a currency exchange, a bus station, a pharmacy or even a video store—where you can use the phone to call home while they time you with a stopwatch. After the call, you pay them in cash. It may take some exploration to locate one of these places, because they are not always in the parts of town where tourists go. Compared to the easy-to-find phones, the cost is much lower—about $1 a minute.

The most economical option is to buy a prepaid long-distance card that works in pay phones marked Ladatel (which stands for Larga Distancia Automática). Many stores sell the cards, including RV parks that cater to "snowbirds." The cost of calling the United States varies with destination and time of day but is usually under a dollar a minute. You can reach an AT&T operator to make a calling-card call on a Ladatel phone by pressing "01," but you need a Ladatel card to operate the phone.

For placing unassisted calls, here are some key numbers to remember. Long-distance operator: 91; international operator (English-speaking): 98; prefixes for dialing direct to the United States, Canada and Europe: 95 (station to station) and 96 (person to person). Area codes in Baja include: Tijuana: 66; Mexicali: 65; Ensenada: 617; San Felipe: 657; La Paz: 112; San José del Cabo/Cabo San Lucas: 114.

OTHER TELECOMMUNICATIONS Because mail was slow and long-distance phone calls were expensive, faxing became the primary mode of business communication in Mexico even before it caught on in the United States. Most hotels and many other businesses can send and receive faxes for you. Larger towns also have storefront fax services. They are by far the least expensive way to send a message home and be sure that it will get there before you do.

Paradoxically, e-mail and the World Wide Web have been slow to reach most parts of Baja. The antiquated phone system in use throughout much of the peninsula won't work with computer modems. Only La Paz and San José del Cabo/Cabo San Lucas currently have reliable Internet service, but this is changing: Telmex officials have announced plans to install digital equipment and fiberoptic cables to many areas soon. There is presently no Internet café or other public access anywhere in Baja, though—at least in Los Cabos—such a service seems long overdue.

▼▼▼▼▼▼▼▼▼▼ Transportation

GETTING TO BAJA

Most visitors travel by road and enjoy the flexibility of going where they want for as long as they want. It is possible to reach some Baja destinations by plane or boat, though the choice of destinations is limited.

AIR There are only a few places where airliners land. The most straightforward plan is to catch a jet to Los Cabos, then rent a car and explore from there. **United, Mexicana** and **Alaska Airlines** offer daily flights from Los Angeles, with connections from other U.S. cities.

Aeroméxico and **Aero California** offer flights to La Paz from Guaymas, Guadalajara and other Mexican cities. Aero California also has a flight from Los Angeles to La Paz.

The most "hidden" spot in Baja that can be reached by commercial jet, the 300-year-old colonial town of Loreto is served by Aero California flights from Los Angeles, with connections from San Diego and Phoenix. Air fares to Loreto are much lower than to La Paz or Los Cabos.

The border cities of Tijuana and Mexicali are served by **Air L.A.** from Los Angeles and **Noroeste** from Las Vegas, Phoenix, Tucson, El Paso and cities of northwestern Mexico.

SEA   Several cruise lines operate weekly trips from Los Angeles to Baja ports. **Royal Caribbean**, with the largest and most luxurious ships, takes seven-day cruises down the Baja coast on the ship *Song of America*, putting in for a day at Cabo San Lucas and continuing to Mazatlán and Puerto Vallarta on the mainland coast before returning to L.A. Lower-priced three- and four-night cruises aboard the *Viking Serenade* go to Ensenada, stopping on Catalina Island for a day en route. ~ 800-327-6700.

Unless you're on your honeymoon, and maybe even then, the big drawback to cruise ship travel is that sailing schedules leave little time to explore ports of call beyond a few blocks of "cruise-ship-approved" galleries and shops. Shipboard luxury is the essence of most cruise experiences, and ports of call are almost incidental. Many passengers never disembark until the end of the cruise. Amenities on the ships—swimming pools, fine dining, showrooms, casinos—rival those of land-based resorts, and the all-inclusive accommodations are priced in the same range per night as the better Los Cabos resorts. Ticket prices vary widely depending on the time of year and on whether you take an inside (windowless) or outside (with portholes) cabin. Discounts and other little-known deals abound, so it's best to enlist the help of a travel agent who specializes in cruises; most of them emphasize this specialty in their Yellow Pages listings.

Travelers can combine a road trip with an all-day or all-night cruise across the Sea of Cortez by entering Mexico on the mainland and taking the ferry from Guaymas to Santa Rosalía or from Mazatlán to La Paz. The ferries are inexpensive for walk-on passengers but rather expensive for motor vehicles, and bringing your car across the border into mainland Mexico involves official inconveniences, described in the next section, that can be avoided by crossing directly into Baja from California.

DRIVING   The Baja Highway—Mexican Route 1, officially called the Carretera Peninsular—extends a distance of 1730 kilometers, or about 1060 miles, from Tijuana to Los Cabos. Other highways go to San Felipe in the northeast and Todos Santos in the southwest, but most Baja destinations are along Route 1 or on unpaved side roads off the main highway. More U.S. motorists drive the Baja Highway than any other road outside the United States.

For driving in Mexico, you'll need a valid U.S., Canadian or international driver's license and Mexican auto insurance. To get that, you need your driver's license and proof of ownership—a current registration certificate or title. Auto insurance policies issued in the United States are not valid in Mexico. An uninsured accident is a crime under Mexican law, which presumes the defendant guilty until proven innocent. This means that if you don't have liability insurance and you are involved in an accident that causes property damage, your vehicle will be impounded until you pay the damage and a fine. If any person is injured in the accident, you will go to jail. Motor vehicle liability insurance costs about $3 a day, with slightly lower weekly and monthly rates. Collision/comprehensive insurance is also available but not required, and many Mexican insurance agencies sell prepaid legal insurance, entitling you to a Mexican lawyer if you get in trouble any time of day or night. At a flat fee of $50, the advisability of buying this coverage depends on how much trouble you're planning to get into.

Many travelers coming from Arizona and points east cross the border at Nogales, drive south on Route 15 to Guaymas, and take the ferry across to Santa Rosalía. This short cut saves about 1250 kilometers over driving to Tijuana and then south. The one-way cost of taking a vehicle on the ferry ranges from about $100 for passenger cars to more than $300 for motor homes. If you choose this option, however, you must comply with the much stricter requirements for taking a vehicle into mainland Mexico. You need a tourist card and a car permit—a window sticker plus a special stamp on the owner or driver's tourist card. Get them at the customs and immigration port of entry on the highway south of Nogales. Here, too, you need proof of vehicle ownership. If the title shows a lien against the vehicle or if it is registered in another person's name or a company name, you need a notarized letter from the lienholder or owner authorizing you to take the vehicle to Mexico for a specified time. The owner or driver who has the car permit stamp on his or her tourist card must be in the car whenever it is being driven.

At this writing, strict regulations designed to stanch the flow of stolen cars from the United States to Mexico are in force. Anyone bringing a motor vehicle into Mexico must carry with them either a major credit card or a collision/comprehensive insurance policy valid for the duration of the stay. Otherwise, the owner can be required to post a cash bond guaranteeing that he or she will return with the vehicle to the United States—through the same border crossing. Mexico keeps pledging to simplify these requirements. To find out whether they've done so yet, contact a Mexican consulate in the United States or the U.S. Embassy in Mexico City. ~ Paseo de la Reforma No. 305, 60500 Mexico, D.F.; 5-211-0042.

None of these formalities apply to driving a car into Baja from California, but you must go through all the same red tape if you take your vehicle on the ferry from Baja to the Mexican mainland.

RENTING A CAR Tijuana, Ensenada, Loreto, La Paz and Los Cabos all have car rental agencies. Rates are lower in Tijuana than in other destinations farther south. International agencies such as Avis and Hertz offer lower rates than most local outfits. You cannot normally rent a car in the United States and take it into Mexico, though some RV rental places will make special arrangements allowing you to take a motor home across the border, especially if you are traveling with a caravan.

When renting a car, the person who signs the contract must be over 25 and have a valid major credit card. You must take out Mexican liability insurance with a $1000 deductible. Collision/comprehensive insurance is optional, and expensive; this kind of protection is good to have on Baja roads, but check first to find out whether you need it. Many credit cards provide the same coverage when a rental is charged to the card. Your personal insurance policy may also provide for rental cars, or you can often add a rider clause providing for rental coverage for much less than paying the rental agency's insurance rates.

Car rental rates fluctuate with the season. Slack tourist seasons mean good deals. Three-day, weekly and monthly rates are almost always cheaper than daily rentals. Cars with standard shifts are generally less than automatics. Compacts are more economical than larger sedans and vans. In Baja, Volkswagen Beetles are by far the most affordable rental cars. Membership in such groups as the American Automobile Association or the American Association of Retired Persons entitles you to a discount at most international car rental agencies.

Four-wheel-drive vehicles are available at premium rates from some agencies. Most resort destinations have places that rent sport vehicles such as ATVs, motorcycles, dune buggies or jeeps.

CARAVANS Caravans of a dozen to fifty or more camping vans, travel trailers or motor homes are such a common sight on the roads of Baja that you're sure to encounter several (except in the heat of summer, when boaters organize caravans). Organizers make campground arrangements ahead of time, and a caravan may fill the whole campground to capacity for a night or two before moving on. Caravanning means RVers tour with the same like-minded people for the whole trip instead of meeting new friends at each campground, and traveling together guarantees help in case of mechanical or medical problems. It is a great solution for people who lack confidence about traveling in a foreign country on their own.

Various kinds of groups organize Baja caravans. Travel clubs charge for membership and provide up-to-date travel information, discounts and low-cost insurance. Most Baja travel clubs also organize caravan tours for members; others provide information on commercial caravan tours and members' cooperative trips. Major Baja travel clubs include **Vagabundos del Mar Boat and Travel** (190 Main Street, Rio Vista, CA 94571; 707-374-5511, 800-474-2252, fax 707-374-6843), **Mex Club** (660 Bay Boulevard, Suite 214, Chula Vista, CA 91910; 619-585-3033, fax 619-420-8133) and **Discover Baja Travel Club** (3089 Clairemont Drive, Suite A-2, San Diego, CA 92117; 619-275-4225, 800-727-2252, fax 619-275-1836).

Independent tour operators also organize Baja caravans using your RV or theirs. **Point South R.V. Tours**, for instance, owns its own fleet of identical white motor homes, which caravan participants rent as part of the tour price—a great option if you want to experience the ultimate RV adventure but don't own one (yet). ~ 11313 Edmonson Avenue, Moreno Valley, CA 92555; 909-247-1222, 800-421-1394, fax 909-924-3838.

Other Baja caravans are offered through national motor clubs, West coast car and motor-home clubs, and owner's groups such as Winnebago and Airstream.

TWO

The Land
and Outdoor Adventures

Baja is a paradise for campers, kayakers and off-roaders. The varied terrain makes it possible to experience all kinds of outdoor adventures. One day you may hike up a secluded canyon with palm trees and waterfalls; the next, you may surf the big waves of the Pacific or snorkel the still waters of a shallow bay on the Sea of Cortez, camping on a gracefully curving beach with only seabirds for company.

In this chapter, we'll take a look at the environments of Baja, its unique and often bizarre plant life, the animals, birds and fish that inhabit its vast wilderness, and the outdoor skills involved in exploring the region. This is no comprehensive study of desert survival; I'm simply sharing my own observations in the hope that it will enhance your Baja experience as well.

GEOLOGY

Baja is the creation of the same slow, ponderous geological movement that causes California's earthquakes today. You could say that the peninsula is the part of California that has already fallen off into the Pacific.

Both Californias began to form more than 200 million years ago, when the North American continent separated from Africa and drifted westward, creating the Atlantic Ocean. Like a cruise liner running aground, the western edge of the continental plate pushed its way over the hard rock crust that supports the Pacific Ocean floor, crushing it down into the earth's superheated interior. As the continent grated and ground its way across the ocean crust, it scraped granite and sediments into a ridge more than 1200 miles long, forming the foundation for the Sierra Nevada. The oceanic crust buckled under the pressure, cracking into huge slabs of rock called batholiths that slanted upward from west to east, then plunged straight down on the east side in jagged, fractured escarpments. The massive geological collision also ruptured veins of magma deep in the earth, and volcanoes began erupting all along the Pacific coast. This geological turmoil continued for more than 100 million years, spanning the age of dinosaurs from dawn to extinction.

The earth fell silent. The two mountain ranges—one on the mainland and the other on the island—slowly eroded. Mountain streams carried sand, soil and sediment down to the sea until it completely filled the trench that separated the island from the mainland, creating Alta California's central valley and merging Baja with the mainland. The new land blossomed into a lush sub-tropical eden where prehistoric mammals grazed. The quiet lasted for 30 million years.

But deep in the earth, pressure was building up from the inexorable westward drift of the continental plate. Something had to give. About 30 million years ago, the Pacific Plate started grinding northward along a crack—which developed into the San Andreas Fault. The land from around present-day Puerto Vallarta to beyond San Francisco started slipping very slowly up the coast. Over 30 million years, the California coast and Baja have moved some 450 miles north along the San Andreas Fault (called the Sea of Cortez Rift when it's underwater). Along the way, the Baja peninsula has peeled away from the mainland to create the Sea of Cortez, one of the most recently formed seas on the planet.

Sixteen million years ago, the climate changed drastically. Rainfall all but ceased, creating a drought without end in the interior and west of the major mountain ranges. Then, as now, rain and snow fell on the highest ranges, Sierra Juárez, Sierra San Pedro Mártir and Sierra de la Laguna, but the water evaporated or soaked into the earth before reaching the lowlands. Over millions of years, vast quantities of fresh water accumulated in aquifers, or underground lakes, beneath parts of the desert, where they remained hidden until the mid-20th century.

Today, the Baja peninsula is about as wide as the sea that separates it from mainland Mexico. It continues to slip north at about an inch a year, grinding its way up the San Andreas Fault, resulting in California earthquakes. Volcanic activity has also continued into recent times. Franciscan priests were there to witness the last eruption of Volcán Las Tres Vírgenes, in the Vizcaíno northwest of Santa Rosalía, in 1746. Tres Vírgenes and possibly other volcanos on Baja are dormant but not extinct.

FLORA   The Desierto Central, Baja's most magical desert, displays the most remarkable profusion of plant life on the peninsula. Almost all the cactuses, agaves and trees found in other desert areas of Baja are here too, along with strange species that exist nowhere else on earth.

The plant that particularly gives the central desert landscape its surreal quality is the *cirio*—"candle" in Spanish. Cirio trees are shaped like giant upside-down carrots, sometimes twisted into whiplike curves, reaching heights of up to 60 feet. Their trunks are covered with thousands of tiny, twiglike branches that sprout leaves after rainy spells. Spring rains also bring out crowns of white flowers on the tips of the trees. Cirios are of no known use to man: They cannot be burned as firewood or cut into boards or posts for construction. They produce nothing edible. They are protected by the Mexican government as an endangered species. A gringo botanist exploring Baja in 1922 burdened the cirio with the whimsical name "boojum tree" after an imaginary species mentioned in Lewis Carroll's *The Hunting of the Snark*; the name is still in common use among North Americans in Baja.

The *ocatillo* grows from the Mojave Desert of Nevada and Arizona south along the eastern side of Baja. The ocatillo has slender, polelike, thorny branches that grow in bursts ten feet tall. A relative of the cirio, it sprouts leaves along its branches after rainy spells and flies sprigs of flamingo-pink blossoms like banners from the branches' tips in April. Another species of ocatillo, found in the south between La Paz and Los Cabos, looks the same except that its branches grow from a central trunk, not directly from the ground.

Country people chop down the woody skeletons of dead *cardones* for use as firewood.

Also unique to Baja is the "elephant tree," called *copalquín* by Mexicans. Its thick, twisted trunk and branches contrast the tufts of tiny twigs that burst from the branches and sprout leaves after rare rainy spells, when it may bloom with tiny pink flowers. A second species of elephant tree, the *torote blanco*, looks almost like the *copalquín*, as its white, papery bark peels away, it is yellow instead of green underneath. A smaller relative, the incense tree or *torote colorado* is most common south of San Felipe; it exudes a fragrant oil and smells like incense when burned. Another common desert tree that is leafless except after rain, the *palo verde* has a green trunk and branches and can blossom in a profusion of tiny yellow flowers in April. An unrelated species, the *palo blanco* is a straight, slender tree with smooth white bark that grows in dense thickets near seasonal waterholes.

The *cardon*, found in abundance through most desert areas of Baja, is the world's largest cactus. It is similar in appearance to the saguaro of Arizona but larger, reaching 40 feet with trunks up to eight feet around. Forests of these tree-sized cactuses are called *cardonals*. Another unique Baja cactus, the creeping devil or galloping cactus, sends out long, wavy branches in every direction. As they grow longer, they eventually touch the ground and put out roots, so that over decades the plants "creep" across the ground from one root system to the next. A single plant can cover an area thirty feet across with an impenetrable tangle of sharp-spined branches that provide protection for small animals and birds. Known to Mexicans as the *pitahaya agria*, this cactus produces a sour but edible fruit. Despite appearances, the creeping devil is closely related to the organ pipe cactus, or *pitahaya dulce*, whose sweet fruit was a staple of Baja's original Indian inhabitants and is considered a delicacy today. The *nopal*, or prickly pear cactus, also produces a tasty fruit, and its leaves are often sliced into strips, cooked and served as a vegetable. Other common cactuses of the Baja peninsula, which also grow in the deserts of the southwestern United States, include the barrel cactus, the jumping cholla, the teddy bear cholla, the candelabra cactus and the old man cactus.

Several species of desert plant have bursts of swordlike leaves with sharp points. Some are yuccas, and others, with wider, thicker leaves, are agaves. Besides the ground-hugging common yucca, sometimes called Spanish bayonet, another yucca that is abundant in some areas is the *datillo*, which grows on a trunk, looks much like the Joshua tree of California, and reaches heights of 20 feet. The most striking agave is the century plant, or *maguey*, whose English name comes from the popular myth that the plant lives for a hundred years, then blooms once and dies. The plants' normal life span is more like 40 years, but the blooming-and-dying part is true. Century plants store growth energy for all those years, then pour it forth in a flowering, branching once-in-a-lifetime stalk taller than a man.

Many colorful wildflowers are native to the Baja deserts. Although they are termed "annuals" (as opposed to perennials), their seeds can lie dormant in the desert sand, awaiting a rainy spell, for twenty years or more. When rains do come—generally in the

◆◆◆

BAJA'S FRUITS AND VEGETABLES

Virtually all agricultural crops come from somewhere else. Three hundred years ago, missionaries brought *las tres hermanas*—corn, beans and squash, the three staple foods of Mexican Indians before the Spanish arrived—and taught their converts how to farm. The missionaries also introduced olive trees and grapevines; olive oil and wine were shipped back to mainland Mexico, where their sale helped to support the missions. Today the major agricultural crop is wheat, grown in vast fields in Baja's northern hills and coastal plain. Most crops are grown for export to the U.S. market and are more familiar to shoppers in American supermarkets than in Mexican produce markets. Asparagus, strawberries and onions are regional specialties.

spring in Baja California and the summer in Baja California Sur—the desert blooms into a carpet of brilliant blossoms.

In the Sierra Juárez and Sierra San Pedro Mártir, juniper, piñon and oak cover vast expanses of rolling foothills and canyonlands. At higher altitudes that accumulate snow in winter, tall evergreen species including bishop pine, lodgepole pine and sugar pine, and white fir form majestic forests that look more like the Colorado Rockies than like most people's idea of Baja. Aspen trees grow in isolated stands amid the evergreens. The Sierra San Pedro Mártir also boasts a unique tree species, the San Pedro Mártir cypress. Columbines, lupines, Indian paintbrush and other mountain wildflowers bloom in early summer.

The mountain vegetation of the Sierra la Laguna, in southern Baja California Sur between La Paz and Los Cabos, is even more remarkable. Desert plants (large cactuses and datillo), mountain trees (oaks and pines), tropical coastal vegetation (palms and madroña trees) and extravagant displays of wildflowers grow side by side in his unique subtropical mountain Eden. Almost unknown (though it is only 45 miles from Cabo San Lucas), the Sierra la Laguna's unique ecosystem is not protected by law, only by its remoteness: it can only be reached by an overnight backpacking trek on rugged foot trails. It is the most endangered environment in Baja today. Water from the sierra's lakes, including the one for which it was named, has been diverted to Los Cabos, reducing evaporation, cloud buildup and rainfall in the mountains, so the luxuriant flora is gradually drying and withering as the arid desert below gradually advances up the slopes of the sierra. As environmentalists lobby urgently for Sierra la Laguna to be granted national park status, other powers want to see the sierra opened up to cattle grazing.

The San Ignacio and Mulegé rivers and other sources of fresh water support an oasis-like ecosystem made up of cottonwoods, willows, tamarisk and palm trees. The tamarisk, or salt cedar, an Asian ornamental bush, was originally introduced to Mexico and California to help stabilize river banks. It thrived and soon ran wild throughout the region's riparian ecosystems. Unfortunately, tamarisks kill off other plants by lowering the water table and increasing the salt content of the soil around them. They grow in impassable thickets along river banks and around waterholes, reaching heights of 25 feet, and cannot be burned or otherwise gotten rid of. At least tamarisks are pretty, with their long, plume-like lavender blossoms and their delicate lacework of leaves that resemble juniper needles at first glance but turn golden in the fall.

The palm trees most commonly seen in southern Baja are date palms, a species introduced by missionaries in the 1700s. They, too, prospered in Baja's hot, sunny climate and spread into the wild. It is estimated that more than 80,000 wild date palms

grow on the peninsula today, along with lesser numbers of coconut palms. The palm trees that are native to Baja are California fan palms and blue fan palms, whose pointed leaves radiate
in flat spreads from long stems. Fan palm fronds are the preferred
material for making palapa thatched roofs.

Subtropical vegetation does not stop at the water's edge. Many
varieties of seaweed grow in the shallow waters off both shores
of the peninsula. Largest of these is giant kelp, which grows along
the Pacific coast in thick underwater tangles, providing shelter
for young fish and many other kinds of sea life. When bunches
of kelp break loose in rough seas and wash ashore, they make
unsightly, smelly piles of rotting vegetation that flies love.

FAUNA   Baja is one of the world's major whalewatching destinations. The
center of attention is the astonishing number of gray whales that
gather each winter in three Pacific coast bays—Scammon's Lagoon
(Laguna Ojo de Liebre), Laguna San Ignacio (Bahía de Ballenas)
and Bahía Magdalena. All three are shallow, protected bays where
water evaporates so rapidly that thick, snow-white crusts of sea
salt crystallize along their shores; the salt content of the water is
much higher than in the open ocean.

A *panga* ride among thousands of gray whales is certainly
one of the most remarkable experiences Baja has to offer, but
veteran whalewatchers know that these waters have an even
bigger thrill in store. The Pacific Ocean off Los Cabos and Todos
Santos, and the Sea of Cortez as far north as Bahía de los Angeles (especially around Loreto and the islands of Monserrate,
Santa Catalina and Santa Cruz), are among the world's best
places to observe blue whales, the earth's largest living creatures.
Reaching lengths of 100 feet and weighing up to 180 tons, the
giant beasts are three times the size of gray whales. Their blow-
holes can spray plumes of water up to 25 feet in the air. Despite
their bulk, they are the fastest of all whales, swimming at up
to 30 miles an hour. These leviathans once numbered about
250,000 and inhabited all the world's oceans; they were hunted
nearly to extinction between 1909, when steam power first
made whaling ships fast enough to catch them, and 1966, when
hunting blue whales was outlawed worldwide. At that time, scientists believed that the whales were technically extinct—too
few in number to find mates and reproduce. In the northern
Pacific, including Baja, blue whales have made a much stronger
recovery than in other oceans, although they still rank among
the most endangered mammals. They now number an estimated
2500.

Other whales that frequent the Sea of Cortez include hump-
backs, orcas, dwarf sperm whales, fin whales, Bryde's whales and

Gentle Giants off the Baja Coast

Gray whales spend the spring and summer months in the Bering Sea off the coast of Alaska, where they feast on huge quantities of tiny organisms called lobster krill and plankton. In November, the female whales migrate southward in small groups, hugging the Pacific coast of Alaska, British Columbia, Washington, Oregon, California, Baja California and Baja California Sur to reach Laguna Ojo de Liebre (Scammon's Lagoon), Laguna San Ignacio and Bahía Magdalena—salty, protected lagoons where the water's buoyancy makes birthing whale calves easier. The calving takes place in January and February. At the same time, the males are making their way down the coast. Arriving at the calving lagoons, they breed with females who are not nursing newborn calves. The males' subtropical vacation is brief. They begin their northward migration on the first day of spring, and all are gone from the lagoons by April 1.

The gray-whale calving grounds were discovered in 1857 by American whaling captain Charles Melville Scammon, and within two years the whales were completely annihilated in Laguna Ojo de Liebre, which forever after would be known as Scammon's Lagoon. By 1900, no whales could be found along the entire Pacific coast, and by 1937, after a generation without whaling in the lagoons, they still numbered fewer than 100. Their numbers began to recover quickly only after 1972, when an international treaty abolished whaling in the open Pacific Ocean. In 1996, the whale population reached 20,000, the estimated number before Scammon's arrival.

Migrating whales can be seen all along Baja's Pacific coast, traveling about four knots per hour and swimming past at an average rate of one every two minutes during peak migration times. They usually travel in small family groups called pods. Male gray whales sometimes venture into the southern part of the Sea of Cortez, joining other whale species that frequent those waters.

Binoculars are better than telescopes for spotting whales. Watch for a cloud of spray above the water. One of these spouts is made when a whale exhales air through its blowhole.

shortfin pilot whales. Dolphins including the common, bottle-nose and Pacific white-sided varieties as well as the endangered Gulf of California harbor porpoise—are also seen in the Sea of Cortez. In the Loreto area and at Bahía Concepción, boaters and beach campers might see as many as 100 dolphins gliding and leaping along the surface.

Seals and sea lions also live in the waters of the Pacific coast of Baja. The most common are harbor seals, California sea lions and huge, grotesque elephant seals. More exotic species include the Guadalupe fur seal, a threatened species. The largest seal and sea elephant rookeries are located on the hard-to-reach ocean side of Isla Cedros, west of Guerrero Negro. Travelers who don't have their own yachts find the seal colony on offshore rocks near Santa Rosalillita and the sea lion colony off Land's End at Cabo San Lucas easier to reach.

Another marine mammal sometimes mistaken for a seal is the southern sea otter, the largest member of the weasel family, which reaches four to five feet in length. The otters were hunted to the brink of extinction in the mid-1800s. In 1874, the U.S. state of California passed the world's first endangered-species law to protect sea otters north of the border, and fur hunters moved their operations to the waters off Baja, where the otters were completely exterminated. A century later, after they were placed under worldwide protection, the otters began to reappear along Baja's Pacific coast.

Endangered species of sea turtle found on Baja beaches include the hawksbill, leatherback, green, loggerhead and olive ridley. The southern Pacific coast and the entire coast of the Sea of Cortez, especially the Bahía de los Angeles area, have been turtle breeding grounds. Local people would go there to gather turtle eggs, which were considered a delicacy, and fishermen would catch adult turtles for food. As the coastal population of Baja grew, overgathering of eggs and overfishing drastically reduced the number of turtles in Baja waters. A Japanese fishing fleet finished the job, killing all the turtles in Bahía de los Angeles to process and ship back to Japan, where the meat has traditionally been prized as a sushi ingredient. The government banned the killing of sea turtles and the taking of eggs in 1990, and Japan signed an international treaty the following year prohibiting the importation of turtle products. A research station has been set up at Bahía de los Angeles to study the best way to restore the wild sea turtles of the Sea of Cortez.

People in Baja are familiar with the consequences of extinction. Once they could choose to spend their time diving for oysters instead of fishing. These made good eating, and there was always a chance that one would contain a pearl like the ones that originally lured Cortés to the peninsula more than four centuries ago. With the invention of diving suits in the 1870s, La Paz quickly became the world's largest source of pearls, But an unidentified mollusk disease struck the oyster beds of La Paz in 1936, and by 1941 the entire oyster population of the Sea of Cortez had been wiped out. Clams, scallops, mussels, crabs and lobsters continue to thrive along both coasts.

Many fish, large and small, live in Baja waters. On the Pacific side, ocean currents cause an upwelling of deep-sea water to the surface along the coast, carrying with it game fish such as marlin and sailfish. The big fish often round the tip of the peninsula to take refuge in the calmer, more sheltered waters of the Sea of Cortez. Sharks, mostly of the small and not-very-threatening variety, infest Sea of Cortez waters and keep them as clean as piscine vultures would. The most spectacular fish of the shallow waters off Baja shores, the manta ray, or devil fish, measures an awesome 20 feet or more across, weighs up to two tons and can leap from the water, gliding and landing with a dramatic *splat*. Smaller species include the bat ray, the mobula, the guitarfish, the butterfly ray and the dangerous stingray.

> Although the sea was overfished to the point of sterility 20 years ago, smaller native fish are returning in large enough numbers to attract billfish.

Largest among the seabirds that inhabit the Baja coast, the California brown pelican (Mexicans know it as *pelicano gris,* or gray pelican) nests in large colonies on many islands both in the Sea of Cortez and along the Pacific coast. The pelicans eat fish, which they scoop from the water using their long, pouched beaks. They often fly in formation just inches above the water surface, but can also dive from heights of up to 200 feet and snatch fish with deadly accuracy. They gather wherever fishermen are to grab discarded trash fish and entrails. Other common seabirds of the Baja coast include seagulls, terns, boobies, cormorants and frigate birds.

The most common large wading bird of the peninsula is the graceful, solitary great blue heron, found any place where there is calm, shallow water, salt or fresh. The heron hunts by stepping so slowly through ankle-deep water that it appears motionless, then shooting its S-shaped neck forward faster than the eye can follow to snap up a fish, crab or frog. Concentrating on its quest for food, a heron may appear completely oblivious to the din of fishing boats, motor homes and soccer players that come within a few feet of it. Great blue herons sometimes live inland near springs, rivers and intermittent waterholes, where they feed on snakes, insects, rodents and smaller birds. Other wading birds often seen in Baja include white herons, green herons, ibis, spoonbills, storks and four kinds of egret, as well as sandpipers and godwits.

Ospreys, or sea eagles, live along both coasts of Baja, especially around protected Pacific coast bays such as Scammon's

Lagoon, where they nest on telephone poles along the main street. These large raptors circle over the lagoon at heights of about 100 feet until they spot a fish near the surface, then dive and snatch it in their talons. During the spring nesting season, both male and female bring back whole fish to rip into strips and feed to their ravenous offspring.

The forbidding Baja interior also provides habitat for many animal species, but most of them are rarely seen. Burrowing mammals such as prairie dogs, ground squirrels and jackrabbits live underground during the day to avoid the brutally hot sun and emerge in the morning and evening hours. Coyotes, which prey on the rodents, are also nocturnal. Intelligent and curious, they can sometimes be spotted around sunset observing campers from a discreet distance.

Although turkey vultures are far from endangered as a species, they are protected under Mexican law because of their vital role in keeping the desert clean.

Wild burros are a common sight in Baja California Sur. They often stand placidly by the side of the highway watching the occasional vehicle speed by. They are the descendants of beasts of burden who proved to have better desert survival skills than their masters. Wild burros have been roaming Baja for at least 200 years, yet they have not developed a noticeable fear of humans. Locals sometimes catch them and domesticate them. More often, they are used for breeding, since wild sires are believed to produce offspring that are stronger and better adapted to the harsh Baja environment. Ranchers let their female burros loose with the wild burro herds to round up later when they are pregnant.

Pronghorn antelope are occasionally seen grazing on high, open plains. Once abundant, they were hunted to the brink of extinction. Today, the Baja pronghorn is listed as an endangered species in Mexico, and it is illegal to kill one. Their numbers are increasing, but they now graze in remote areas far from roads.

Deer abound in the northern Baja sierras. You're likely to see them in the high country of Parque Nacional San Pedro Mártir, where they are protected from human hunters and less vulnerable to attack by their other major predator, the mountain lion, which stalks the dense scrub oak woodlands in the foothills of the sierras. The most common denizens of the foothills are javelinas, or peccaries, piglike animals that root in packs and can be dangerous to hikers. Other wildlife of the sierra includes squirrels, skunks, raccoons, and the occasional bear.

Twenty species of birds of prey patrol the skies of Baja. Besides the osprey, they include golden eagles, peregrine falcons, hawks, harriers and owls. Turkey vultures, known in Mexico as *zopilotes,* are the most commonly seen large birds in the Baja interior. They are the size of eagles but soar with their wings in a V instead of straight out and have small, bald, red heads. They are everywhere in Baja, sunning themselves in groups of a dozen or so on giant cactuses, gliding in lazy circles overhead, huddling around road kill. The unique power of the vulture is its natural immunity to botulism, salmonella and other poisonous bacteria, allowing it to eat the most disgusting things. In the southern part of the peninsula, they are joined in their scavenging by caracaras. The head of this big tropical carrion eater looks much larger because of its sweeping black and white feather crest—like a vulture with a bad toupee.

Many songbirds, including meadowlarks, orioles and blackbirds, migrate to the deserts of Baja in the winter. Perhaps the most common desert bird is the cactus wren, a brownish bird with a spotted breast. It builds its nest in a tall cactus and feeds on insects and worms. White-winged doves, another common desert bird, nest near springs and waterholes; people have survived in the desert by following the doves to water. Other common desert birds include roadrunners, mockingbirds, ravens and ladderback woodpeckers.

The most conspicuous mountain birds are several species of jays, including the piñon jay, which is sky-blue and robin-sized with no crest, the Gray's jay or camp robber, and the Stellar's jay with its long black crest. Other common mountain birds include flycatchers, juncos, nuthatches and woodpeckers. More than two dozen hummingbird species migrate to Baja in the winter. Some, such as the black-chinned hummingbird and rufous hummingbird, are found throughout the northern sierra; many more species gravitate to Baja California Sur's lush Sierra la Laguna.

Outdoor Adventures

With its magnificent beaches, bays and national parks, Baja is a wonderland for campers and water sports enthusiasts. Adventures of every description await, from whalewatching excursions to canyon hikes to all-day desert excursions on rugged, unpaved four-wheel-drive tracks or horse trails. The Pacific coast boasts some of the world's great surfing beaches, such as those on the Islas de Todos Santos near Ensenada, and near the towns of San Quintín and Todos Santos.

Mexican boating restrictions are generally at least as strict as those in the United States. Authorities recently prohibited sea kayaking among the whales in Magdalena Bay and Scammon's Lagoon, putting an end to one truly unique Baja experience. Today, most sea kayaking is done on the Sea of Cortez side of the peninsula, especially in spring and fall. While kayaking is feasible anywhere along the east coast, the most popular area (and the one where most rental kayaks and guided trips are available) is south of Mulegé at Bahía Concepción, where curious dolphins often approach kayakers and whales can sometimes be seen in the distance.

FISHING   Deep-sea fishing in the waters off Baja is some of the best in the world. Cabo San Lucas is renowned for sailfish, swordfish, blue marlin and white marlin. Japanese and domestic overfishing with drift nets exterminated billfish in the Sea of Cortez during the 1970s, but their numbers are recovering; today sailfish and marlin are often caught around La Paz and Loreto and as far north as San Felipe. Commercial fishing is prohibited in much of the Sea of Cortez, and tourist sport fishing is being promoted as more environmentally friendly and profitable than catching fish for market. Though it is not legally required, boat operators and federal officials urge catch-and-release sport fishing.

On the Pacific side, Ensenada's charter fishing boats go out in search of yellowtail and tuna. Other Pacific coast game fish include albacore, barracuda and bonito. Local fishermen along both coasts catch sharks for food, and it is easy to arrange a shark-fishing trip. In most settlements along the Sea of Cortez, independent fishermen who own *pangas*—long, open wooden motorboats that ride low in the water like rowboats—prefer taking gringos out for a day of sport fishing over going out to catch fish for the local restaurants: It pays better.

Deep-sea fishing is a pricey sport, since charter boats capable of handling a billfish cost several hundred dollars a day. Surf fishing offers more affordable angling thrills, especially in the Los Cabos area, where roosterfish feed close to shore. These big, silver fish reach 65 pounds, and since they live in the surf, they are powerful swimmers skilled in using the breaking waves and undertows to their advantage, giving them a reputation as formidable fighting fish. They are edible but not very good. The idea is to battle the fish for 20 to 30 minutes, land it, have your picture snapped with your catch, and release it into the surf before it gasps its last.

The best months for fishing on either Baja coast are mid-June through mid-November, peaking in September when water temperatures are warmest. Big fish are still caught sometimes in January and February, but much less often.

On a boat from which anyone is fishing, every passenger—children included—must have a Mexican sportfishing license. The licenses cost between $15 and $30 each, depending on their duration and the size of the boat. Snorkelers and scuba divers also need the license for spearfishing. A license is required for fishing in streams, rivers and lakes, but not for surf fishing from the beach or rocks without a boat. The easiest way to get one is to contact the California office of the **Secretaría de Pesca Mexicana**, 2550 5th Avenue, Suite 101, San Diego, CA 92103-6622; 619-233-6956. There are also Secretaría de Pesca offices in many of Baja's major coastal towns, and fishing outfitters along the Tijuana border and in all tourist areas sell fishing licenses.

The waters of Baja invite swimming, boating, scuba diving, fishing, kayaking, surfing and other recreational activities. Whether you're out for a short swim, a day of angling for roosterfish or a sea trek in a kayak, it is prudent to be aware of the ocean's risks. Baja's Pacific coast gets big waves and high winds, especially during the winter and spring, while the more sheltered Sea of Cortez coast usually has a gentler surf. Enter the water on the Pacific side with extreme caution. There may be overpowering waves and, in some places, treacherous undertows.

In summer, except during rare but devastating tropical storms, waves in the Pacific subside until they can't be ridden on a surfboard, and the Sea of Cortez becomes as flat as glass. The major hazards are from marine life. If you step on a sea urchin, soaking the affected area in very hot water for 15 to 90 minutes will draw the toxin out. Another remedy is to apply undiluted vinegar, ammonia or even urine. The same remedies work equally well with jellyfish stings. If these preliminary treatments don't work, consult a doctor.

A far more painful injury, and one that always calls for medical treatment, can be inflicted by the poisonous tail spine of a stingray. These creatures are not aggressive and prefer to bask peacefully on shallow, sandy sea floors. They will strike if a bather kneels or steps down on them directly, so when walking in shallow water, shuffle your feet in a way that will send stingrays scooting off to safety.

The heat of the desert can be fatal if you are stranded without sufficient water. A well-acclimatized human adult needs at least one gallon of water a day to survive in the Baja desert. Motorists are wise to stock up on all the water they have room for; buy five or more gallon jugs of drinking water at a time, and replenish whenever your supply falls to less than two jugs per person. Salt tablets cause water retention and can help prevent dehydration and heat exhaustion. Beer and other alcoholic beverages are not a substitute for water. In fact, alcohol increases your body's rate of water loss.

Rattlesnakes, tarantulas and scorpions are found in all parts of Baja except the high mountains. All three are poisonous and can be deadly in rare instances, but none is aggressive toward humans. They can tell that you are too big to eat and will only bite or sting in self-defense, so the best way to avoid bites is to make a lot of noise while hiking in the desert and be alert to avoid putting your hands or feet where you can't see them. Most scorpion stings and spider bites happen at night from rolling over on a poisonous insect while sleeping. If you are tent camping, be sure to keep the tent zipped shut whenever it is set up to prevent insects from entering. Scorpions sometimes live in the thatch roofs of camping palapas and drop down on sleeping campers in the night, so it's a good idea to thrash the roof with a stick as you're moving in to shake loose any lurkers. Finally, whether you're camping or sleeping in hotels, it is prudent to avoid unpleasant surprises by shaking your shoes or boots out before putting them on in the morning.

In the event of a bite, get to the nearest medical clinic as fast as possible. Like bumblebee stings, tarantula bites are rarely fatal except to small children and people with heart problems, insect bite allergies or other medical conditions, but they are quite painful. Rattlesnake bites are rarely life-threatening. The snakes can control how much venom they release from the poison sacs behind their fangs, and when striking in self-defense they tend to inject a low dose or even none at all. Unfortunately, there is no way to be sure until the poison takes effect, so don't wait—head for the nearest town and medical help. Scorpions cannot control their poison dosages as snakes can, and some are lethal while others are merely painful. Take no chances; seek medical treatment immediately. Some people carry snakebite kits in their emergency survival gear, even though doctors disagree on the advisability of using them. If you slice open a snakebite wound and suck the poison out, the risk of infection may be greater than the risk of death from the venom, and the person who sucks the venom out can become poisoned in the process.

CAMPING   Whether you camp in a tent, in a van, under a shell on a pickup truck or in a motor home the size of a city bus, you'll find Baja a camper's paradise. Hundreds of beach campgrounds along both coasts are operated by individuals or rural collectives called *ejidos*. The campgrounds' amenities vary widely. A top-of-the-line RV park has "full hookups"—water, electric and sewage—and sometimes television cables. Level concrete pads are provided for motor homes, and campsites may be suitable for tenting. Parks often have a swimming pool and restaurant and may be protected by a high wall and a guarded gate. Designed for long-term "snowbirds," these places can take much of the fun out of on-the-road camping. Per-night prices typically run about $25 in season. Most of these places are found in or near major towns, including Ensenada, San Felipe, Loreto and Los Cabos.

Mid-range private campgrounds have central restrooms with flush toilets and showers, sometimes hot. Sites are usually on or near the beach; the packed sand is suitable for tents and RVs; they'll have sheltered picnic tables and (often) fireplaces. They typically have electric hookups and a sewage dumping station. These places are not walled, but the owners live on the premises. Sites cost $10 to $12 a night in season.

A third category of beach campgrounds, often run by *ejidos,* has only the most primitive facilities. Sites usually have a palapa, or palm-thatched shelter, for shade, and that's about it. There may be fiberglass portable restrooms or makeshift outhouses nailed together out of scrap lumber. The good news is that they are located on many of Baja's most magnificent beaches, and the cost is minimal—typically $5 or less per night. There is no security and no real crime problem either.

Finally, many remote beaches can be reached via unpaved side roads, some of which may require four-wheel-drive. Unofficial tent and truck camping areas have evolved in many of the most beautiful spots. Camping is unrestricted and free away from developed areas. It's up to you to bring your own water, food and shelter, to dig your own latrine and to haul away your own trash. Camping is also allowed on all offshore islands that have suitable beaches.

Away from the coast, just about the only campgrounds are in the national parks—Parque Nacional Constitución de 1857, Parque Nacional Sierra San Pedro Mártir, Cataviña in the Desierto Central Natural Area and San Ignacio on the southern edge of El Vizcaíno Biosphere Reserve.

HIKING

For the casual vacationer, hiking will consist of long walks on seemingly endless beaches and short desert walks on four-wheel-drive roads near the main highway. The difficulty of carrying enough water to meet your needs in the sunbaked desert prevents long-distance trekking in most areas.

The best hiking and backpacking possibilities are found in two mountainous areas of the interior. Parque Nacional Sierra San Pedro Mártir has an extensive, though poorly marked, network of alpine hiking trails starting from the road to the Mexican National Observatory; 10,000-foot Picacho del Diablo can be climbed either from this approach or from Diablo Canyon on the San Felipe side of the mountains. Even more spectacular—and even harder to get to—is the Sierra de la Laguna, an area of lush mountains north of Los Cabos in the rugged interior of the lower peninsula.

THREE

History and Culture

THE INDIANS In the remote canyons of the Desierto Central, under huge rock overhangs, murals in burnt sienna and black depict deer, mountain lions, desert bighorn sheep—and the people who originally inhabited the Baja peninsula. Experts think the giant paintings were made over a thousand-year period from A.D. 500 to A.D. 1500, but little is known for certain about their meaning or about the people who made them, who are called simply "the Painters"; their relationship (if any) to the Cochimí people, who lived in the area when the Spanish landed but had no apparent artistic tradition, is a topic for endless academic argument. When 18th-century Spanish missionaries asked the Cochimí about the cave art, they claimed the murals had been painted long ago by an extinct race of giants. Today, the Cochimí no longer exist, and it is unlikely that the mystery of the paintings will ever be definitively solved.

Here's what anthropologists do know about the ancient people of Baja. A single arrowhead found recently in the vastness of the Desierto Central is of a type used 12,000 years ago to hunt mammoths and giant bison. The first people to set foot in Baja may have followed big game animals as they moved south ahead of the creeping glaciers that marked the onset of the last Ice Age. Stone tools and other artifacts found throughout the peninsula show that people lived there by 8000 B.C. Ancient clamshell middens 20 feet high remain as evidence that fishing villages existed along the Pacific coast as early as 6000 B.C. We know nothing of the relationship, if any, between the people of the coast and whoever made the cave paintings in the remote canyons of the interior. They wore little or no clothing, and their possessions were minimal. They lived softly on the fragile land and left few clues for modern scientists.

Millennia passed. When the first Europeans arrived, they found the Baja peninsula populated by an estimated 50,000 nomadic Indians who traveled in small bands. They were skilled hunters, and some scratched out small cornfields in the mountains; for the most part, though, they lived by harvesting shellfish from the sea and plants from the desert.

The Indians were separated into more than a dozen language groups. Major among them were the Pericú people in what is now the Los Cabos area, the Guaycuro in the region of La Paz and Loreto, the Cochimí in the central desert, and the Yumano in the mountains of northern Baja. The four groups were divided by ancient hostilities. Deadly raids and ambushes were commonplace along the fringes of their territories. The violence claimed so many lives that adult women outnumbered adult men by a wide margin, and it was usual for a husband to have several wives. Clans, the central unit of Indian society in Baja, were essentially polygamous extended families.

At the time of European contact, none of the four groups had tribal leadership. All were guided by shamans, who lived in remote locations and practiced herbal medicine and magic. An enigmatic account by one early missionary reports that the Guaycuro worshiped an entity known as "the man who came from the sky."

THE EXPLORERS   Spanish conquistadors first came to Baja as a result of the rivalry between two would-be rulers of colonial Mexico, Hernán Cortés and Nuño de Guzmán. Cortés, the discoverer of Mexico in 1519, had conquered the Aztec capital of Tenochtitlán in 1522, demolishing the ancient city and rebuilding it as Mexico City. Cortés then set out on a 20-month expedition to Honduras. In his absence from Mexico City, his enemies spread false news of his death and seized his property. Upon his return, Cortés was arrested and taken back to Spain to stand trial on false charges that had been made to stop him from reclaiming his property.

While Cortés awaited trial, the King of Spain appointed an *audencia*, or tribunal, to govern Mexico temporarily until the court case was resolved. But one after another, the members of the audencia died mysteriously, leaving Guzmán, a former slave trader and the most despised villain in Mexican colonial history, notorious for corruption and cruelty to Indians, as the de facto dictator. His rule lasted less than a year before he outraged his subjects by physically attacking the Bishop of New Spain during church services. On the Bishop's complaint, the King of Spain sent a new audencia to relieve Guzmán of his post. Hearing that they were on their way, Guzmán decided to get out of town before they arrived. He mounted a private army and set forth to conquer the west. In a brutal campaign of terror, he swept through Michoacán, Jalisco, Nayarít and Sonora, massacring the local Indians wherever he went. Guzmán's reign as warlord instilled in the Indians of western Mexico such hatred of the Spanish that for more than a century afterward, no one who traveled overland in the region returned alive.

Meanwhile, acquitted of the charges against him, Cortés returned to Mexico to reclaim his place as the rightful governor; but the king had other ideas. He decided that henceforth the colony would be ruled by a viceroy—a surrogate for the king himself. Cortés lacked the noble lineage to qualify as viceroy of the land he had conquered. Instead, the king sent him to Cuernavaca, where he built a castle and reigned as the Marquis of Oaxaca, with dominion over the southern territories all the way to Guatemala, but had few responsibilities and no real power.

With excess time on his hands, Cortés decided to outfit an expedition in hopes of parlaying his personal fortune into a new empire. His plan was to explore the unknown west coast of North America in search of a navigable passage between the Atlantic and the Pacific. He established a shipyard near modern-day Zihuatanejo, transporting the metal fittings, rigging and other components for his vessels 400 miles over the mountains from Veracruz on the Gulf of Mexico.

Cortés did not go along on the early expeditions, though he financed them. The first ship, commanded by Cortés' cousin Diego Hurtado, set out in 1532, but encountered pirates led by Nuño de Guzmán near the mouth of the Sea of Cortez. The ship was seized, and the crewmen were either executed or put ashore at the mercy of hostile Indians.

The following year, Cortés sent out a second exploration party in the newly built ship *Concepción*, for which the magnificent Bahía de Concepción would later be named. This expedition, too, was doomed. The captain was murdered by mutineers led by the ship's pilot, Fortún Jiménez, who made the first Spanish landfall on the Baja peninsula in 1534. The mutineers had little opportunity to bask in the glory of their accomplishment. While refilling their water casks at a spring near what is now La Paz, they were attacked by Indians. According to Mexican legend, the Indians were enraged when the Spanish tried to rape their women. Jiménez and the crew members who had accompanied him ashore were killed. The men who had stayed aboard ship escaped, but lack of fresh water forced them to land on the opposite shore of the Sea of Cortez, where Guzmán's soldiers captured them and their ship. A single survivor escaped and eventually journeyed on foot down the west coast to Cortés' port with the first report of a huge "island" where pearls were found in abundance.

Spanish exploration of the Americas in the 1500s was characterized by the notion that human imagination was divinely inspired, and therefore, every place that was described in a legend, novel or epic poem must actually exist. Visionary tales of golden cities in the wilderness sent conquistadors off in futile quests for such nonexistent empires as El Dorado, Quivira and Cibola. A popular Spanish novel of the time, *Las Sergas de Esplandián* by

Garcí Ordóñez de Montalvo, mentioned "an island on the right hand of the Indies very near the terrestrial Paradise, peopled by black women among whom there was not a single man . . . Their island was the most impregnable in the world with its cliffs and headlands and rocky coasts. Their weapons were all of gold, because in all the island there was no metal except gold." The fictitious island was named California after its ruler, Califia, queen of the Amazons. As reports began to filter back of a huge island off the North American west coast, Cortés and others easily convinced themselves that they had found the fabled California.

Enthusiastic over the prospect of treasure, Cortés decided to finance a third expedition. This time, he decided to lead it himself and confront his nemesis, Guzmán. He set off with three ships, 500 soldiers and sailors, 37 families and 130 horses, planning to establish a permanent colony on the shore of Bahía de la Paz. He never met Guzmán, who, hearing the news that Cortés was on the way with a sizable army, fled across the rugged Sierra Madre to the Gulf of Mexico, where he was arrested by the viceroy's soldiers.

Cortés built Santa Cruz, a sturdy little village with stone houses and a church, at the site of present-day Pichilingue near La Paz. There he found the remains of the mutineer Jiménez and his unfortunate followers. He also found a handful of the pearls that he was seeking. But he did not find the Amazon warrior women or their gold. Burdened with too many soldiers and too few farmers, plagued by drought, storms, and disease, Santa Cruz never became self-sufficient, and after two years Cortés and his colonists abandoned it and returned to Mexico.

Obsessed with the hope of redeeming his failure by discovering an Atlantic-Pacific passage, Cortés applied to the viceroy for permission to organize a fourth journey of exploration to California. When permission was denied, he went ahead and invested the remainder of his fortune in an illegal 1539 expedition, sending two ships up the Pacific coast under the command of Francisco de Ulloa. The ships traced and mapped both the mainland and Baja shores of the Sea of Cortez. Then, having determined that Baja was not an island, they rounded the tip of the peninsula and continued up the Pacific coast. When they reached Isla Cedros, an island off the tip of Baja's Vizcaíno Peninsula, Ulloa dispatched the smaller of his ships southward to report his discoveries to Cortés, while he continued north in his other ship. Ulloa was never heard from again. His fate and those of his crew and ship remain unknown to this day.

Destitute but for the money from selling the surviving ship, Cortés returned to Spain, where he died five years later at 63. The sea that separated Baja from the mainland was named in his honor—the Mar de Cortés. Centuries later, after Mexico gained its independence from Spain, history would be revised to paint Cortés as a villain, and the name of the sea would be officially changed to the Golfo de California, but Mexicans still prefer the more evocative name Sea of Cortez.

Viceroy Mendoza commissioned one more sea exploration of the west coast two years after the Ulloa voyage. Unlike his predecessors, Portuguese-born sea captain Juan Rodriguez Cabrillo bypassed the Sea of Cortez and, after stopping to replenish the expedition's water supply at what is now Cabo San Lucas, sailed up the coast to Isla Cedros and the Bahía de Todos Santos. Cabrillo and his crew went on to anchor at the sites of present-day San Diego, Catalina Island and Santa Monica. While exploring the Channel Islands off Santa Barbara, he slipped, fell from a cliff and died from his injuries, but not before claiming the entire Pacific coast of North America in the name of the King of Spain.

The Manila galleons were the largest ships ever built until the 20th century.

Cabrillo's pilot, Bartolomé Ferrelo, continued the mission, sailing as far north as Oregon before returning to Mexico. Unfortunately, he brought back no treasure, and Cabrillo's and Ferrelo's discoveries were dismissed as insignificant. There would be no more Spanish expeditions up the Pacific coast for more than 50 years. Instead, the viceroy would turn his attention to developing trade with Asia, and this enterprise would eventually lead to the colonization of Baja.

THE MANILA GALLEONS Centrally located on the Pacific Rim, the Philippines had been a hub for trade between the merchants of China, Japan, Indonesia, Malaya, Indochina and India for centuries. Ferdinand Magellan had reached the Philippines in 1521 and claimed the islands for Spain. Soon afterward he died there, fighting alongside his new ally, the Rajah of the Philippine city of Cebu, against the rajah's enemies. Magellan's fatal heroism earned Spain an alliance with the rulers of the Philippines that would endure for centuries.

If Spain could establish commerce with the Philippines, it would break Portugal's monopoly on the lucrative spice trade in Europe. From the new port of Acapulco on Mexico's southern coast, Spanish ships could easily ride the prevailing winds and ocean currents across the Pacific Ocean to the Philippine Islands in about three months. The problem was getting back. After several failed attempts, a 1542 Spanish expedition led by Ruy López de Villalobos made the crossing from Acapulco, but he could not find a return route and finally surrendered his ship and crew to the Portuguese.

The return route was not found until 1564, when Miguel López de Legazpi navigated far northward to the latitudes of Japan.

Westerly winds and the North Pacific current carried him back across the ocean to California, where it was an easy matter to follow the Baja coastline south to Acapulco. Instead of three or four months, this circuitous return route took at least seven months and often as much as a year, but the rewards were awesome.

The Philippine trade, which soon shifted from Cebu to the more accessible port of Manila, proved to be one of the biggest coups of the Mercantilist era. Instead of carrying silver from the mines of Mexico back to the king's treasury in Spain, merchants shipped the silver to the Philippines for trade with the Chinese, who needed it for coinage to expand their own trade empire. In exchange, the Spanish received huge quantities of silk, cotton, oriental rugs, jade, ivory, porcelain and precious gems, as well as pepper, cloves and cinnamon. The Chinese were so eager for Mexican silver that they even exchanged gold bullion for it. When these goods went back through Mexico to Spain, they were sold throughout Europe at many times the worth of the silver they were bought with. Suddenly, Spain was the most prosperous nation in Europe.

Spain expanded its Manila fleet by hiring Chinese shipwrights in the Philippines to build new galleons in exchange for the abundant Mexican silver. This international partnership resulted in ships that combined elements of European sailing vessels and of Chinese junks. The new galleons were built bigger and bigger; eventually they had more than three times the cargo capacity of the ships that traveled between Spain and Mexico.

The need for a Spanish colony on the Baja coast was clear to captains of the Manila galleons: They were often critically short of food and water by the time they sighted California. A resupply point at the tip of the Baja peninsula would have done much to alleviate the hardships of the trip. But the Mexican viceroy, remembering Cortés' failures, could not be interested in another attempt to colonize Baja. It was the British, not the Spanish, whose ships next made landfall there.

Francis Drake was a privateer—a freelance warship captain chartered by the British government to commit piracy against Spanish ships in the Caribbean. As word got out about the incredible riches of the Manila galleons, Drake decided to rob one. He sailed around Cape Horn and north to the tip of Baja, where he lurked in wait for the Spanish ships. His attack came as a complete surprise, since no British ship had ever entered the Pacific Ocean before. Drake returned to England with all the treasure he could carry.

A few years later, another British privateer, Thomas Cavendish, anchored at Cabo San Lucas and robbed the Manila galleons again. He, too, made it safely back to England with his loot.

By 1598, British privateer ships were pouring into the Pacific and gathering around Los Cabos to wait for their prey. By 1615, Dutch pirate ships had joined the pack, setting up their own stronghold in the Bahía de la Paz. The viceroy belatedly realized that a colonial presence on the Baja Peninsula was essential to the security of the Manila galleons. But colonizing the Baja was easier said than done. Expeditions in 1596, 1644 and 1663 ended in failure. The token colony of San Bruno, near present-day Loreto, lasted for 19 months but was abandoned when the colonists' supplies ran out. A resupply station on Baja finally became a reality in 1730, thanks to Jesuit priests.

The Manila galleons crossed the Pacific every year for two and a half centuries, until just a few years before Mexican independence. During most of this time, pirates ruled the seas off the coast of Baja. Fighting them became a predictable part of the arduous return trip from the Philippines.

THE MISSIONS   The first successful settlements in Baja were established at the end of the 17th century by the Jesuits, a Catholic order that had been founding missions across mainland Mexico for a century. Inspired by an encounter with Father Keno, the legendary mission builder of northern Mexico, Jesuit priest Juan María de Salvatierra applied for permission to start a mission in Baja. Considering the many failed attempts to colonize that barren, waterless peninsula, neither the viceroy nor the Mexican Jesuit leadership was willing to finance another attempt. But Father Salvatierra's enthusiasm impressed Jesuit officials in Europe; in 1697, with 21 other priests and some soldiers, he began construction of a mission church at Loreto to convert the local Guaycuros to Catholicism.

Father Salvatierra presided over the Loreto mission until his death 20 years later. During that time, he built four other missions, at San Javier, Ligui, Mulegé and Comomdu. Each mission was comprised of a church, clerical residences and an adjoining pueblo where Indian converts lived. The people worked on church land and shared in the crops. Under Spanish law, a mission was to last for only ten years, and then the land was to be turned over to the villagers, partly as private farms and partly as *ejido* land. In Baja, the Jesuits never quite got around to signing their land over to the Indians, but then again, they never succeeded in growing much on it. All through the missionary era, the priests and their Indian followers survived on food donated by wealthy patrons on the Mexican mainland.

Father Salvatierra's successors built 15 more missions in southern Baja during the 18th century, spanning most of Baja California Sur. The most important of these was San José del Cabo. Built in 1730 on a natural harbor, it was ideally situated to resupply the Manila galleons with fresh water from nearby springs. From then on, the ships put in at San José each year.

In 1733, outraged by a church prohibition against polygamy, the Pericús revolted against the four southern missions—San José, Todos Santos, Santiago and La Paz—killing several priests and all six guards assigned to the missions. When the Manila galleons sailed into San Jose, only to find the port in the hands of angry Indians, they hastened to report the uprising to the viceroy, who sent in the army. San José del Cabo became as much a military garrison as a mission, with soldiers outnumbering priests.

During the Jesuits' 70 years of mission work in southern Baja, the peninsula's total population fell to 7000. More than 85 percent of Baja's native people had died from epidemics of European diseases such as smallpox and measles, to which they had no natural immunity.

The arrival of soldiers and sailors at San José brought with it the beginning of a horror that would destroy the missions of southern Baja. Measles, syphilis and smallpox quickly spread from San José through the land of the Pericú. By 1748 the entire tribe was dead, and the missionaries had refocused their attention among the Cochimí, who were just beginning to experience the epidemics.

In 1767, suspecting that the missionaries might be amassing personal fortunes through fundraising and failing to turn mission land over to the villagers, the king ordered the Jesuit order expelled from the Spanish Empire.

With the expulsion of the Jesuits, Franciscan missionaries under the leadership of Father Junipero Serra took over the mission headquarters at Loreto for a few years. Soon, however, the king of Spain decreed that California would be divided between two religious orders—the Franciscans to do missionary work in Alta California, and the Dominicans in Baja. It was this decree that originally defined the boundary between the two Californias.

The Dominicans established half a dozen new missions in Baja California, from Santo Tomás with its vineyards and olive orchards to San Pedro Mártir, deep in the rugged mountains of the interior. They relocated Indians from the north to revive the southern missions. But wherever the missionaries went, fatal diseases accompanied them.

Mexico attained independence from Spain in 1821. Soon thereafter, the new government secularized missions throughout the country and confiscated their agricultural land. The only exceptions were the Dominican missions of northern Baja. These were allowed to continue as usual because, as the only settlements in the region, they provided way stations for travelers between the towns of Alta California and those of southern Baja. The missions' original purpose became little more than a memory, as there were hardly any Indians left to convert.

THE INVADERS   At first, the few people who cared one way or the other in Baja, like their counterparts in the other remote territories of Texas and Yucatán, generally favored the idea of being an autonomous republic. They changed their minds after British privateer Lord Thomas Cochrane, who had sailed around the tip of South America plundering isolated towns all along the Mexican coast, seized San José del Cabo and then attacked Loreto. Cochrane's landing party was repulsed by the city's military guard, which consisted of 15 soldiers. He returned to raiding the Mexican mainland and never bothered with Baja again. The people of both cities pledged their loyalty to Mexico in 1824. To reduce the power of the church, the capital was moved from Loreto, the headquarters of the Dominican missions, to La Paz.

With scarcely any population, mineral wealth or arable farmland, the national government took little interest in the peninsula. Instead, the few Mexican pioneers who crossed over from the mainland found that gringos coveted Baja far more than Mexico did. In the 1830s, Texas won its independence from Mexico. About the same time, U.S. diplomats initiated fruitless attempts to buy California from Mexico. As the pressure of western migration increased, the United States agreed to annex the Republic of Texas as a state. Mexico and the United States had radically different ideas about the location of Texas' southern border; the annexation touched off a military confrontation between the two nations. Texas was the excuse for the Mexican War, but California was the prize.

In May of 1846, when news arrived that fighting had started along the Rio Grande, a small fleet of American warships that had been stationed at the Mexican port of Mazatlán to protect the U.S. consulate there headed up the Pacific coast to seize San

WHY THERE ARE TWO CALIFORNIAS

History records differing versions of why Baja, which was still occupied by U.S. troops and was initially part of U.S. negotiators' demands after the Mexican War (1846–48), was not included in the final settlement. Mexican students learn that their country balked at turning Baja over to the United States for reasons of national pride and security—it would have relinquished control of sea lanes to the mainland ports of Guaymas and Mazatlán. *Norteamericano* schoolbooks say that after U.S. military command in Baja reported the peninsula to be worthless and uninhabitable, negotiators decided to take New Mexico instead. There is probably some truth in both versions. In any case, in 1848 the partition of Baja and Alta California became permanent.

Diego, Monterey and San Francisco. There was no fighting. As U.S. Marines took control of the Alta California ports, the fleet returned southward to take control of Baja California.

U.S. Navy gunships blockaded the mouth of the Sea of Cortez. They then sailed to La Paz, where the American commodore informed the Mexican governor that he was placing Baja under U.S. control. There was no demand for surrender; instead, the authorities in La Paz were merely asked to pledge "neutrality" in the war—meaning that they would remain in charge of local affairs but would not resist U.S. military occupation. Six months later, U.S. ships took control of San José del Cabo under the same kind of neutrality agreement. Officials were happy to avoid a military confrontation: After all, there was no telling which nation would own Baja after the war. Baja's loyalty to Mexico had never been particularly strong, and it had eroded as the Mexican government had changed leadership no less than 50 times in 26 years, usually by assassination or military coup. Echoes of this "neutral" attitude toward both Mexico and the United States have helped shaped Baja's unique character ever since.

In September of 1847, the Mexican government ordered a small group of officers under the command of Capitán Manuel Pinada to cross the Sea of Cortez from Guaymas and land in Mulegé, north of the area held by the U.S. forces, now supplemented by two companies of infantry. Pinada did not bring many soldiers; every available man was needed for the last-ditch defense of Mexico City, which fell to an expeditionary force of U.S. Marines the same week that Pinada landed in Baja. Instead, the captain brought crateloads of rifles and conscripted the able-bodied men of Mulegé, Comondú and San Ignacio—about 300 in all—into a citizens' army to fight the gringos. After a skirmish at Mulegé, Pinada and his troops besieged La Paz, but after 12 days of fierce fighting the Mexicans ran out of ammunition and had to withdraw.

The Mexicans turned their attention upon San José del Cabo, which was occupied by a far smaller U.S. force, and fighting raged there for more than a month before American reinforcements arrived to save the day for the U.S. The final battle, near Todos Santos, ended in the surrender of Capitán Pinada and his troops. In all, the war in Baja involved fewer than 1000 soldiers on both sides. Sadly, the battles of San José del Cabo and Todos Santos took place after Mexico's surrender on February 2, 1848; news that the war was over had not yet reached the commanders of either side in the Baja conflict.

The treaty that ended the war ceded almost half of Mexico, including the modern-day states of California, Arizona and New Mexico as well as portions of six other western states, to the

United States. In return, the U.S. agreed to pay Mexico a sum that was slightly less than negotiators had offered for California alone before the war.

Soon after Alta California became U.S. territory, the discovery of gold there brought a wave of more than 80,000 squatters and prospectors west from the United States to northern California. Alta California became simply California, the 31st U.S. state, in 1850. Suddenly an oppressed minority, many Hispanic Californians moved south to Baja, but few stayed; most eventually went to mainland Mexico. By the end of the 19th century, Alta California's population would be only 2 percent Spanish-speaking, and Baja's population would be even smaller than it had been before the Mexican War.

Civil violence between liberal and conservative elements continued in mainland Mexico but rarely affected the Baja Peninsula; the biggest threat continued to be invaders from *el norte*. In 1853, backed by a group called the Knights of the Golden Circle, whose purpose was "to promote the benefits of slavery," American soldier of fortune William Walker and an army of mercenaries sailed into La Paz and seized the capital. Walker planned to establish Baja as the independent Republic of Sonora and Baja California, with himself as President, and then petition to be annexed by the United States. Mexican troops soon arrived to recapture La Paz, and Walker's army retreated first to Cabo San Lucas, then grudgingly northward along the Pacific coast, fighting battles at El Rosario, San Quintín and Ensenada. Walker finally returned to the United States, where he was arrested for violating the federal Neutrality Act of 1818.

Walker was later acquitted, and national press coverage of the trial earned him widespread support, including backing from newly elected U.S. President James Buchanan. He would invade Costa Rica and Nicaragua before he was executed in Honduras in 1860. An estimated 20,000 people died during Walker's forays, nearly matching the death toll of the entire Mexican War. Walker's tombstone reads, "Glory to the patriots who freed Central America of such a bloody pirate! Curses to those who brought him and to those who helped him."

Speaking of pirates: the wildest part of the Baja coast was invaded in 1857 by another kind of unscrupulous profiteer. American sea captain Charles Melville Scammon followed migrating gray whales to their calving waters in Laguna Ojo de Liebre. Using explosive harpoons, his men slaughtered more than a thousand of the whales and filled his ship to the brim with whale oil. But when Scammon returned to San Francisco with his huge haul, it could not be kept secret. The following year, Scammon's Lagoon became a scene of slaughter on an unprecedented scale as more than 50 whaling ships "harvested" thousands of whales. By the end of the 1859 season, no more gray whales could be found around Scammon's Lagoon. Nor would they be seen along the California coast until 1900, and Baja's gray whale population would not reach pre-whaling levels until 1996.

THE LAST WILDERNESS   After centuries of failed attempts to conquer Baja, investment began to accomplish what military might could not. As the population of southern Baja's few small settlements dwindled, businessmen from north of the border eyed the possibilities for exploiting the peninsula. Unscrupulous real estate operators dealt in dubious mining claims and acreages. The biggest of these frauds got its start in 1863, when Mexican president Benito Juárez leased the northern two-thirds of Baja to an American promoter, who turned around and sold his claim to an investment cartel, which gave "free California farmland" to new arrivals from the East. The company made its profits on ship passage to the new land and on selling supplies—construction materials, for instance. And fresh water. Settlers soon found that their 160-acre "farms" were located along the salt-encrusted shoreline of Bahía Magdalena. Within a few years, the most tenacious settlers had abandoned their holdings, and the Mexican government revoked the lease.

The idea of leasing the Baja wilderness to foreigners for hard currency was reinvented in 1883, when the Mexican government under President Porfírio Díaz passed the *ley de colonización*. The law allowed the government to replenish its treasury by opening up vast Baja land concessions for sale to American and European corporations. They would then theoretically help tame the frontier and develop a viable economy on the peninsula.

Foremost among these would-be developers was the International Company of Mexico, a Connecticut-based investment group, that envisioned a wheat-farming empire on northern Baja's Pacific coastal plain, from Ensenada to San Quintín. American farmers bought land and began to develop the plain, but when their first year's crop died from lack of rain, most decided that they had been duped and went back to the United States. The shareholders sold the International Company of Mexico to a British corporation with still more grandiose plans. Bringing shiploads of English farmers—who would not find it so easy to quit and go back home—they not only established a large flour mill and a shipping pier at San Quintín but even started construction on a railroad that, if completed, would have linked San Quintín with San Diego. But as it became obvious that the drought that had destroyed the American colony was not just a bad season but a permanent condition, the English farmers, too, abandoned Baja.

More successful were several mining concessions, especially the copper mine at Santa Rosalía started by a German company in 1885. The world's largest copper mine, it was later sold to the

French, but a German shipping company retained a monopoly on transporting the copper back to Europe. The foreign companies shaped the economy and architecture of the area, and many local residents today claim German or French ancestry.

Most of the concession holders in Baja did little to promote economic development. By the last years of the 19th century, Baja theoretically belonged to two dozen or so *ranchos* owned by wealthy Californians who rarely, if ever, set foot there. In fact, so many hundreds of acres of the parched and largely unexplored landscape were required to support a single steer that the Mexican cowboys who ranged this desert landscape were less herdsmen than bring-'em-back-alive hunters.

The discovery of gold in the northern mountains of Baja fueled the development of Ensenada, a port that was readily accessible from California but not from mainland Mexico; but the ore played out within a few years. Four centuries after its discovery, Baja remained Mexico's Alaska, irresistible to adventurers and almost impossible to live in.

THE HIGHWAY   The peninsula languished in the desert sun. The Mexican Revolution brought a brief flurry of action in 1911, when an independent rebel group known as the Magonistas joined forces with labor activists from the United States in a grandiose plan to seize Baja and form a leftist border republic. The rebels captured Mexicali and Tijuana with ease, but were soon forced to retreat into the mountains as Mexican army reinforcements arrived.

During the early 20th century, the border between the United States and Mexico was "open," without immigration restrictions. In 1920, the United States adopted the 18th Amendment, prohibiting the possession, sale and use of alcoholic beverages. Californians responded by hastening across the border to the saloons and dance halls of Old Mexico. The first luxury resorts were built in Rosarito and Ensenada, along with a plush gambling casino, and Hollywood celebrities flocked there. Tijuana, meanwhile, started earning a reputation for easy-to-find vice that has persisted to the present day. The tourist boom lasted only 12 years before Ensenada's high life was dealt a double blow: Prohibition was repealed in the United States, and gambling was declared illegal in Mexico.

Tijuana's sleazy side continued to thrive, especially after 1941, when World War II brought hundreds of thousands of young men to the naval base in San Diego, just a short bus ride from the border. But fears started to grow that Mexicans would take American fighting mens' jobs and women while they were overseas. In Los Angeles' 1943 Zoot Suit Riots, Anglo soldiers and sailors assaulted hundreds of Latinos in the streets while the police stood by and arrested the victims. The U.S. government closed the Mex-

Where the
Commons Survive

The biggest factor that shaped Baja in the first half of the 20th century was land reform. As you drive the Baja Highway today, you'll see many signs for place whose names are preceded by "EJ." This cryptic abbreviation stands for *ejido*, the Spanish word for "common." In rural Spain at the time Mexico was colonized, villagers used community land ("commons") owned by the church for grazing livestock and gathering firewood. The system was carried over to the New World by missionaries, and these *ejidos* fostered the growth of Indian villages near the missions until 1840, when church land was confiscated by the government. (The commons had largely been privatized out of existence in Europe by this time.) The *ejido* concept was revived in another land reform movement in 1930, when the government distributed millions of acres to landless *campesinos* for communal use.

The system has served to encourage settlement of Baja California, as irrigation wells have created more arable land. In recent years, such settlements have provided at least a small safety valve for Mexico's explosive population pressures, as thousands of Indians from the poor southern state of Oaxaca have taken the government up on offers to relocate to Baja.

New *ejidos* are created when rural people form a group and petition the government to grant them land that is currently not in use. The government finances the purchase of equipment and seeds, as well as the cost of drilling irrigation wells, through a chain of special banks called Banco Rural; the villagers pay the loans back with a share of the crops. The government's share is sold throughout Mexico in federally operated CONASUPO stores. In some areas today, *ejido* land is used for other purposes. Many tourist campgrounds along both coasts of Baja are owned and operated by *ejidos*.

All *ejido* land was owned by the government, and the people who lived and worked there were merely its custodians, until 1993, when the law was changed to give legal title to the *ejido* members; they could decide by majority vote whether to keep the land as community property or divide it among themselves as private property. The idea was to make it easier for *ejido* farmers to borrow money to modernize. Opponents have claimed that the privatization is a plot to expose *ejido* lands to the threat of bank foreclosure. So far, many *ejidos* in Baja are prospering in enterprises that range from cotton plantations to tourist campgrounds; others have not been so fortunate.

With the population growth brought by the *ejido* system and irrigation, Baja California achieved statehood in 1952.

ican border, passed a series of stringent immigration laws, and deported from the border states large numbers of Mexican Americans who could not prove that they had been born in the U.S.A. The deportations more than doubled the size of Tijuana. Ever since, it has been easy for United States citizens to enter Mexico but very difficult for Mexicans to come to the U.S. legally.

In 1952, the United States installed a radar station at San Felipe and built a highway (now Route 5) there from Mexicali. It was the first paved road into the Baja desert, opening Sea of Cortez beaches to travel-trailer campers, the RVers of that era.

The rugged, rocky road that linked Ensenada and the San Quintín Valley to the southern towns of Loreto, La Paz, San José los Cabos and Cabo San Lucas remained the kind of journey that legends are made of—a 2000-mile round trip with few food and water stops, no reliable gasoline supply and no tow trucks. Today, the rusted shells of abandoned cars and trucks from the 1950s are a common site along the highway, relics of the days when many vehicles that started off across the Baja wasteland never came back. The custom of caravanning in groups started in the early days of the Baja Highway to provide a way out of the desert in case of a breakdown. The Baja 1000, originally a motorcycle race from Tijuana to La Paz (since rerouted and expanded to include cars, trucks and all-terrain vehicles) and first held in 1967, brought the Baja Highway into the U.S. public consciousness.

Paving of the Baja Highway was completed in 1972, about the same time that motor homes were enjoying their greatest vogue in the United States. The flow of RV adventurers and "snowbirds" was immediate and enthusiastic. It has never slowed down. At the same time, the highway made farmering on southern Baja's coastal plain feasible—since there was now a way to get crops to market—and spurred the development of new population centers at Ciudad Constitución and Ciudad Insurgentes. Farming and tourism have made Baja one of the most prosperous areas of Mexico in recent years.

Baja California Sur, the southern half of the peninsula, was granted statehood in 1973; it was the last territory in Mexico to become a state.

▼▼▼▼▼▼▼▼▼▼
Culture

PEOPLE

Inhospitable terrain and lack of water severely limited the population of Baja until recent years. If all the various peoples—American Indian, Spanish, Anglo American, British, German, French and Japanese among them—who settled on the peninsula at one time or another had stayed, Baja would be a cultural melting pot on the same order as Alta California, its neighbor to the north. But instead, the population of Baja is made up of three ethnicities: mestizo, Indian and Anglo.

Mestizo (commonly called *mexicano*), the dominant race of Mexico, is a synthesis of Spanish and indigenous Indian cultures mingled over nearly five centuries. More than 95 percent of Baja's two million residents are mestizo. Seventy-five percent of the peninsula's people live along the border with the United States, and fewer than half of them were born in Baja. Newcomers are drawn by job opportunities in *maquiladoras* (duty-free factories) along the border, and by prospects of seasonal farm work on both sides of the border. People also move from mainland Mexico to Baja to be close to relatives living in California and to enjoy the peninsula's *tranquilo* way of life.

Few of the peninsula's native Indian people survived the epidemics that wiped out entire tribes in colonial times. Their only descendants are a few hundred Paipái Indians living in the Sierra de Juárez southeast of Ensenada. The Indian population of Baja today comes from the southern state of Oaxaca, where people have been encouraged by the government to relocate to Baja *ejidos* to alleviate tribal poverty and overpopulation. While most work on farms, growing numbers of Indians sell trinkets or beg in resort areas, and others travel from beach to beach selling souvenirs and provisions from the backs of trucks. Indians account for about 2 percent of Baja's permanent population. The polite word for American Indians in Mexico is *indígen* (pronounced almost like "Indian" in English), not the pejorative *indio*.

Although Anglos from the United States, Canada and England have sometimes accounted for a large part of the peninsula's population in the past, those not born in Baja were expelled following the Mexican Revolution of 1910–12. Today, official census figures show that only 2 percent of Baja's population is Anglo. But this is misleading, since most retirees and other expatriates who make their homes in Mexico legally reside in the United States; they are officially tourists, even though they may live in Baja year-round and return to the U.S. for a few days once or twice a year.

The regional cooking of Baja begins and ends with seafood. Shrimp *(camarones)*, lobster *(langosta)*, crab *(cangrejo)*, clams *(almejas)*, scallops *(callos)*, octopus *(pulpo)*, squid *(calamar)*, along with many varieties of fish *(pescado)* are ubiquitous ingredients all over Baja.

CUISINE

Baja tacos are wrapped in corn tortillas, but that is the extent of their resemblance to the familiar taco found in the United States. The Baja version will contain strips of stir-fried fish, crab or other seafood, salsa, guacamole and a cabbage marinade similar to cole slaw. Tacos are served at beachfront stands, open-air fast-food eateries called *comedores,* and inexpensive restaurants in all coastal areas of Baja.

Shrimp, crab and octopus are often served as cocktails *(cokteles)*—uncooked, marinated in lime juice, vinegar, oil, cilantro and spices and served in a tall glass. Similarly, fish is chopped or grated and marinated to make *ceviche*.

Shrimp is commonly served in garlic sauce *(al mojo de ajo)* or breaded *(empanizados)*. Prawns *(gambas)*, like shrimp but larger, may be sliced open and stuffed *(rellena)* with cheese, crabmeat or other fillings. Crabs are typically steamed *(al vapor)* or deviled *(al diablo)*. Stone crab claws come cracked and sauteed in butter.

Pacific spiny lobsters, the kind commonly caught off the Baja coast, are sliced in half lengthwise with a big, sharp knife and grilled with butter, garlic and spices. This way of preparing lobster, called *estilo Puerto Nuevo* after the major lobster-fishing port south of Rosarito, is favored throughout Baja.

Clams of several varieties are among the most common foods along the Sea of Cortez coast. Chocolate clams (pronounced "cho-co-LA-tay") are not to be missed. These fat clams in dark brown shells are almost the size of hamburgers; order a half-dozen and you may need a doggie bag. They are steamed and sliced in half inside the shell before serving.

Menus often say just "pescado" and serve whatever white-fleshed fish the sea provides that day—typically snapper *(huachinango)*, yellowtail *(jurel)*, mackerel *(sierra)*, tarpon *(sabalo)* or halibut *(lenguado)*. These are prepared in many ways—in garlic sauce *(al mojo de ajo)*, in a salsa of chopped tomatoes, onions, olives, cilantro and spices *(veracruzano)*, in a savory fish stew *(guisado)*, or cleaned, breaded and fried whole *(empanizado entero)*. Order one of these and you'll often get a red snapper big enough to feed a whole family. Better restaurants feature steaks from large fish such as tuna *(atún)*, swordfish *(pez espada)*, shark *(tiburón)* and the most delicious of all fish in Baja waters, mahi-mahi *(dorado)*.

Baja lacks the abundance of tropical fruits and vegetables available in other parts of Mexico. Though much of northern Baja California is farmland, most of its produce is exported to the United States. If a restaurant serves vegetables other than the standard side dishes of beans and rice, they usually come out of a can. During harvest times, which vary depending on the crop, vendors sell local produce at roadside stands. Surplus crops are also sold from the backs of trucks that make the rounds of beaches in areas inhabited by campers. One week the crop may be tomatoes, the next week strawberries or onions. *Elotes*—steaming hot ears of corn served with chili powder, lime and cream—are a specialty at some roadside stands.

The Mexican food served in restaurants is much the same as you would expect to find in a typical "Mexican" restaurant in the United States. Since many more gringo tourists than locals eat in restaurants, the menus focus on the dishes that are most familiar north of the border—tacos, enchiladas, tamales and burritos. *Chiles rellenos*, a popular dish in Baja restaurants, are different from their U.S. counterparts. Poblanos—large, mild, dark green chiles shaped like bell peppers—are filled with cheese or seafood, breaded and fried.

The Mexican food served in most restaurants is not as *picante* as elsewhere in Mexico. The *salsa fresca* that comes with tortilla chips is fresh, as the name implies, but usually not very hot. If you request *salsa picante*, you will invariably get Tabasco sauce bottled in Louisiana. Another concession to gringo tastes? No: imported Tabasco is the kind of hot sauce most often found in Baja grocery stores. Like most things, it's cheaper and easier to get hot sauce from southern California than from the Mexican mainland.

The language barrier between English and Spanish should never be perceived as an obstacle to visiting Baja. Locals have a long history of contact with gringos and may even have one or two in their family trees. Surrounded by bilingual and tourist-oriented signs, and bombarded by American television, even locals of limited education understand a fair amount of English, though they may be self-conscious about trying to speak it. In fact, "Spanglish"—a crazy-quilt mix of Spanish and English words with elastic rules of grammar—approaches the status of an unofficial "official language" in Baja. So many people like to practice speaking English that the language barrier you're most likely to run into is when you find yourself in a lengthy conversation *in English*—and can't understand a word.

LANGUAGE

Today, more and more Baja residents come from the mainland, where English is not heard as much. Mexican students are required to attend school until the age of 14. Unless they drop out, they are required to take two years of English in high school. The dropout rate is high in some poor regions of Mexico, but not in Baja. Students in Mexican universities must be reasonably fluent in English to graduate. So in general, educated middle-class Mexicans speak English well; unskilled laborers do not. Indian children who grow up on tribal land are not required to attend school, so adult Indians rarely understand English and sometimes cannot even speak much Spanish.

Speaking fluent Spanish enhances any trip to Mexico, of course. But what if, like most people who live in the United States, you don't? Many people who have never studied Spanish worry more than they ought to about traveling south of the border. One of the fundamental lessons of foreign travel is that people can communicate even though they don't know a word of each other's languages. Words help, but your tone of voice, the expression on your face, and gestures or sign language often count for more.

Even though English is widely understood, people will relate to you better if you attempt to speak Spanish, no matter how poorly. It pays in smiles if you study for your trip by practicing a few useful phrases like *"¿Cuánto vale esto?"* (How much is this worth?), *"La cuenta, por favor"* (the check, please), *"¿Tiene usted una habitación para la noche?"* (Do you have a room for the night?) and *"¿No habría modo de resolver el problema de otra manera?"* (Isn't there another way to resolve this problem?). If your comprehension of Spanish leaves something to be desired, try to ask questions that can be answered with a yes or no, with one word, or with a number. It can be very frustrating to ask for directions and receive a cheerful reply that's so long, fast and complicated that you can't make sense of it. Better to ask questions like "Is this the right way to _____?" "How many blocks?" "On the right or left?"

Of the many books available for studying Spanish on your own, the one I have found most helpful and friendly is *Spanish Lingo for the Savvy Gringo* by Elizabeth Reid, who spent eight years teaching English to Mexicans in Rosarito. Her Spanglish approach to vocabulary building is ideal for Baja travelers. The book is available in many southern California and Baja bookstores or from In One EAR Publications, 29481 Manzanita Drive, Campo, CA 91906-1128; 800-356-9315.

Many people who have studied Spanish in school find themselves helpless when it comes to actually communicating in Mexico. Once you've learned it, the vocabulary stays stored in the deep recesses of the mind, but it's often hard to bring it to the surface after years of disuse. Before you leave for Baja, a few weeks using aids such as cassette tapes can help attune your ear and tongue to the language. A painless way to tune into Spanish is to spend your TV-viewing hours watching Spanish-language cable channels or rented videos. The Mexican motion-picture industry is undergoing a renaissance these days; internationally acclaimed films such as *Como Agua Para Chocolate (Like Water for Chocolate)* are well worth watching in Spanish with or without the English subtitles. Most U.S. video stores can order Mexican films and Spanish-version videocassettes (subtitled or dubbed) of almost any popular Hollywood film.

MUSIC   In many restaurants, especially in Ensenada, La Paz and Los Cabos, you will be approached by groups of strolling musicians. They play at tables for a fixed rate per song, often cutting the restaurant in for a small amount. In Baja, the going rate is about five pesos per song for each band member. In dollars, a romantic trio gets about US$2 for a song, and a large *mariachi* or *conjunto norteño* may get up to about $6 a song.

The most familiar Mexican musical groups are mariachis, the ensembles of musicians dressed in big sombreros and tight clothes decorated with gold or silver piping. The bands, made up of five to eight or more guitar, *guitarrón* (bass guitar), violin and trumpet players, originated in Guadalajara in the 19th century, and their ornate outfits represent the suits worn by *charros*, or cowboys, of that era on formal occasions. Though Guadalajara is still the mariachi capital, all parts of Mexico have good mariachis. Their music follows traditional forms, especially *rancheras*, cowboy songs that usually have to do with love or drinking, and *corridas*, folk songs that tell stories, often with patriotic, topical or tragic themes. Most of the standard rancheras sung by mariachis today were composed from the 1920s to the 1950s. The most famous and prolific of ranchera composers, José Alfredo Jiménez, is memorialized by a larger-than-life statue in Mexico City's Plaza Garibaldi. Musicians continue to write corridas, though.

In the border region, it's not unusual for the newer *corridas* (folk songs) to tell how brave drug smugglers met their sad fates.

Conjuntos norteños are the traditional musical groups of the Mexican border states. Neither as large nor as formal as mariachis, a norteño group usually numbers from three to five members, dressed in cowboy hats, boots, jeans and western shirts. Though they may look like *norteamericano* country-western bands and play many of the same standard rancheras and corridas as mariachis do, the norteños have a distinctive style that people in other parts of the country sometimes ridicule as provincial but which Mexicans from both sides of the border adore. Besides guitars and a guitarrón, common norteño instruments include the accordion and the snare drum, neither of which is ever used by mariachis, as well as the violin.

Tríos románticos usually wear modern business suits and consist of a guitar player, a *requinto* player (the instrument looks like a miniature guitar and sounds like a mandolin) and a percussionist who plays *maracas* and other small rhythm instruments. Their repertoire typically includes contemporary Mexican pop music, translations of American easy-listening tunes set to latin rhythms, and traditional Mexican songs.

Listen to any Mexican musical group playing requests in a tourist restaurant, and you may get the impression that the only songs they know are "Guantanamera," "Cielito Lindo" and "El Rancho Grande." In fact, hundreds of traditional Mexican songs are included in the repertoire of every strolling musician. Get familiar with a few others and impress your companions when the musicians come around to your table. For starters, try "Las

Laureles" (The Laurels), a classic Mexican love song that few gringos know, or the haunting "Peregrina" (Traveler), written to honor a blonde American reporter with whom Mexican governor Felipe Carrillo Puerto had fallen in love.

FOUR

The Border

Coils of razor wire top the 150-mile-long chain-link steel fence, nicknamed the Tortilla Curtain, that stretches from the Pacific Ocean to the Colorado River delta, separating the state of California from the state of Baja California. Most of Baja's population lives within seven kilometers of the border, enticed from all over Mexico by the promise of steady factory jobs in the *maquiladoras*, the dream of crossing the border for better pay in southern California or, in some cases, the fast-money gamble of smuggling drugs or guns. Rich with opportunity, wracked with poverty and desperation, the California–Baja border forms a sociological fault line between two lands that are utterly unlike one another.

Although it seems unlikely that many readers would opt to spend their vacations in the high-stress border zone when so many fantastic beaches and fascinating hideaways lie farther south, crossing the border—twice—is unavoidable. Fortunately, it's also easy. Crossing northward, however, takes considerably longer.

This chapter contains complete information on crossing the U.S./Mexican border in both directions at each port of entry between California and Baja California. It shows you how to appreciate Baja's largest cities, Tijuana and Mexicali, as well as the smaller border towns of Tecate and Algodones. Along the way, dirt-road side trips can take you to two hidden destinations in little-known Parque Nacional Constitución de 1857, far removed from the border cities—Laguna Hanson, Baja's only natural lake, and the secluded hot springs of Cañon de Guadalupe.

Tijuana

Tijuana is a city of paradoxes: one of the wealthiest cities in Mexico, brimming with free-trade economic opportunities—yet sobered by the suffering of hundreds of thousands of people living in desperate poverty. All Spanish-speaking "undocumented workers" found in California, Nevada, Oregon and Washington are deported to Tijuana, regardless of their state or country of origin. According to unofficial estimates, as many as half a million Tijuana residents either are on their way to the United States or have recently been expelled from there. If you wander too far from the main drag, you may find where they live—in makeshift huts of cardboard and salvaged plywood without electricity or plumbing, jammed haphazardly onto vacant lots around the industrial zone. It's an aspect of "hidden" Tijuana that most visitors are content to leave undiscovered.

Tijuana got its start in 1889 as a customs house on the edge of a large cattle ranch called Rancho Tia Juana, meaning "Aunt Jane." The outpost was of little importance until the 1920s, when Prohibition sent hordes of Californians across the border for liquor, as well as horse races, casino gambling and sleazy nightclubs featuring stage shows whose depravity has passed into legend. In the early thirties, Prohibition was repealed in the United States, and casino gambling was banned in Mexico. Tijuana's fortunes floundered.

President Lázaro Cárdenas sought to rescue the city's economy by declaring Baja a free-trade zone, a move designed to stimulate retail sales of imported goods to southern California shoppers at tax-exempt discount prices. The plan initially met with only limited success, as the Great Depression strangled the flow of free-spending shoppers across the border. When economic salvation finally arrived, it came in the form of World War II, bringing a huge U.S. naval force to San Diego, just 18 miles north of Tijuana. A hectic red-light district flowered overnight as hookers and street hustlers from all over Mexico were drawn to Tijuana like pelicans to a fishing fleet.

Tijuana earned its reputation as the quintessential badass border town, and it has yet to live down that reputation. Half a century later, many Americans' mental picture of Tijuana is a city brimming with dark-alley easy, slightly slimy, sticky-fingered guilty pleasures. The fact is, today you can find more lowlife and scary cops in Los Angeles than in Tijuana.

CROSSING THE BORDER

Tijuana's port of entry, San Ysidro, is said to be the world's busiest border crossing. More than 60 million people cross here each year—pedestrians and bus riders as well as motorists in 15 million private cars.

Crossing south into Tijuana is easy. Route 5 from San Diego takes you directly to the border, where Mexican officials normally wave cars with U.S. plates right through. Keep to the center lanes as the freeway takes you over the Río Tijuana, a deep concrete ditch that flows northward into the United States, on the rare occasions when it flows at all. Right on the other side of the river, you'll find yourself in a dizzying three-level freeway interchange. Follow the signs to "Downtown/Centro" to reach the

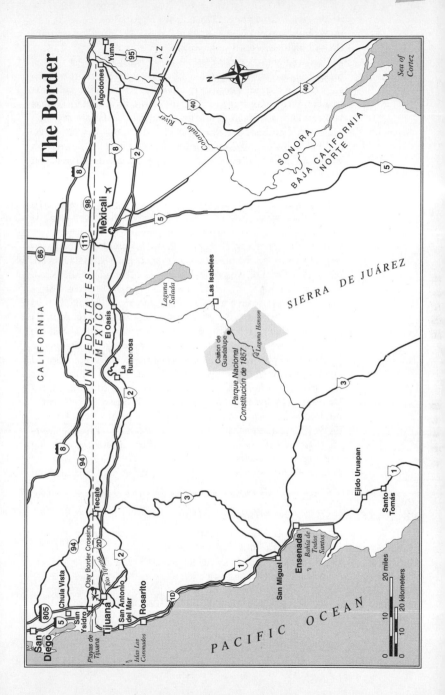

downtown tourist zone, "Paseo de los Héroes" to reach the cultural center and public market, and "Mex 1-D Cuota" to get onto the toll highway south to Ensenada.

Reentering the United States is a different story. Even though most gringos get through U.S. Customs with no more than a glance and a couple of cursory questions, every car must still come to a complete stop; this obstructs the traffic flow enough so that you can expect to wait in line for an hour or so before reaching the gates. The lines are longest on Sundays and U.S. holidays, and the wait can be as much as four hours. Lines are shortest on weekdays before 10 a.m. and after 10 p.m.; at those times you can often get across the border in as little as 20 minutes.

Here's a secret for those who simply must brave the border at rush hour: The U.S. inspection area has 24 gates, of which 16 are open at any given time. They are evenly divided between the east and west sides of a center median filled with street vendors' stalls. The west lanes come from Highway 1, downtown and Paseo de los Héroes—all the places gringo tourists go. The east lanes are fed by Via Oriente, Paseo de Tijuana and Avenida Padre Kino, the main thoroughfares on the northeast side of the river. Rarely used by visitors from the U.S., these lanes typically take half as long as the west lanes. To reach them, cross the river on Avenida Independencia, which runs between the Centro Cultural and the Palacio Municipal, and turn left on any of the three main streets.

A second port of entry, the Otay Border Crossing, is located 20 minutes east of downtown Tijuana's San Ysidro crossing, past the airport. It often takes half as long to cross into the United States at Otay because there is markedly less private car traffic. Located in a major industrial zone, it is the border's truck route, used by most tractor-trailer rigs and many passenger buses. Hours are 6 a.m. to 10 p.m., and the trucks stack up for the morning opening; traffic clears after midmorning. To get there, take the *libre* highway from Rosarito or Boulevard Agua Caliente from

✔ CHECK THESE OUT—UNIQUE SIGHTS

- Wander through a miniature Mexico, complete with tiny skyscrapers and Mayan temples, at **Mexitlán** in Tijuana. *page 65*
- Plunge into **Mercado Hidalgo**, the busy public market in the Zona Río, for Tijuana's most authentic cultural experience aside from bullfighting. *page 69*
- See how **Tecate** beer is made—and sample the product—in the town of the same name. *page 74*
- Explore Mexico's largest Chinatown, **La Chinesca**, just a few blocks' walk from the border in downtown Mexicali. *page 80*

downtown Tijuana, continuing on Avenida Cuahutémoc (beware the dizzying *glorieta*, or traffic circle, around the statue of the Aztec leader for whom the avenue is named) and following the signs to "Airport" and "Otay Border Crossing." Sounds easy, but a co-pilot is almost essential for navigating the *glorietas*.

Visitors who cross the border into Tijuana on foot can walk directly from the customs and immigration area through **Viva Tijuana**, a mall full of curio shops and restaurants, then over a pedestrian bridge that spans the Tijuana River, and be in the downtown tourist zone in a matter of minutes. It's so easy that you might consider leaving your car at one of the huge parking lots on the U.S. side while you check out downtown Tijuana, then reclaiming it when you're ready to hit the highway south.

SIGHTS

As you cross the border by car, look for the giant glass piñata that marks the entrance to **Mexitlán**, a rooftop museum above a parking garage. Although located just south of the Tijuana River, a three-block walk from Avenida Revolución, this park remains "hidden"—albeit in plain sight—because gringo tourists rarely venture away from the main drag to see it. Business has been so slow at this highly touted attraction that its promoters sometimes threaten to move it to Mexico City. Too bad—it's a mini-spectacle worth seeing. Elaborate dioramas contain more than 200 scale models of ancient temples, colonial buildings, historic sites from all over Mexico, including a replica of the country's tallest skyscraper and a replica of the 1968 Olympic Stadium in Mexico City, complete with 100,000 tiny, handcarved spectators. Admission. ~ Avenida Ocampo at Calle 2; 38-41-01.

◄ *HIDDEN*

Avenida Revolución, the heart of the tourist zone, runs south from the border for 11 blocks. Visitors crossing the pedestrian bridge get there by walking two blocks along Calle 1, encountering many street vendors along the way. Motorists cross the river a few blocks to the east and immediately find themselves in an amazing multilevel traffic whirl. The Calle 2 and Calle 3 exits lead to Avenida Revolución, where parking lots are plentiful if not cheap. Curio shops, boutiques and galleries share the avenue with nightclubs, sports betting parlors, hotels and restaurants, all packed with Americans. Along Avenida Revolución, the sleazy character of old-time Tijuana has been transformed for better or worse by international chains; within a couple of blocks are a Jack-in-the-Box, a KFC, a Burger King and a Hard Rock Café. Older buildings converted to mini-malls house hundreds of small shops side-by-side with chic international designer outlets, all vying to assist tourists with their duty-free shopping needs.

Running diagonally away from the border crossing and Mexitlán along the west bank of the Tijuana River, the **Zona Río** represents contemporary Tijuana in sharp contrast to the traditional tourist zone. Interspersed among financial institutions, upscale hotels and stylish retail stores line the broad Paseo de los Héroes. Even though a 30-foot-tall bronze statue of U.S. President Abraham Lincoln presides over the paseo from a traffic circle, local government has been largely unsuccessful in its strategy of enticing American tourists to this flashy urban redevelopment area.

The main attraction of the Zona Río is the **Centro Cultural Tijuana**, the hub of the city's performing arts scene, nicknamed "La Bola" because of its shape, which resembles the world's largest golf ball. The symphony orchestra, the ballet folklórico, repertory companies and lecturers use the center's 1000-seat theater. Also in the cultural center are an art exhibition gallery that presents changing shows by local artists, an astronomy room, and the big, round IMAX theater that gives the center its distinctive shape; it shows wraparound movies in English and Spanish. The highlight for many visitors is the **Museo de las Identidades Mexicanas**, an anthropology museum that explains the complex cultural heritage of the Mexican people. Admission to museums. ~ Avenida Paseo de los Héroes at Calle Mina; 84-11-11.

If you drive south from the tourist zone, Avenida Revolución curves around to the east to become **Boulevard Agua Caliente**, lined with big, modern hotels and shiny new restaurants. The **Toreo de Tijuana** (see "Sed, Sangre y Sol" in this chapter), the older of the city's two bullrings, marks the beginning of the hotel strip. Route 1 *libre*, the free highway to Ensenada, turns off to the south at the bullring.

At the east end of the hotel zone is **Caliente Race Track**. Formerly called the Hipódromo de Agua Caliente, the famous race track for which the boulevard was named ended live horse racing in 1993. Greyhounds race there nightly as well as Saturday and Sunday afternoons. There is also betting on closed-circuit horse race broadcasts from California, viewed on television monitors in the track's sports club. ~ Boulevard Agua Caliente at Avenida Salinas; 81-78-11.

LODGING   The tall, Art Deco-ish **Hotel Nelson** has 92 clean, plain rooms with carpeting and private baths. You can take your choice of a windowless, dungeonlike interior room or a pricier, noisier one that has a TV, a phone and a window overlooking the heart of Tijuana's tourist zone. ~ Avenida Revolución 501; 85-43-03, fax 85-43-02. BUDGET.

The **Hotel Caesar** is an atmospheric old-timer from Prohibition days. The 42 clean, comfortable, air-conditioned rooms have the kind of character that comes with age, and the halls are decorated with framed photos and posters of bullfights. ~ Avenida Revolución 827; 88-16-66. BUDGET.

Down-and-dirty budget travelers might consider the **Villa Juvinil Tijuana.** Set in a parklike athletic complex, this unaffiliated and generally unkempt youth hostel across the river from Tijuana's action has dormitory-style sleeping rooms with school-style lockers and co-ed rest rooms down the hall. The good news is that rates are about $5 a night. The bad news? Curfew is 10 p.m. ~ Avenida Padre Kino 22320; 84-75-10. BUDGET.

The six-story **Hotel Lucerna** was a showpiece of the Zona Río district's redevelopment in the 1970s. When the tourist boom in the Zona Río failed to materialize, the hotel began to suffer from inattentive maintenance. The 179 guest rooms and suites have a lived-in look and a resort feel, making for a good deal at the lower end of the moderate range. Most look out over the

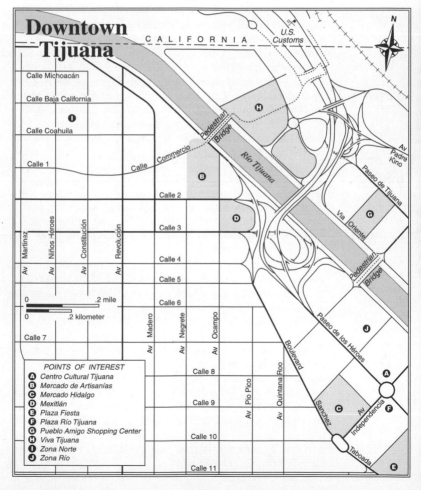

Downtown Tijuana

CALIFORNIA

U.S. Customs

N

Calle Michoacán

Calle Baja California

O

Calle Coahuila

Pedestrian Bridge

Río Tijuana

Av Padre Kino

Calle Commercio

Calle 1

Calle

H

Paseo de Tijuana

B

Calle 2

Via Oriente

G

D

Calle 3

Pedestrian Bridge

Av Martinaz

Av Niños Héroes

Av Constitución

Av Revolución

Calle 4

Calle 5

0   .2 mile
0   .2 kilometer

Calle 6

Calle 7

Av Madero

Av Negrete

Av Ocampo

Paseo de los Héroes

J

Boulevard

Av Pio Pico

Av Quintana Roo

A

POINTS OF INTEREST
A *Centro Cultural Tijuana*
B *Mercado de Artisanías*
C *Mercado Hidalgo*
D *Mexitlán*
E *Plaza Fiesta*
F *Plaza Río Tijuana*
G *Pueblo Amigo Shopping Center*
H *Viva Tijuana*
I *Zona Norte*
J *Zona Río*

Calle 8

Calle 9

Calle 10

Calle 11

Sanchez

Av Independencia

C

F

Taboada

E

swimming pool and the lush gardens that surround it. ~ Paseo de los Héroes 10902; 34-20-00, fax 34-24-00. MODERATE.

To find out where the boulevard and race track got their name ("hot water"), spend a night at the **Holiday Inn Express—Tijuana Agua Caliente**, where the facilities include a large whirlpool tub fed by natural hot springs, as well as a swimming pool, sauna and exercise room. Guest rooms are spacious and nicely furnished, and most have one queen-size or two double beds. ~ Paseo de los Héroes 18818; 34-69-01, fax 34-69-12. MODERATE.

Most upscale hotels in Tijuana are found along Boulevard Agua Caliente. The largest and finest, the **Gran Hotel Tijuana** has 422 light, spacious rooms splashed with fiesta-color accents in twin 25-story towers that are Tijuana's tallest buildings. In-room amenities range from cable TV to computer data ports. The hotel has a heated pool, tennis courts and a jacuzzi. The higher the room, the better the view and the steeper the rate. ~ Boulevard Agua Caliente 4500; 81-70-00, fax 81-70-16, or 800-472-6385 in the U.S. DELUXE.

HIDDEN ▶ For lower-priced accommodations in the Agua Caliente area, try the **Motel Padre Kino**. There is nothing special about the plain, almost drab motel rooms, but for lodging within walking distance of the race track and country club, the prices—in the $25 range—are unbeatable. ~ Boulevard Agua Caliente 3; 86-42-08. BUDGET.

DINING

Along Avenida Revolución are dozens of budget-priced places for lunch—many of them hauntingly familiar. For something completely different from the international burger franchises, try **La Especial**, a busy taco-and-enchilada eatery that still feels like a typical Mexican *comedor*. ~ Avenida Revolución 718; 85-66-54. BUDGET.

Pedrin's, across from the jai alai fronton, ranks high among Tijuana seafood restaurants. *Camarones* (shrimp), *langosta* (lobster) and *cabrilla* (sea bass) are specialties. You can dine alfresco in a second-story garden setting overlooking the busy tourist zone below. ~ Avenida Revolución 1115; 85-40-52. DELUXE.

One of the longest-established and best-known restaurants in the tourist zone, **Tia Juana Tilly's** is packed with noisy gringos morning, noon and night. There's a good reason. Tilly's serves big portions of some of the best Mexican food on the border—not only familiar dishes but also more exotic ones from distant parts of Mexico—*cochinita pibil* (pork barbecued in a Seville orange marinade), *pollo en mole* (chicken in chile-and-chocolate sauce) and enchiladas *suizas* (chicken enchiladas in a tangy sauce with ranch cheese melted over them). ~ Avenida Revolución at Calle 7; 85-60-24. MODERATE.

The Caesar salad was invented at **Caesar's**. As atmospheric now as in Prohibition days, the restaurant still serves salads made according to the original recipe (though not by the same chef). Dinner only. ~ Avenida Revolución 827; 88-27-94. MODERATE.

Restaurant prices drop steeply even one block off Avenida Revolución. Discover the **Café Pekín**, a long-established, unpretentious restaurant one block south of Revolución where they serve distinctively Baja-style Chinese-Mexican fare—egg rolls, stir-fries and heaping bowls of fried rice enlivened with hot chiles. ~ Avenida Constitución 1435; 85-24-30. BUDGET.

◄ HIDDEN

The dozens of fast-food stalls at **Mercado Hidalgo**, the city's main public market near the Zona Río, offer a varied choice of inexpensive dishes from all over Mexico. For a dollar or two, you can buy a fistful of fish tacos or pineapple tamales, a grilled pork sandwich, a steaming bowl of *posole* stew or a plastic plate of beans and rice with an egg on top, and eat it at a picnic table at a little distance from the market fray. ~ Avenida Independencia at Boulevard Sanchez Taboada. BUDGET.

The penetrating stare of a huge portrait of Salvador Dali—sets the stage for the artsy atmosphere of **Gypsys**. This long, narrow restaurant specializes in Spanish-style *tapas* and also serves full meals, such as Spanish *tortillas*—an omeletlike egg-and-potato dish, no relation to the Mexican tortilla. The restaurant is in a shopping center just half a mile from the San Ysidro border crossing. Closed Monday. ~ Pueblo Amigo Shopping Center; 83-60-06. MODERATE.

In the Agua Caliente area, **La Leña** is a clean, modern steak house serving thick mesquite-broiled slabs of beef and northern Mexico ranch specialties such as *carne asada*—beef strips barbecued in a spicy red-chile marinade—and *gaonera,* a steak sliced down the center and stuffed with guacamole and cheese. ~ Boulevard Agua Caliente 4560; 86-47-52. MODERATE.

You'll find an abundance of fresh produce, along with meat stalls that may convert the squeamish to vegetarianism, at the big, busy **Mercado Hidalgo**, the city's main public market, located a block from the Centro Cultural Tijuana. ~ Avenida Independencia at Boulevard Sanchez Taboada.

GROCERIES

The major supermarket chain in Tijuana and all of Baja California is **Calimax**. There are branches on Avenida Constitución between Calles 1 and 2; on Avenida Revolución between Calles 9 and 10 on Paseo de los Héroes at Avenida Cuahutémoc; and the flagship store on Boulevard Agua Caliente across from the Caliente race track. All are open 24 hours a day. ~ 88-08-94.

Look for Mexican and imported gourmet foodstuffs at **Ley**, located in the Pueblo Amigo. ~ Via Oriente 9211; 84-27-71.

SHOPPING It doesn't get much more touristy than Tijuana's **Mercado de Artisanías**, located where visitors step off the pedestrian bridge from the border over the Tijuana River. Here, vendors display Mexican "arts and crafts"—mostly factory-made curios and gift items —along with a fair selection of Guatemalan clothing. The main purpose in establishing this open market was to keep street vendors from clogging the sidewalks of Avenida Revolución. ~ Calle 2 between Avenidas Ocampo and Negrete.

A better bet is the shopping area at **Mexitlán**, where fixed-price retail shops offer authentic folk art—fine silver jewelry, ceramics, woodcarving and weaving from all parts of Mexico. ~ Avenida Ocampo at Calle 2; 38-41-01.

Avenida Revolución is so shopper-friendly that you'll find an array of possibilities for every taste and budget here. You may have to fend off youths whose job is to steer you into their families' stores, and you may have to dig through endless clutters of onyx elephants and huge, brocaded mariachi sombreros, but in the end you'll most likely find something that tugs at your purse-strings. Leather goods, from boots and belts to suitcases, are the best bargain in Tijuana, and there are plenty of others. A wooden dance mask from Michoacán? A delicately embroidered Oaxaca wedding dress? Guess jeans or Ralph Lauren sportswear? Avenida Revolución is the place to look.

Start your shopping spree at **Tolán**, reputedly Tijuana's finest Mexican folk art gallery. Prices here may be high, but the quality and selection of both museum-quality indigenous work and contemporary ethnic paintings, jewelry, sculpture, weaving and ceramics set the standard for comparison in Baja gift shopping. ~ Avenida Revolución between Calles 7 and 8; 88-36-37.

Nearby is **Sanborn's**, part of the nationwide department store chain that is the Mexican counterpart of Macy's. Sanborn's has responded to the invasion of international discount stores like Wal-Mart and Sam's Club by stocking higher-quality merchandise to attract a more upscale clientele. In Tijuana, with its free-trade status, this policy has translated into attempts to tantalize American tourists with quality imports, from Japanese consumer electronics to French perfume, at prices somewhat lower than you'd expect to find in San Diego or L.A. ~ Avenida Revolución at Calle 8; 88-14-62.

Though you'd never know it if all you saw was ultra-touristy Avenida Revolución, Mexicans too come from far and wide to indulge in Tijuana shopping sprees. **Pueblo Amigo**—within easy walking distance of the border crossing—and **Plaza Río Tijuana** and **Plaza Fiesta** farther along Paseo de los Héroes are landmarks in the Zona Río. All three indoor shopping malls contain an improbably large number of stores selling silver jewelry from Taxco, the famous silversmithing center in the southern Mexico state of

Guerrero. There are also many stores featuring quality European and Asian imports—as well as imports from the United States, aimed at Tijuana's growing young urban professional market.

From the sleazy to the ultrachic, nightlife is one of the main attractions that lures visitors over the border to Tijuana. Many never get farther than Avenida Revolución, which becomes a bright, loud, touristy dance club scene after dark. Street barkers will try persistently to lure into their clubs any gringo male who looks like he has money to spend. You know you're not drunk enough yet if you find yourself trying to figure out why you went to another country just to hang out in a **Hard Rock Café**. ~ Avenida Revolución at Calle 2; 85-25-13. For something a little more un-American, check out **Red Square**, with its vaguely Kremlinesque facade and its rooftop bar overlooking the main street. ~ Avenida Revolución at Calle 6; 88-27-82. The last of the old-timers, **Bar San Marcos** dates back to World War II and entertains its patrons with lavish mariachi productions. ~ Avenida Revolución at Calle 5; 88-27-94. **Disco Salsa** blares high-energy Latino dance music until dawn. ~ Avenida Revolución between Calles 1 and 2; 34-86-15. Bars and discos along Revolución typically stay open until 3 a.m. on weekdays, 5 a.m. on weekends.

Just off Avenida Reforma are a number of "hidden" places that you don't have to be a tourist to go to. You'll find Latino dance rhythms, cheap tequila and plenty of usually amiable Mexican rowdiness at **La Estrella**. Cover for men. ~ Calle 6 east of Avenida Revolución; 88-13-49. The pedestrian alleyway that starts by the tourist information office at Avenida Revolución and Calle 1 and runs diagonally to Avenida Constitución is lined with no-name, hole-in-the-wall bars showcasing mariachis and marimba groups in a ceaseless battle of the bands.

Another side of Tijuana nightlife can be found in the Zona Río, the recently redeveloped commercial district around Paseo de los Héroes and Calle Diego Rivera, east of the traditional downtown tourist zone. Discos here tend to be sleek and trendy, catering to upper-class Mexicans as much as to gringos. Many have dress codes and are selective about who they allow in. One of the longest-established clubs in the area, **¡OH! Laser Club** still has the splashiest light show in town. Cover. ~ Paseo de los Héroes 56; 84-02-67. **Baby Rock**, part of a chain of chic Mexican rock-and-roll clubs found mostly in beach resort towns, is frequented by the city's young, moneyed, and fashionable. Cover. ~ Calle Diego Rivera 1482; 84-94-38. **Jala la Jarra**, next to the Guadalajara Grill, is another popular disco, always packed on weekends. Cover. ~ Calle Diego Rivera at Paseo de los Héroes; 34-30-65.

Tijuana has the liveliest gay scene between the border and Puerto Vallarta. Things get started late. **Mike's Disco**, a prominent club in the heart of the tourist zone, draws mostly male crowds with its nightly Mexican female impersonator stage shows. They start at midnight and continue until nearly dawn. ~ Avenida Revolución 1220; 85-35-34.

Tijuana's red-light district is the **Zona Norte**, between Calle Comercio (Calle 1) and the Tijuana River, within walking distance of the pedestrian bridge from the border crossing. The district centers on Calle Coahuila between Avenida Martinez and Avenida Niños Héroes, which run one-way in opposite directions for convenient cruising. No-nonsense gay bars, strip joints and sordid little establishments of every description pack this self-consciously seedy district where for a price you can get anything you want and (if you're not careful) more. Assume that everyone you meet here, regardless of gender or putative sexual preference, is a trained professional.

If gambling is your preferred vice, there are ten branches of **Caliente Race & Sports Books** around the city, including the big **Centro Caliente** on Revolución, where you can bet on televised sporting events daily until midnight. ~ Avenida Revolución at Calle 4; 88-34-25. Or you can phone your wagers in to **Caliente Phone Bet** (82-84-48) and watch the game on a big-screen TV at **Yuppie's Sports Café** in the Zona Río. ~ Paseo de los Héroes at Calle Diego Rivera; 34-23-24. Another option is jai alai, a fast-as-a-horserace game played by teams hurling a hard rubber ball at speeds up to 160 miles an hour according to rules guaranteed to bewilder the ignorant. You can watch it, and place parimutuel bets, at the **Palacio Fronton**, an entertainment complex that also houses three restaurants and a disco. Cover. ~ Avenida Revolución at Calle 8; 38-42-42. There's video horse racing and live greyhound racing nightly and on weekend afternoons at the **Caliente Race Track**, an 11-kilometer drive or bus trip south of downtown. You can't miss its grandiose Moorish-style entrance, which dates back to 1916. ~ Boulevard Agua Caliente; 81-78-11.

BEACHES & PARKS

PLAYAS DE TIJUANA 🏃 This string of narrow beaches, where Route 1-D, the toll highway south to Ensenada, reaches the Pacific coast and turns south, is fronted by Tijuana's nicest residential area. The concrete and chain-link border fence runs across the north end of the beach. Although the beaches are open to the public, neighborhood security and border patrols make sunbathing uncomfortable and camping unthinkable. Most visitors pass by Playas de Tijuana in favor of the developed resort area of Rosarito, ten minutes' drive farther on (see Chapter Five). ~ Paseo Playas de Tijuana, off Route 1-D less than a kilometer north of the tool booths.

Sed, Sangre y Sol

The poetic turn of speech "silk, blood and sun" is often used to refer to bullfighting, a spectacle that is popular throughout Mexico, and nowhere more so than along the Baja California border. Latinos who live across the border in California and Arizona, where bullfights are illegal, flock to the *corridas de toros* in Tijuana and Mexicali on Sundays. Mexicans and Mexican-Americans believe that gringos misunderstand the nature of bullfights, unable to see beyond the horror and cruelty of hacking livestock to death with barbed darts, spears and swords.

Though the rules and trappings of bullfighting originated in 18th-century Spain and came to Mexico in the last years of colonial rule, it also mirrors the ritual public sacrifices of the Aztecs and Toltecs in earlier times. Mexicans see each bullfight as display of courage—not a sport like boxing or riding in *charreadas* (rodeos), but a ritual that links them to heritage and primal instinct. Several mounted *picadores* and *banderilleros* on foot participate in the first half-hour of a fight, but the *matador* (literally, "killer") is the star of the show, so icy of nerve that he—or she—cannot only stand within inches of a charging thousand-pound behemoth with horns that can rip a horse apart or toss a man in the air, but at the same time execute customary cape passes with the precision and grace of a ballet dancer. The bull, too is judged on its courage. Though hand-selected at an early age for belligerence and trained in the art of fighting on a special ranch for four years, there is no predicting how a bull, bloodied and tormented, will face the certainty of death.

Any gringo who wishes to understand the Mexican people on their own terms must attend at least one *corrida de toros*. A word of caution, though: Take care not to give voice to feelings of horror or disgust unless a human is gored. Mexican spectators take offense at negative reactions by gringos at bullfights, and they may bring various nasty substances to throw at disgraced *matadores*—or rude tourists.

Six bulls are fought in an afternoon's *corrida*, which lasts about six hours. Tijuana has two bullrings—the older **Toreo de Tijuana** (Boulevard Agua Caliente 100; 86-15-10) and the larger **Plaza Monumental** (Route 1-D; 80-18-08). Bullfights are held every Sunday from May through September at one ring or the other—in August at both. Mexicali's bullfights are held every other week from October through May at the **Plaza Calafia** (Calle Calafia; 57-06-81). Admission at all three bullrings is around $15 for seats in the sun and $25 in the shade.

ISLAS LOS CORONADOS ⚓ 🛶 ⛵ Seven miles off the coast of Playas de Tijuana lies a chain of four tiny desert islands, occupied by the ruins of a Prohibition-era resort hotel and a small Mexican Navy detachment that enforces the law prohibiting humans from setting foot on the islands. Boaters can circle around and between them, though, for fishing, diving and wildlife watching. Los Coronados host one of the largest pelican rookeries on the Baja coast, along with a large sea lion colony and smaller groups of elephant and harbor seals. ~ Accessible by fishing *panga* from San Antonio, south of Playas de Tijuana on the toll highway.

▼▼▼▼▼▼▼▼▼▼

Tecate

The industrial mountain town of Tecate, 32 miles southeast of San Diego, offers a simple alternative to crossing the border at Tijuana—and that's about all. The distance to Ensenada is about the same from Tecate (116 kilometers) as from Tijuana (109 kilometers). There is not much advantage to crossing at Tecate on the way south, and you miss the gorgeous coastal drive from Tijuana to Tecate. Northbound, it's another story. Tecate is a quick, easy, relatively traffic-free place to enter the United States practically any time.

Tecate is set at an elevation of 1690 feet in a bowl-shaped valley surrounded by jagged, rocky hills. Picacho Tecate (Tecate Peak, 5884 feet), part of the coastal mountain range, towers above the town. Tecate's permanent population is 45,000. The major industry is making beer.

Baja's oldest border town, Tecate got its start in 1831 as the private ranch of a wealthy Peruvian who went on to become governor of San Diego while it was still part of Mexico. When farmers flooded into the rich Valle de Guadalupe in the 1880s to grow wine grapes, olives and wheat, the ranch headquarters became first a supply station and then a full-fledged town. In 1915, the completion of a railroad between Tijuana, Tecate, Mexicali and Tucson, Arizona, made Tecate an important shipping center as it opened United States markets to local growers.

A few years later, when the United States imposed Prohibition, Tecate businessman Alberto Aldrete built a whisky distillery that employed most of the townspeople. It was as hard for U.S. agents to stop bootleggers from smuggling liquor through the mountains and canyons along this part of the border as it is to catch unauthorized immigrants here today. The whisky distillery went out of business when Prohibition ended in the United States, but its huge malt factory was converted to manufacturing beer, the town's most famous product today.

Several U.S.-based companies have built *maquiladora* manufacturing plants on the border outside of Tecate's city limits. Factory workers, who live in *colonias* of tiny, identical cinderblock houses near the plants, account for about half the valley's population but are not included in the official census figures for Tecate because most *maquiladora* laborers are categorized as temporary residents whose families and permanent homes are in rural areas of central and southern Mexico.

Considering its location at San Diego's mountainous back door, you might expect Tecate to be a smugglers' haven. Although you'd probably be right, so far Tecate has not experienced the disastrous rise in gun violence that has accompanied increased drug and firearm smuggling in other border cities. Built around a peaceful town plaza, Tecate is the most typically Mexican town on the Baja border. It is also, in all likelihood, the town with the most dentists per capita in North America. Many San Diego residents visit Tecate routinely for dental work at a fraction of southern California prices.

CROSSING THE BORDER

The border crossing at Tecate has but two U.S. Customs booths and a tiny Mexican *aduana*, or customs office, that apparently is never open. An average of 1500 cars and trucks a day cross the border here in each direction, or fewer than 100 an hour when the border crossing is open—daily from 6 a.m. to 10 p.m.

Crossing southward, you probably won't have to stop at all. Stay on the same street, Calle Lázaro Cárdenas, for four blocks and you'll reach the Plaza. Jog left one block to Calle Ortiz Rubio and you'll soon find yourself crossing the river and heading out of town on the road to Ensenada.

Returning northward, you'll learn why so many experienced Baja buffs like the Tecate border crossing. It's easy to find, and there is rarely more than a ten-minute wait. Saturday is the busiest day. Sunday is quiet.

SIGHTS

The **Cervecería Cuauhtémoc-Moctezuma**, the biggest building in town, fills up to 1600 bottles a minute with two of Mexico's best-known export beers, Carta Blanca and Tecate. (Only bottled Cerveza Tecate is actually made in Tecate; the canned beer is made at the original Carta Blanca brewery in the mainland city of Monterrey.) The beer is made differently depending on whether it is headed for Mexico or the United States.

Tecate beer sold in Mexico has a slightly higher alcohol content, more hops and a stronger taste than the export version. Group tours of the factory, which individuals can join, are given on most Saturday mornings, and parties of five or more can usually arrange a tour on weekdays. Either way, advance reservations are essential. Located one block south and four blocks west of the plaza. ~ Avenida Hidalgo and Calle Carranza; 4-2011

◄ HIDDEN

High in the Sierra de Juárez east of Tecate, the open-air **Museo El Vallecito** offers a chance to explore an archaeological site adorned with pictographs by nomadic Yumano Indians as much as three thousand years ago. The rock paintings, done on protected cliff surfaces in hues of red, black and white made from pulverizing colored stones, consist mainly of human figures and geometric patterns. Both the designs and their locations probably had shamanic significance, and some have been found to possess astronomical implications. Crude artifacts—grinding stones, arrowheads and tool fragments—have also been found in the area, which served as a temporary campsite for hunters and gatherers for thousands of years. Admission. ~ Located three kilometers off Route 2 on an unpaved road that turns off near the Restaurant El Chipo in La Rumerosa and passes the Rancho Santa María del Oro before reaching the site; no phone.

LODGING   The main downtown hotel is the modest **Hotel Tecate**, located on the southwest corner of the plaza. Its 24 guest rooms are clean, though slightly frayed around the edges, with double or twin beds, ceiling fans and private baths; some have TVs. There's no heat, so this hotel is a dubious option in winter. ~ Calle Libertad at Avenida Presidente Cárdenas; 54-11-16. BUDGET.

The more comfortable **Motel El Dorado** has 41 spacious rooms with one queen-size or two double beds, wall heaters, air conditioning, in-room phones and cable color TV. ~ Avenida Benito Juárez 1100; 4-13-33. MODERATE.

Although a stay at **Rancho La Puerta**, five kilometers west of Tecate, may be beyond the means of most casual vacationers, the curious traveler can get a peek at the grounds by visiting the all-vegetarian café near the entrance for lunch or just a latté and biscotti. Simultaneously elegant and rustic, the resort has no TVs or phones in the guest casitas. It *does* have some of the best fitness facilities anywhere, including a complete spa, tennis courts and swimming pools, enough exercise equipment to train an army, and more than 20 miles of jogging trails through spectacular foothills. Celebrities such as Oprah Winfrey and Barbara Streisand

---

✔ CHECK THESE OUT—UNIQUE LODGING

- *Budget:* Sleep as cheap as you're willing to at Mexicali's **Hotel Mexico**, where even the best rooms are budget-priced. *page 80*
- *Moderate:* Bask in a whirlpool fed by natural hot springs at Tijuana's **Holiday Inn Express—Tijuana Agua Caliente**. *page 68*
- *Deluxe:* Take a room with a view in Tijuana's tallest building, the **Gran Hotel Tijuana**. *page 68*
- *Ultra-deluxe:* Work out until you collapse into the lap of luxury (for a minimum of a week) at **Rancho La Puerta** near Tecate. *page 76*

Budget: under $35   Moderate: $35–$70   Deluxe: $70–$105   Ultra-deluxe: over $105

come here to relax and restore their minds and bodies. The minimum stay is a week, from Saturday to Saturday, at a cost of about $200 per person per night, double-occupancy. Guests can arrange complimentary transportation across the border to the resort from Lindberg Field in San Diego. Reservations should be made up to a year in advance. ~ Route 2; reservations c/o The Golden Door, P.O. Box 463057, Escondido, CA 92046; 619-744-4222, 800-443-7565, fax 619-744-5007. ULTRA-DELUXE.

Look for first-rate resort accommodations at surprisingly affordable prices at the **Hacienda Santa Veronica**, a half-hour's drive east of Tecate on the highway to Mexicali. The resort's condominium-style mini-suites have contemporary furnishings, private patios and fireplaces. There are six tennis courts, an outdoor swimming pool and mountain trails for hiking, jogging and horseback riding, as well as race tracks for motorcycles and all-terrain vehicles. The activity that makes this resort unique is bull-fighting lessons; the hacienda was originally a bull-breeding and -training ranch, and you can pit your nerve and skill against a sharp-horned training cart or, if you dare, a small yearling bull. ~ Route 2; reservations c/o Hacienda Santa Veronica, 74818 Vellie Drive, Suite 4, Palm Desert, CA 92260; 85-97-93 in Tijuana, or 619-341-9811 in the U.S. MODERATE.

The often noisy, no-frills **Jardín Tecate** on the south side of the main plaza serves tasty, low-priced soups, salads and fish dishes, as well as *comidas corridas*—fast-service daily specials. Locals outnumber tourists, and there's sidewalk dining in hot weather. ~ Andador Libertad 274; 54-34-53. BUDGET.

DINING

El Passetto, in an alleyway on the westside of the plaza, specializes in traditional Italian food and also has a few Mexican and seafood selections. The owner serves his own homemade red table wine. ~ Callejón Libertad 200; 54-13-61. MODERATE.

La Carreta is a cool, dim sit-down restaurant featuring *norteño* Mexican cooking—the familiar burritos-and-enchiladas fare, typical of Mexico's northern cattle ranching region and often called Tex-Mex in the United States. ~ Avenida Juárez 270; 54-04-62. BUDGET.

Panadería El Mejor Pan has, as the name claims, some of the best bread in Baja. The little bakery is located two blocks east of the plaza. Open 24 hours. ~ Avenida Juárez 331.

GROCERIES

PARQUE NACIONAL CONSTITUCIÓN DE 1857 🏃 This 12,400-acre park surrounds Laguna Hanson, the only natural lake in Baja and an important refuge for migratory water birds (though it does not always contain water). The lake is in the heart of the Sierra de Juárez, a pine-covered mountain highland that separates the Mex-

PARKS

icali Valley and Colorado River delta from the Pacific coast. ~ Laguna Hanson is located midway along an unpaved 100-kilometer road that runs between Route 2 and Route 3. From Route 2 between Tecate and Mexicali, high-clearance vehicles can take the park road that turns off to the south four kilometers west of the tiny roadside village of La Rumerosa at the highest point along the highway—this is challenging for passenger cars because of a rocky stretch just inside the park entrance. Most vehicles, including cautiously driven motor homes, can get to the lake by driving north from Route 3 at kilometer 55 east of Ensenada.

On the other side of the park, Cañon Guadalupe offers natural 105°F hot springs shaded by palms at the base of the sierra's steep eastern escarpment. Guides take hot-springs visitors to nearby waterfalls, Indian caves and petroglyphs. Snow may make areas of the park inaccessible in winter. ~ To reach the canyon and hot springs, take the unpaved, wide but washboard road that turns off Route 2 to the south near kilometer 27 east of Mexicali; it's a 57-kilometer trip to the hot springs. An alternate route, more suitable for large vehicles but treacherous if there has been recent rain, turns off at kilometer 25; the sign says "Laguna Salada."

▲ Camping around Laguna Hanson is informal and free. There is no water, so bring your own drinking water. At Cañon Guadalupe, there is a commercial campground by the hot springs. Sites range from $15 to $30 per night; no hookups. Reservations, a good idea at the hot springs on weekends, can be made through Guadalupe Canyon Hot Springs and Campground, P.O. Box 4003, Balboa, CA 92661; 714-673-2670.

▼▼▼▼▼▼▼▼▼▼
Mexicali

Formerly so arid that humans could not survive there, the Valle Mexicali came to life in 1902 with the completion of the Imperial Canal, which diverted water from the Colorado River on the U.S. side of the border to irrigate California's Imperial Valley as well as the desert around Mexicali, which was controlled by the Colorado River Land Company, a consortium of U.S. businessmen who had leased vast holdings from the Mexican government. The company brought thousands of Chinese laborers who had helped build the canal to farm the Mexicali Valley as sharecroppers. The population of early-day Mexicali was 93 percent Chinese.

Mexicans came gradually to the Mexicali area—first for the fast money to be made from Prohibition-weary Americans, then for the vast areas of *ejido* farm acreage made available when land reform swept through 1930s Mexico, cancelling the leases of foreign landholders like the Colorado River Land Company. Land reform also disenfranchised many Chinese farmers, forcing them to look for work in the thriving capital. Today, Mexicali's La Chinesca district is the largest Chinese-Mexican community in the entire country. A unique dialect of border Spanish mixed with Chinese is often heard in shops and restaurants.

Mexicali's economy turns on agriculture, not tourism. An elaborate irrigation system connected to Morelos Dam, on the Colorado River just south of the border, has transformed more and more arid desert into fields green with crops for export to U.S. and Canadian supermarkets. *Maquiladora* factories lure thousands of workers from areas of mainland Mexico where jobs are hard to find. "Temporary" *maquiladora* workers swell Mexicali's official population from 775,000 "permanent residents" to more than a million. Though surrounded by the squalid housing projects that go along with *maquiladora* plants, the long-established parts of the city are more befitting the capital of Baja California —palm-lined boulevards, monumental statues, flower-filled parks, fountains and quiet residential neighborhoods with manicured lawns.

CROSSING THE BORDER

You can see the smoggy orange glow of city lights at night from U.S. Interstate 8, a mere 11 miles north of the border crossing, but you won't find much civilization north of the line between San Diego and Yuma. It exists for wheat and vegetable shipments to U.S. supermarkets from the farms of the Valle Mexicali. It only makes sense for tourists to use the Mexicali border crossing if they are going to San Felipe.

Baja California's sprawling capital city is so far from anything on the U.S. side that the crossing is rarely very busy. It's open 24 hours a day, so there is no early-morning truck stack-up, and it's easy to follow fast, four-lane Calzada López Mateos from the border diagonally across the city to the junction of Route 2, west to Mexicali or east to San Luis Colorado and the Mexican mainland, and Route 5 south to San Felipe.

Heading north, it's easy to stray from Calzada López Mateos onto Boulevard Benito Juárez, a main drag that marks the east edge of the city. Stay on it and you'll eventually come to the low concrete walls and high chain-link-fence that mark the border. Avenida Cristóbal Colón parallels the border for miles and eventually brings you to the port of entry.

SIGHTS

Parque Niños Héroes de Chapultepec, Mexicali's formal downtown plaza, is located three blocks east of the border crossing and less than one block south of the border. From here, the downtown area continues eastward for almost two miles, though it is only four blocks wide. ~ Between Avenidas Cristóbal Colón and Francisco Madero and Calles Ayuntamiento and Altamirano.

The graceful **Catedral de la Virgen de Guadalupe**, the city's primary house of worship, is located a block east and a block south of the plaza. Most of the old, historic churches of Baja had crumbled into memory long before this 20th-century Spanish Mission Revival–style edifice was built. ~ Avenida Reforma at Calle Morelos.

La Chinesca, the Chinese district, is "on the other side of the tracks," along Avenida Altamirano a few blocks south of the plaza across the diagonal Calzada López Mateos and the train tracks that run alongside it. The mainly residential district has a scattering of the exotic little shops and mysterious signs you'd expect in a Chinatown, along with dozens of inexpensive Chinese restaurants.

The **Universidad de Baja California** has several facilities around the city. The administration buildings, on the main campus two miles east of the center of downtown, occupy the most historic building in town—the original Palacio de Gobierno or state capitol. ~ Avenida Reforma at Avenida Sebastian Lerdo de Tajada; 54-04-00. The Colorado River Land Company's corporate headquarters once occupied another impressive office building just north of the former capitol. ~ Avenida Reforma at Calle F.

The University's top attraction, the **Museo Regional (Museo Hombre, Naturaleza y Cultura)**, is eight blocks east of the main campus. The biggest and best museum on the peninsula—almost by default—its eight galleries contain exhibits on geology, fossils and the mission churches of Baja. The main focus is on anthropology, especially the Yumano and other nomadic peoples who inhabited the Sierra de Juárez and Sierra San Pedro Mártir in pre-Columbian times. All interpretive signs are in Spanish. ~ Avenida Reforma at Calle L; 52-57-17.

The **Teatro del Estado**, Baja's largest performing-arts theater, presents Mexican plays, dance concerts and musical events. Schedule information is available across the street at the Comité de Turismo y Convenciones (COTUCO) office. ~ Calzada López Mateos at Avenida Castellanos; 64-07-57.

Baja California's governor, state legislature and judiciary are housed in separate buildings of the **Centro Civico-Comercial**, an ambitious urban renewal project on the south edge of the city near the Plaza de Toros Calafia bullring. There's not much to see. ~ Avenida Los Héroes.

LODGING   The **Hotel del Norte**, with its distinctive architecture—Art Deco meets Santa Fe—is near the border crossing. Its 52 well-maintained rooms are comfortable and full of personality, though traffic noise can be a problem. Some rooms have air-conditioning and color TV. ~ Calle Melgar 205; 52-81-01. BUDGET TO MODERATE.

One of the most affordable places to stay in the downtown area, the **Hotel Mexico** caters mainly to Mexican families. The rooms are spotless but show signs of severe wear and tear. Guest accommodations (and rates) vary from spartan rooms with a bed and not much else to attractively furnished ones with private baths, TVs and air conditioning. All rooms have one thing in common: pink walls. ~ Avenida Sebastian Lerdo de Tejada 476; 54-06-09. BUDGET.

The **Hotel La Lucerna**, located in the southeast part of the city on the road to San Felipe, has 192 air-conditioned rooms, suites and individual bungalows in a lush garden setting that makes it one of Mexicali's prettiest hotels. Many rooms have balconies that overlook the two swimming pools and the fountains and palm trees surrounding them. Guest facilities also include an exercise room. ~ Boulevard Benito Juárez 2151; 66-10-00, fax 66-4706. MODERATE.

Top of the line in Mexicali is the **Holiday Inn Crowne Plaza**, with 158 spacious, colorfully decorated guest rooms that are up to the standards of better motor inns in the United States. The air-conditioned rooms have phones, cable color TV and even computer modem ports. Located seven kilometers south of the border, just off the highway to San Felipe. ~ Avenida de los Herdes 201; 57-36-00, fax 57-05-55. MODERATE.

Mexicali's youth hostel, the **Instituto de la Juventud y el Deporte**, has dormitory accommodations designed more for the use of visiting sports teams than gringo travelers. Its location, a long way from the border, the bus depot or anyplace you might want to visit, makes it a doubtful choice. There is no food service. ~ Calle Coahuila 2050; 57-61-92. BUDGET.

DINING

About half the restaurants in Mexicali are Chinese. In the Chinese district south of Calzada López Mateos, check out **Alley 19**, the granddaddy of them all, operated by the same family in the same location since 1928. The menu presents a choice of stir-fries, mostly beef and vegetarian dishes, served over heaps of fried rice. Try the *chau men*, which contains different vegetables from the

✔ **CHECK THESE OUT—UNIQUE DINING**
- *Low budget:* Feast on fish tacos or pineapple tamales at one of the many *comedores* in Tijuana's **Mercado Hidalgo**. *page 69*
- *Budget:* Chow down like the locals on the *comida corrida* at the **Jardín Tecate** on Tecate's town plaza. *page 77*
- *Moderate:* Feast on beef and broccoli at **La Misión Dragón**, Mexicali's Spanish Colonial–style Chinese restaurant. *page 82*
- *Deluxe:* Savor the sea bass at **Pedrin's**, home of the best seafood in Tijuana. *page 68*

Budget: under $5   Moderate: $5–$10   Deluxe: $10–$18   Ultra-deluxe: over $18

familiar American-style chow mein. ~ Avenida Benito Juárez 8.
BUDGET.

HIDDEN ►   **Restaurant Buendía,** a hole-in-the-wall eatery also in La
Chinesca, offers an authentic taste of Mexicali's unique Chinese-
Mexican cuisine—items like stir-fried beefsteak with vegetables,
and spicy egg rolls that bear a striking resemblance to burritos.
The prices are worth walking a few extra blocks for. ~ Avenida
Altamirano 263; 52-69-25. BUDGET.

More upscale is **El Dragón,** atmospherically Asian in a pagoda-
shaped building on the east side of town. The elegant restaurant
serves shrimp and lobster dishes as well as exceptional presenta-
tions of local standards such as beef broccoli and *chau men.* ~ Calzada Benito Juárez 1830; 66-20-20. MODERATE. The same management also operates **La Misión Dragón,** where the food meets
the same high standard and the ambience strikes a strange synthesis of classic Chinese and Spanish Colonial mission styles that
expresses Mexicali's unique Chinese-Mexican character perfectly.
~ Boulevard Lázaro Cárdenas 555; 66-44-00. MODERATE.

Several blocks south of the main Universidad de Baja Califor-
HIDDEN ►   nia campus, the **Cenaduría Selecta** is a little off the beaten path,
but that does not stop a mostly Mexican clientele from packing
the place most evenings. In business since 1945, the restaurant
serves an assortment of Mexican combination plates and thin,
Mexican-style beefsteaks. ~ Calle C 1510; 62-40-47. MODERATE.

The place to go for great seafood is **Los Arcos,** in the Centro
Cívico-Comercial. The menu includes the Baja California favorite,
Puerto Nuevo style lobster, along with sea bass, shrimp sauteed
in garlic, and a wealth of other culinary delights. The light, somewhat sterile atmosphere seems to have been created with business
lunches in mind. ~ Avenida Calafia 454; 56-09-03. MODERATE.

SHOPPING   One of the few shopping spots that rises above downtown Mexicali's usual run of curio shops is the **Galería de la Ciudad,** a large,
privately owned art gallery that displays works by contemporary
Baja artists. ~ Calle Obregón 1209; 53-50-44.

Desarrollo Artesanal de Mexicali, a government-sponsored
store, sells arts and crafts handmade in Baja California. Prices are
good. It's too far to walk there from the border, though. ~ Boulevard Lázaro Cárdenas 1190; 61-64-44.

NIGHTLIFE   Although a few sleazy bars and strip joints survive as reminders
of bygone days when Mexicali hoped to lure rich gringos across
the border with various vices, most of the city's scant nightlife
these days is in the plush, flashy discos at the better hotels. Check
out **La Capilla,** a dance club in the Hotel La Lucerna that's a favorite hangout for the young and prosperous. Cover. ~ Calzada
Benito Juárez 2151; 66-10-00.

BOSQUE DE LA CIUDAD This large city park contains a lake **PARKS** surrounded by forest, a zoo, carnival rides and a miniature train that takes visitors on a quick tour of the park. Admission is three pesos. Closed Monday. ~ Calle Alvarado, north of Boulevard Lázaro Cárdenas on the southwest side of the city; 55-28-33.

▼▼▼▼▼▼▼▼▼
Algodones

The small town of **Los Algodones** (usually just called Algodones), located off U.S. Interstate 8 where the California–Arizona state line meets the Mexican border, is the obvious port of entry for travelers from points east who are bound for the San Felipe area. It is also theoretically possible to cross the border here and continue west on Mexican Route 2 through Mexicali and Tecate to Tijuana, though the slowness and complexity of the road network in the Colorado River Delta makes Algodones a poor alternative to other border crossings farther west.

Named for the cotton fields that surround it, Algodones is the commercial center for residents of the agricultural area near the mouth of the Colorado. The town, with its narrow, nameless dirt streets, covers an area of just one square mile and has a population of 12,000. Yet during the winter months, an average of 15,000 visitors from the United States come through each day.

You can't take fresh fruits or vegetables from Baja California Norte to Baja California Sur because of Mexican agricultural regulations designed to control fruit flies and other pests.

Most visitors pay to park in the huge lot on the U.S. side of the border and walk across, avoiding the problem of searching for one of the free but scarce parking spaces on the streets of Algodones. During the hot months, when visitors from the U.S. are rare, almost all activity in Algodones shuts down, though the border remains open.

The border crossing is open from 6 a.m. to 10 p.m. Algodones **CROSSING** is in the Pacific time zone (barely). Mexican auto insurance, a must **THE** for those driving their own cars into Baja, is available from **Insur-** **BORDER** **ance Agency Francisco Navarrete.** ~ Calle 1 at Mariano Ma Lee; 1-70-65.

As you drive east from Algodones, following the signs that mark **SIGHTS** Route 3 on its circuitous path to join Route 5 to San Felipe, you pass through the eastern part of the **Valle de Mexicali,** Baja's largest agricultural area. Irrigated by water diverted from the Colorado River at Morelos Dam, about two miles south of Algodones, the area has seen explosive population growth in recent years.

Roads linking Algodones and the many small farming communities of the valley with Mexicali were unpaved until the early 1990s. Poverty is more obvious here than in most other parts of

Baja. Most people who live here are essentially sharecroppers who struggle along on subsistence farms and work seasonally, harvesting crops at large farms on both sides of the border. Watch to the north and you'll glimpse the **Algodones Dune Field** beyond green fields of alfalfa. More than a hundred feet high in places, the huge expanse of sand sprawls across the border and is inaccessible from the Mexican side.

LODGING   There is little reason to consider spending the night in Algodones, since you'll find motels and motor inns galore just off U.S. Interstate 8 in Yuma, Arizona, just a few miles east of the Algodones border crossing.

DINING   Numerous vendors sell tacos, *elotes* (corn on the cob) and fruit salads on the streets of Algodones during the winter.

For a sit-down meal, **El Rancherito**, a tourist-oriented place two blocks south of the border crossing, serves typical border cuisine: burritos, enchiladas and several varieties of tamales. ~ Calle 1.

GROCERIES   **Carlota's Bakery**, in the Real Plaza del Sol mini-mall two blocks south and a block east of the border crossing, tempts travelers with breads and sweet rolls. A small open-air café serves continental breakfasts and snacks.

Almost any time is harvest time for one vegetable or another in the Valle de Mexicali, and many small farmers make extra cash by carrying veggies in to Algodones to sell to gringo tourists. Don't be surprised if every third person you meet offers to sell you a bundle of asparagus. Another week, it could be onions. Most vegetables can be taken across the border into the United States, though without a special permit you can't bring in avocados, potatoes (including sweet potatoes and yams) or sugar cane.

SHOPPING   The main draw in Algodones is affordable pharmaceutical drugs. Mexican law permits the sale of most drugs without a prescription, and manufacturers often "dump" surplus drugs south of the border at prices much lower than in the United States. Signs in front of most of the 35 pharmacies in town quote bargain prices on antibiotics, nicotine patches, Valium and Rogaine. United States law requires that anyone bringing prescription drugs into the country have a doctor's prescription in their possession, though senior citizens who come to Algodones regularly report that enforcement of the law is fairly lax. The town also has 35 dentists and 15 optometrists, whose prices are often less than half as much as those charged in Arizona.

Most of the vendors who line the streets of Algodones offering curios and trinkets from all over Mexico are itinerant, migrating to the Mexican mainland or to Tijuana or Ensenada in the summertime.

Near Tijuana, **Islas los Coronados** is a favorite area for yellowtail, sea bass, halibut and barracuda. Charters can be arranged informally at San Antonio del Mar.

▼▼▼▼▼▼▼▼▼▼▼▼
Outdoor Adventures

FISHING

Islas los Coronados is an enormously popular area for scuba diving. Although the islands may not look like much from the surface, they are the summits of a cluster of steep underwater mountains whose rock faces, like coral reefs, teem with sea life. The best dive areas lie 60 to 90 feet below the surface and can be hazardous for inexperienced divers. A popular spot for easy diving is the kelp forest off the southern tip of the southernmost island. There are no regularly scheduled commercial dive trips, and most scuba enthusiasts come in their own boats.

DIVING

Tennis courts are hard to find in Tijuana; most visitors who are inclined toward gringo sports head for the resorts at nearby Rosarito. The best bet for Tijuana tennis is the **Gran Hotel Tijuana**, which has two hard-surfaced courts for guest use. ~ Boulevard Agua Caliente 4500; 81-70-00.

TENNIS

Mexicali has a number of municipal and semiprivate *clubs deportivos* that have tennis courts as well as swimming pools and other facilities. The lowest fees are at the **Ciudad Deportiva**, where you'll find four hard-surfaced courts available on a first-come, first-served basis, along with a public swimming pool, baseball diamond, running track and jai alai fronton. ~ Boulevard Cuahutémoc; 55-30-25. Visitors can rent courts at the private **Club Raqueta Britania**, which also has a workout room and spa. ~ Boulevard Anahuac at Calle Mar Baltico; 57-13-07.

◆◆◆

✔ CHECK THESE OUT—UNIQUE OUTDOOR ADVENTURES

- Scuba among the moray eels that inhabit the underwater cliffs off the Islas los Coronados. *page 85*
- Play tennis at Mexicali's Ciudad Deportiva, which also has a swimming pool, running track and jai alai fronton. *page 85*
- Tee off within shouting distance of the border at the Tijuana Country Club. *page 86*
- Hike through the pine forests that surround Laguna Hanson, Baja's only lake, in the Parque Nacional Constitución de 1857. *page 86*

GOLF   The semiprivate **Tijuana Country Club** (also called the Club Social y Deportivo Campestre) has a long 18-hole course that sometimes hosts the Mexican Open Golf Tournament. ~ Boulevard Agua Caliente; 81-78-55, 81-78-63.

The **Club Deportivo Campestre de Mexicali** is another 18-hole semiprivate country club course, so similar to Tijuana's that the two courses must have shared the same designer and possibly the same blueprints. ~ Route 5 south; 61-71-30, 61-71-70.

HIKING   The cool pine woods that surround Laguna Hanson in the **Parque Nacional Constitución de 1857** are one of the best hiking areas in Baja. A well-defined trail makes its way around the lake (which does not always contain water). A complete circuit of the lake involves more than 20 miles of walking, all fairly level. Other trails wander off into the forest. Those who venture out of sight of the lakebed should be sure to take a compass, since the secondary trails are unmapped and can be confusing.

▼▼▼▼▼▼▼▼▼▼▼▼

Transportation

AIR   **Air L.A.** has frequent flights to Tijuana International Airport from Los Angeles. **Aero California** also has flights from Los Angeles to Tijuana, Loreto, La Paz and Los Cabos. **Mexicana** has flights between Tijuana and Los Cabos, and **Aeroméxico** links Tijuana with Guadalajara and several other major cities of western Mexico. The airport is located east of Tijuana near the Otay Border Crossing.

Mexicali International Airport has daily **Air L.A.** flights from Los Angeles. **Aviación del Noroeste** flies between Mexicali and other northwestern Mexico cities, including La Paz and Mazatlán. **Mexicana** offers daily service to Mexicali from Mexico City and Guadalajara.

Tecate and Algodones do not have commercial airports.

CAR   Tijuana's San Ysidro Border Crossing is at the end of U.S. **Interstate 5** south from San Diego. The Otay Border Crossing is reached via the last exit from U.S. **Interstate 805** before it merges into I-5 at the border.

Tecate is 32 miles southeast of San Diego. To get there, exit Interstate 5 or 805 at Chula Vista and follow **Route 94.**

Mexicali is on Route 111, 11 miles south of Interstate 8 near El Centro, California.

Algodones is also just off Interstate 8. Take the Andrade exit, three miles west of Yuma, Arizona; it is about three miles south to the border crossing.

CAR RENTALS   Car rentals are easy to come by in Tijuana. At Tijuana International Airport, try **Avis** (83-23-10), **Budget** (83-29-05), **Dollar** (83-18-61), **Hertz** (83-20-80) or **National** (82-44-33). Most of these chains also have locations in the Zona Rio and Agua Caliente hotel zones.

In Mexicali, rental agencies are found along the Boulevard Juárez strip near the border crossing. They include **Budget** (Boulevard Juárez 2220; 66-48-40), **Dollar** (Boulevard Juárez 1000; 65-62-62), **Hertz** (Boulevard Juárez 1223; 68-19-73) and **National** (Boulevard Juárez 1004; 68-39-63).

The **San Diego Trolley** shuttles passengers from downtown San Diego to and from the San Ysidro Border Crossing, within walking distance of downtown Tijuana, every 15 minutes from 5 a.m. to midnight.

BUS

Greyhound operates bus service across the border from San Diego to Tijuana and from Calexico to Mexicali. **Autotransportes de Baja California** has frequent bus service along Mexican Route 2 between Tijuana, Tecate, Mexicali and Algodones.

Ferrocarriles Nacionales de Mexico operates daily passenger service to and from Mexicali on a spur line that merges with the Ferrocarril Pacífico (Pacific Railroad) at Benjamin Hill, Sonora, and continues southward to Guaymas, Mazatlán, Tepic and Guadalajara, a 36-hour trip. For current schedule information, write FNM, P.O. Box 231, Calexico, CA 92231 or call 57-23-86 in Mexicali. Primera Especial (special first-class) coaches are quite comfortable. Second-class coaches are funky and can be fun— I've been on some where impromptu parties broke out, complete with guitars and tequila—but theft has become a common problem in second-class.

TRAIN

Tijuana's colorful, modern buses run to all parts of the city and make it easy to reach Zona Río and Agua Caliente district attractions from Avenida Revolución.

PUBLIC TRANSIT

Mexicali's old-fashioned public buses run from a central downtown loading zone on Calzado Justo Sierra, two blocks from the border crossing, and go to every part of the city.

Besides private taxis, both Tijuana and Mexicali have *combis* (also called *taxis de ruta*), shuttle vans that travel specific routes and cost more than a bus ride but less than a taxi cab.

Both Tijuana and Mexicali have many independent taxis. Look for them around the border crossings and the major hotels. Cab rates are regulated and authorized fare cards are supposed to be posted. Price gouging is common on border pickups, though, so it is a good idea to ask first what the fare will be. Some taxi drivers like to drive tourists across the border to U.S. Customs— where Mexican price controls do not apply—and then ask for an outrageous amount.

TAXIS

TOURS   The **Comité de Turismo y Convenciones de Mexicali** offers all-day tours of the city from the tourist office near the Monumento Vicente Guerrero in Mexicali or from the tourist office in Algodones. ~ Calzada López Mateos at Calle Camelias, Mexicali; 57-23-76 or 57-25-61.

▼▼▼▼▼▼▼▼▼▼▼▼▼▼▼▼▼▼▼▼▼▼
Addresses & Phone Numbers

Hospital: Tijuana: 84-09-22; Mexicali: 57-37-00

Police: Emergencies (all cities): 134

United States Consulate, Tijuana: Avenida Tapachula 96, Colonia Tipódromo, 681-74-00, fax 681-8016

Secretaría de Turismo del Estado de Baja California Norte: Tijuana, 81-94-92; Mexicali: 56-10-72 or 56-11-72; Tecate: 4-19-05; Algodones: 7-77-06

Comité de Turismo y Convenciones de Tijuana: 84-05-37 or 84-05-38

Comité de Turismo y Convenciones de Mexicali (Mexicali Tourism and Convention Bureau): Lopez Mateos at Calle Camelias, Mexicali; 57-23-76 or 57-25-61

Green Angels (Federal roadside repair and assistance units): Tijuana: 23-38-77; Mexicali: 54-04-43

FIVE

Northern Baja

A cool morning fog drifts in off the ocean to shroud the hills behind the port city of Ensenada. On the other side of the peninsula, dust devils spin crazily across the sunbaked Desierto de San Felipe, one of the driest places on the continent. Northern Baja is a land of striking contrasts, where the fertile farmland of the Pacific coastal plain, the evergreen forests and granite peaks of the Sierra de San Pedro Mártir, and the stark desert shoreline of the Sea of Cortez exist within 90 miles of one another.

The two most popular tourist areas in the state of Baja California—Ensenada and San Felipe—have one feature in common. Both are close enough to the border for a weekend getaway from San Diego, Los Angeles or Phoenix. Beyond that, they couldn't be more different. Ensenada, the third-largest city in Baja, accommodates cruise ships with the biggest, busiest tourist-oriented shopping district between Tijuana and Los Cabos. The lazy little sportfishing village of San Felipe, by contrast, rarely sees any vessel larger than a shrimp boat, and every store in town seems to sell the same T-shirts. The Pacific coast around Rosarito and Ensenada is the setting for numerous luxury beach resorts; San Felipe provides beachfront campsites for astonishing numbers of motor homes and other recreational vehicles.

The hidden aspect of northern Baja awaits discovery in the high sierra between the two coasts, a magnificent wilderness of oak and piñon hill country and the highest mountains on the peninsula. The drive in is beautiful, and hiking or biking the trails of Parque Nacional Sierra de San Pedro Mártir is even more so. But not all the hidden spots in northern Baja involve long backroad expeditions. Some of the nicest Pacific beaches in Baja California are just a few miles off the Baja Highway, near the farm town of San Quintín. The elbow-to-elbow party atmosphere that characterizes the weekend beach scene around Rosarito and Ensenada rarely reaches as far south as San Quintín, and you're likely to find that you have the whole beach to yourself.

▼▼▼▼▼▼▼▼▼▼
Ensenada Area

Steep hills on the landward side and a ten-mile-long peninsula on the ocean side protect the Bahía de Todos Santos from storms, making it the best location for a shipping port on the entire Pacific coast of Baja. The exclusive gringo neighborhoods that blanket the hillsides swell the port's population to a quarter of a million full-time residents; it is Baja's largest city that is not on the border.

Spanish ships first dropped anchor in the bay in 1542, and over the centuries it sheltered both the Spanish Empire's treasure galleons from Manila and the pirate ships that preyed on them. In the 1700s, Todos Santos became a favorite hunting area for whalers. The one obstacle to settlement was the absence of fresh water.

Relying on rain catchments and intermittent streams from the eastern mountains, ranches sprang up during the early 1800s, but it was not until 1872, when gold was discovered in the Sierra de Juárez, that a port settlement began to flourish. Ten years later, Ensenada was declared the capital of the Territory of Baja California. But in time, the mines played out and Ensenada faded into oblivion. In 1915, the territorial capital was relocated to Mexicali, leaving Ensenada as nothing more than an obscure fishing village.

Prosperity returned in the 1920s, as Prohibition in the United States drove Hollywood's party set south of the border. The Playa Ensenada Hotel and Casino opened as the most lavish resort in Baja, but this playground of the rich and famous lasted less than a decade before the Mexican government outlawed casino gambling and closed it down. Ensenada's dependence on tourism and foreign money, however, has continued to the present day.

Today, one out of every four U.S. residents who travel to Baja is a Californian on a brief getaway to Ensenada. The city's shipping port hosts several cruise ships from Los Angeles each week, spilling stampedes of daytrippers into the curio shops that line Avenida López Mateos. Thousands of gringo retirees and expatriates have swelled the city's permanent population to a quarter of a million. This is not a place where people retire to live cheaply; the property prices and overall character of the *norteamericano* Chapultepec Hills district are not much different from comparable neighborhoods in San Diego or Orange County. A major reason gringos move here, rather than someplace farther down the peninsula, is that Ensenada has the best medical facilities in Baja, including the only hospital that accepts U.S. medical insurance instead of requiring patients to pay cash and file for insurance reimbursement on their own. Mexicans from all parts of the peninsula also travel to Ensenada for health care.

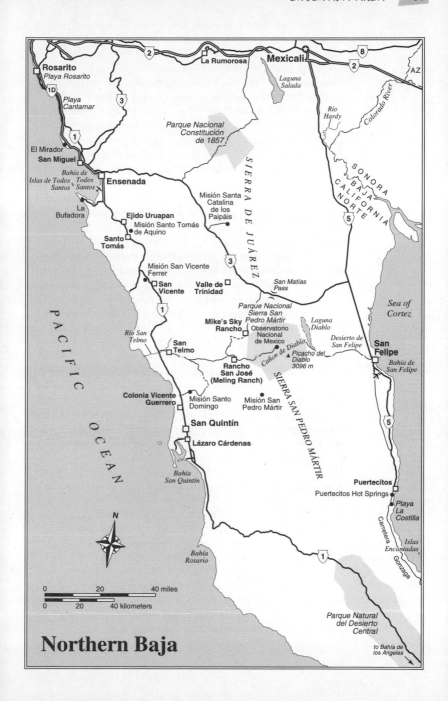

Northern Baja

SIGHTS   The **Carretera Escénica**, or scenic route, from Tijuana to Ensenada covers 190 kilometers, hugging the coastline the whole way. Two roads follow the same route—the *cuota*, or toll highway, which speeds you from the border to Ensenada in less than an hour and costs around $6, and the traffic-clogged *libre*, or free highway, which serves the coastal resorts and takes three times as long.

Between **San Antonio del Mar**, on the southern outskirts of Tijuana, and **San Miguel**, just over the hill from Ensenada, once-upon-a-time fishing villages now merge in an unbroken strip of beachfront hotels, restaurants and condominium complexes. The epicenter of all this beach fun is the string of towering ocean-view condos at the south end of **Rosarito**. The Hotel California is located directly across the highway from Rock'n'Roll Taco in this whitewashed, red-tile-roofed strip town of 50,000 sandwiched between the beach and the Route 1 *cuota*. Rosarito has signs not only in English but also in Spanish. This is because resorts in the area enjoy a modest summer season of visitors from mainland Mexico. In the winter, Rosarito is overrun by hordes of rich gringos every weekend, laid-back and mainly Mexican during the week.

El Mirador, high on a rocky promontory north of Bahía de Todos Santos, is the most scenic rest area between Rosarito and Ensenada. Whalewatchers throng to this place during migrations, and at any time of year the sunset view is as magnificent as any on the Pacific coast.

Entering the city on Route 1, motorists find the **Comité de Turismo y Convenciones** tourist information office at the crowded intersection near the port entrance gate. ~ Boulevard Costero 540; 8-24-11. Road access to the **Port of Ensenada**, on a spit of land that juts into the bay parallel to the waterfront, is restricted. Passengers from the cruise ships that dock at the port's wharf take a shuttle to the downtown shopping district.

✔ **CHECK THESE OUT—UNIQUE SIGHTS**

- Watch for whales in Ensenada's Bahía de Todos Santos from **El Mirador**, an overlook on the way to the sea geyser La Bufadora. *page 92*
- Climb the long stairway to the **Virgin of Guadalupe Shrine** for the best view of San Felipe and miles of surrounding beaches. *page 109*
- Journey into the high country of **Parque Nacional Sierra San Pedro Mártir**, where deer and bears inhabit the evergreen forests. *page 118*
- Visit the **Old English Cemetery** in Puerto San Quintín to glimpse a little-known chapter in Baja history. *page 119*

Located two blocks west of the tourist information office, a 19th-century Mexican customs house has been resurrected as the **Museo de Historia y Antropologia**. The museum does not have much in the way of permanent displays of artifacts from the local area. Instead, it provides space for touring exhibits from the Instituto Nacional de Antropologia y Historia, which has jurisdiction over all of Mexico's historical districts and ancient ruins. If you stop here on your way south, you may find an exhibit on the colonial missions of Baja California, for instance, and then discover on your northbound return trip that it has been replaced by Mayan sculptures or Empress Carlotta's furniture. Exhibits are captioned in Spanish only. Closed Monday. ~ Calle Uribe and Avenida Reyerson.

Three blocks south of the tourist information office on Boulevard Costero is the **Plaza Cívica**, nicknamed Tres Cabezas ("three heads") because the broad paved square contains 12-foot-tall busts of three revered Mexican historical figures: priest-turned-rebel-leader Miguel Hidalgo, organizer of the 1810 rebellion that would lead to Mexico's independence from Spain; President Benito Juárez, who led the fight to drive the French imperialist government of Emperor Maximillian out of the country in 1867; and President Venustiano Carranza, who reigned over the constitutional convention that created modern Mexico in 1917. ~ Boulevard Costero at Avenida Alvarado.

The best view of the city is from the **Colinas Chapultepec**, which enclose the downtown area on the west. The Spanish name sounds more poetic than its English translation—"Grasshopper Hills." Admire the panorama while cruising slowly through this exclusively gringo hillside suburb. To get there, follow Calle 2 west from downtown; it immediately starts climbing into the hills. There is an overlook where the street joins Avenida Alemán, which loops all the way around the hills before returning you to the same overlook.

From downtown, museum buffs can follow Avenida Obregón north (away from the waterfront) for 14 blocks to visit the **Museo de Ciencias de Ensenada**. Situated in a two-story house, the science museum emphasizes oceanography and marine biology. Its educational displays on environmental protection and endangered species are aimed more at school classes than tourists. This museum is one of the best places to learn about the California gray whale and its migrations—if you can read the Spanish-only explanations. Admission. ~ Avenida Obregón 1463; 8-71-92.

◄ HIDDEN

The **Centro Cívico, Social y Cultural Riviera del Pacifico** was originally built in 1930 as the Playa Ensenada Hotel and Casino, the most elegant hotel in Baja for a few years. Managed by retired prizefighter Jack Dempsey, the resort played host to Holly-

wood's beautiful people until 1938, when the government outlawed casino gaming. Today, municipal government has restored
the venerable hotel as a cultural center, used for everything from
weddings to film festivals. Visitors can stroll through the Moorish-
style lobby with its striking murals, the ballroom with its dazzling
wrought-iron chandelier, the chapel where eloping movie stars
used to tie the knot, and the old casino, which recently inspired
Ensenada residents to petition the Mexican federal government
to legalize gambling again in the Baja free trade zone as an economic stimulus; to date, however, the government has shown no
inclination to consider the idea. Donations accepted. ~ Boulevard
Lázaro Cárdenas at Avenida Riviera; 6-43-10 or 6-42-33.

Ensenada's best-known sight is **La Bufadora**, a sea geyser at
a rocky point across the bay from the city. Its name comes from
bufa, Spanish for "snort" and colloquial Mexican for bison; La
Bufadora is commonly translated as "the buffalo snort." This
waterspout is created by the entrance to a long, narrow cavern
just above sea level, between steep cliffs that narrow to a "V."
When a wave rolls in, water crashes over the cavern's mouth, com-
pressing the air inside. As the surf subsides, the air trapped in the
cave blasts the water back out with amazing force, beginning with
a low rumble and climaxing with a plume of sea spray that can
reach almost 100 feet. The phenomenon is at its most spectacular
with a high tide and big waves. La Bufadora becomes extremely
crowded on weekends. There is a parking charge. ~ Carretera
Punta Banda.

La Bufadora is at the end of the long, narrow **Peninsula Punta
Banda**, which shelters the Bahía de Todos Santos from the open
ocean. It's a 40-kilometer trip from Ensenada. The well-marked
road to La Bufadora turns off Route 1 south of the city and runs
along a ridge high above the bay. Several parking areas along the
road provide fantastic views—especially during the southward
whale migration, December through mid-February. Gray whales
are bottom feeders, so they travel close to shore. Many of them
veer into the bay and must swim the length of the Peninsula Punta
Banda to find their way back to the open ocean. This is one of
the best whalewatching spots in Baja California Norte.

HIDDEN ▶   Just outside the mouth of the bay are the **Islas de Todos Santos**.
The smaller northern island contains a Mexican navy base and is
off-limits to civilians, but you can visit the larger southern island
by tour boat or sea kayak. Pelicans, ospreys and many other bird
species nest there, and sea caves and grottos dot the island's south
end. Surfers say the Todos Santos waves reach 30 feet in height.
The islands are said to have inspired the setting for *Treasure Island*
—Robert Lewis Stevenson wrote his famous novel while living at
the north end of the bay.

Mexico's Finest Wineries

The most enduring legacy of the Spanish missionaries who first colonized Baja is vineyards. Just as Alta California is regarded as having the United States' best wineries, so northern Baja has a well-deserved reputation for producing Mexico's finest wines.

Situated in the northern part of Ensenada, **Bodegas de Santo Tomás** makes wine from some of the oldest vines in California. The vineyards themselves are down in the Valle de Santo Tomás, 51 kilometers south of the city on Route 1, where Dominican brothers founded a mission in 1791. There they planted cuttings from grape vines that had originally been brought to the Baja peninsula by Jesuits more than a century earlier. Underground springs and coastal fog helped create an exceptionally good environment, and the vineyards flourished until 1840, when the Mexican government seized all agricultural land owned by the church, and the grapevines were abandoned. Spanish immigrants bought the the old vineyards and revived them in 1888, and Russian immigrants later brought new strains of grapes.

The winery was moved to Ensenada in 1937 to make shipping easier. Today, Bodegas de Santo Tomás produces fine Pinot Noir, Cabernet Sauvignon and Chardonnay varietal wines, which are exported to Europe as well as to the Mexican mainland but are not sold in the United States. Guided tours of the winery, including tastings, are offered several times daily. Admission. ~ Avenida Miramar at Calle 7; 8-25-09 or 8-33-33.

Wine, whether red (*tinta*) or white (*blanco*), is properly called *vino de uva* (grape wine). The more generic *vino* is used to refer to all types of alcoholic beverages, and low-quality tequila is sometimes called *vino blanco*.

From Ensenada, paved two-lane Route 3 runs 250 kilometers across the Baja's mountainous spine to San Felipe, climbing gradually along a series of high, cool agricultural valleys separating the Sierra de Juárez from the Sierra San Pedro Mártir. Pygmy forests of juniper and piñon shelter vast fields of hay and pastures where dairy cows graze.

Ninety kilometers into the trip, an unpaved road turns off to the north and goes about ten kilometers to the adobe ruins of **Misión Santa Catalina de los Paipáis**. Only adobe wall fragments remain of this mission church. Built in 1797 to minister to the Paipai Indians, the mission lasted for more than 40 years but did not prosper. The high altitude made conditions less than ideal for growing crops, and the priests were often forced to turn to the Indians for food to survive harsh winters. In the end, the Indians' resentment erupted into violence, and the missionaries were driven from the valley in an 1840 uprising. Several hundred Paipai Indians live around the old mission and in tiny villages scattered through the wilderness to the north; they are the last surviving indigenous people of Baja. Farther on, past the fast-growing farming town of Valle de Trinidad, the highway crosses 5000-foot San Matias Pass and begins its descent into the San Felipe Desert.

LODGING Beachfront hotels from Rosarito to Ensenada fill up on Friday and Saturday nights, so reservations are advised. Except during the mid-July to mid-September peak season, there is no problem finding vacancies on weeknights, when room rates drop as much as 30 percent. Note that kilometer markers on Route 1 north of town indicate the distance from Tijuana, while south of town they show the distance from Ensenada.

The **Rosarito Beach Hotel and Spa** is one of the few remnants from the days when Rosarito was a tiny, hard-to-reach fishing village on a great beach where silent-movie stars went to hide from the outside world. Built in 1926, this elegant hotel originally had only 12 rooms; it was the only hotel in town with running water. Expanding with each road improvement and corresponding tourist influx, the hotel has grown to 275 rooms. The exterior of today's big, white Mediterranean-style hotel is typical of the beach resort complexes toward the south end of Rosarito; inside, the restored lobby, dining rooms and ballroom ooze Roaring Twenties ostentation. The mix of old and new buildings offers a full range of room choices, from older, very affordable and relatively plain rooms (some without air-conditioning) facing away from the ocean to spacious luxury suites with private balconies overlooking the beach at triple the cheap rooms' price. All guests have the use of facilities that include two heated swimming pools, tennis and racquetball courts, jacuzzis and a steam room. ~ Boulevard

Benito Juárez, Rosarito; 2-01-44, fax 2-11-25, or 800-343-8582 in the U.S. MODERATE TO ULTRA-DELUXE.

Queen of Ensenada's casually elegant small resort hotels is **Las Rosas**, magnificently located on a bluff overlooking the beach at the north end of Bahía de Todos Santos. Downtown is a short drive away. All of the two-story hotel's 31 spacious, pastel-hued rooms and suites have balconies with ocean and pool views, and many have jacuzzis and fireplaces. There is a two-night minimum stay. ~ Route 1, Km. 105; 74-43-10, fax 74-45-95. DELUXE.

Quintas Papagayo Resort is farther east, where the beach dwindles into the port area. That means it's closer to town, within walking distance of the port and shopping district. This old-timey cluster of 50 units, built in 1947 by the owners of Hussong's Cantina, is rapidly being eclipsed by the highrise hotels springing up around it. Still, it's hard to beat for charm and location, and rates here are less than half of those charged at other resorts on the same

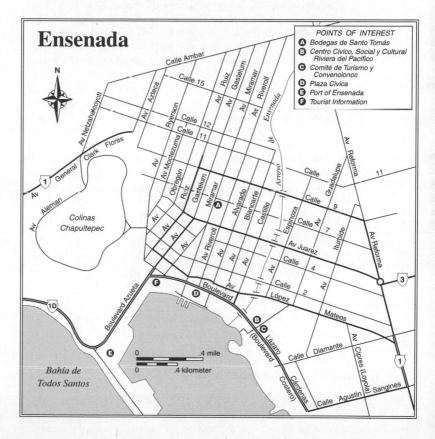

Ensenada

POINTS OF INTEREST
- Ⓐ Bodegas de Santo Tomás
- Ⓑ Centro Civico, Social y Cultural Riviera del Pacifico
- Ⓒ Comité de Turismo y Convenciones
- Ⓓ Plaza Civica
- Ⓔ Port of Ensenada
- Ⓕ Tourist Information

beach. Guest rooms and beach bungalows have decks overlooking the bay, Mexican tile floors and handcarved furniture; the bungalows have kitchenettes and fireplaces. Amenities include a swimming pool and tennis courts. ~ Route 1, Km. 110; 74-41-55, or 619-491-0682 in the U.S. MODERATE.

Centrally located between the main shopping and restaurant street and the Centro Artesanal next to Tres Cabezas Plaza, the 12-story **Hotel Villa Marina** is within easy walking distance of everything downtown, and there's no problem finding your way back—it's the tallest highrise in town. The upper floors on the ocean side offer great views of the port and bay, though on weekend nights the din from the nightclub on the top floor can make guests wish they'd settled for a lower angle of view. Other rooms overlook Avenida López Mateos and the heart of the downtown tourist zone. The 175 cozy, cool and contemporary guest rooms are decorated in shades of blue, and most have narrow private balconies. ~ Avenida López Mateos at Avenida Blancarte; 78-33-21, fax 78-33-51. MODERATE.

A little farther south on López Mateos and a little more affordably priced, the Mediterranean-style **Hotel El Cid** offers standard motor inn accommodations in 52 guest rooms (many with queen-size beds) that are individually decorated to represent the state capital cities of Mexico. There's a heated swimming pool, plus cable TV, phones and air-conditioning in every room. Room rates plunge almost into the budget range during the winter/spring off-season. ~ Avenida López Mateos 993; 78-24-01, fax 78-36-71. MODERATE.

The **Estero Beach Resort** fronts on a secluded stretch of sand at the south end of Bahía de Todos Santos, far from the pandemonium of downtown Ensenada. This beautifully landscaped complex has 106 light, modern guest rooms, ranging from small, bungalow-style units and spacious, modern one- and two-bedroom

---

✔ **CHECK THESE OUT—UNIQUE LODGING**

- *Budget:* Spend a night or two at **Mike's Sky Rancho**, a hideaway for motorcycle enthusiasts (and others) deep in the mountains. *page 99*
- *Moderate:* Escape to a desert oasis in the guise of **Hotel & Suites Las Misiones San Felipe.** *page 112*
- *Moderate to ultra-deluxe:* Savor the traditional luxury of the **Rosarito Beach Hotel and Spa**, a favorite Hollywood haunt in the Roaring Twenties. *page 96*
- *Deluxe:* Hang your hat and enjoy the breathtaking ocean view at **Las Rosas**, perched on a bluff near Ensenada. *page 97*

Budget: under $35   Moderate: $35–$70   Deluxe: $70–$105   Ultra-deluxe: over $105

units with balconies overlooking the ocean to large suites, equipped with kitchens, that can sleep four adults. There are no phones in the rooms. Outdoor sports are the best reason to pick this resort. There are tennis courts and a boat ramp, and you'll find saddle horses, fishing equipment, Wave Runners, kayaks, canoes and bicycles for rent. The resort sits at the edge of an estuary that attracts abundant pelicans, cormorants, egrets and hawks. It's quite a ways into town, but the resort has a restaurant and nightclub. ~ Route 1, Km. 10.5; 76-62-30, fax 76-69-25. MODERATE.

The **Hotel Joker,** south of Ensenada near the turnoff to La Bufadora, adds a touch of whimsical fun to what would otherwise be a routine hotel stay. The 40 guest rooms are contemporary and plain, with balconies overlooking the pool and very white walls and furnishings, but the exterior is a riot of eccentric architecture. Tudor gables and latticework and Gothic towers fill the facade of this essentially ordinary two-story motel to overflowing, and the crenelated turret of a medieval castle stands by the swimming pool and Jacuzzi, rising ten feet above the roofline and affording an ocean view. ~ Route 1, Km. 12.5; phone/fax 76-72-01. BUDGET.

There are no lodging accommodations along Route 3 between Ensenada and San Felipe. Well . . . actually there's one, but **Mike's Sky Rancho** is a little off the beaten track, at 4000 feet elevation on the northern boundary of Parque Nacional San Pedro Mártir, surrounded by mountains, waterfalls and pine forests, with a trout stream running right through the camp. Established by the late Mike Leon, a pioneer Baja 1000 racer, the Sky Rancho has traditionally been the private domain of dirt bikers and other off-roaders for one good reason: getting there requires a 35-kilometer drive on an unpaved road. These days, the resort is getting more family vacation trade, though the families often bring off-road vehicles with them. The road to Mike's, which turns off to the south from the main highway at the summit of San Matías Pass (near kilometer marker 138), is graded and well maintained during the summer months, though it can deteriorate badly over the winter. A passenger car capable of climbing steep hills can usually make the cautious journey from the highway in about two hours. Accommodations are in about a dozen rustic motel-like rooms, electricity is furnished by a gasoline-powered generator, and there are no phones. Moderately priced meals are served family-style in a central dining room. There's a swimming pool. ~ Reservations: P.O. Box 1948, Imperial Beach, CA 92032; 85-49-95 in Tijuana, or 619-428-5290 in the U.S. BUDGET.

◄ HIDDEN

The place to go for elegant dining in Rosarito is **Chabert's Restaurant.** Located at the Rosarito Beach Hotel and Spa, in the mansion

DINING

of the hotel's founder, the restaurant evinces nostalgia for the opulence of the 1920s. The French and Continental cuisine may be the best in the Baja. ~ Boulevard Benito Juárez, Rosarito; 2-01-44. DELUXE.

For more casual fare, **Ortega's Place** in Rosarito offers $1.99 breakfasts and an all-you-can-eat soup-and-salad bar. The specialty in this upstairs restaurant is *langosto estilo Puerto Nuevo* —lobster sliced in half lengthwise, fried in a pot of boiling oil and served with butter, lime and salsa. The Ortega family also operates several lobster restaurants under the same name in Puerto Nuevo. ~ Boulevard Benito Juárez 200, Rosarito; 2-27-91. BUDGET TO MODERATE.

Puerto Nuevo, often called "Newport," just down the road from Rosarito, is a fishing village turned food court. Prime lobster waters lie just offshore, and roadside vendors started selling fried lobster here soon after the road to Ensenada was built. Today, the lobster stands have evolved into a complex of more than two dozen permanent, full-service restaurants. Ranging in appearance from slightly funky to nearly fancy, all serve the same thing —fried lobster—as well as shrimp and fish when available. Most of the families who operate these restaurants catch their own lobsters during the October-to-March season; the rest of the year, the restaurants serve lobsters imported from Australia. Reservations are not taken. ~ Route 1, Km. 44. MODERATE.

As you approach Ensenada from the north, watch for **Enrique's Restaurant** on the ocean side of the highway. Long a local institution, this hole-in-the-wall place got its start as a roadside fried-shrimp stand. Over the decades, it has expanded into a romantic restaurant with a great view of the port. The menu has expanded, too, highlighting exotic Continental dishes like frog legs and glazed quail, but it's still the shrimp that justify the restaurant's reputation. ~ Route 1, Km. 101; 78-24-61. MODERATE.

Ensenada's **Mercado de Mariscos**, at the north end of the waterfront near the tourist information office and sport-fishing docks, is surrounded by open-air stands selling fish tacos—sticks of fresh fish battered, deep-fried and wrapped in a corn tortilla. Condiments range from guacamole to sliced radishes. ~ North end of Boulevard Costero. BUDGET.

The downtown tourist zone is packed with overpriced Mexican restaurants with menus so unimaginative that you might as well be back home at a Taco Bell. Locals who work downtown join the tourist throngs in **El Charro**, which offers some of the best prices around on enchiladas, burritos and chiles rellenos. The specialty is *pollo asado*—whole chickens roasted on spits in the restaurant's front window. ~ Avenida López Mateos 475; 78-38-81. BUDGET.

One of the longest-established restaurants in Ensenada, **El Cid** serves a full range of less familiar Mexican specialties, such as *pescado veracruzano* (fish in a tangy salsa) and *chiles Gertrudis* (a special kind of stuffed chile), as well as international gourmet dishes like quail in rosé sauce and the restaurant's award-winning "Oscaritos"—baby squid stuffed with clams. The atmosphere is shadowy, candlelit and Spanish. ~ Avenida López Mateos 993; 78-24-01. MODERATE.

El Rey Sol has been serving authentic French cuisine in Ensenada since 1947, when the restaurant was opened by a Frenchman and his Mexican wife; they met while working as chefs in Paris. Under their family's management ever since, El Rey Sol maintains the highest standards in food and service. Stained glass and heavy, dark furniture set the mood. The menu is built around fish and seafood selections, including such exotica as filet of manta ray. Besides using freshly caught fish, the chef uses produce from the owners' farm in Santo Tomás. Bread and pastries are baked on the premises. ~ Avenida López Mateos 1000; 78-17-33. DELUXE.

The exterior of **Bronco's Steak House** proclaims "¡LA NUEVA COSTUMBRE MEXICANA—DE COMER STEAKS!" ("The new Mexican custom—of eating steaks!") In fact, many local Mexican families who would never set foot in a downtown tourist restaurant come to Bronco's to celebrate birthdays and other holidays. The interior is wood-paneled and decorated with ranch memorabilia, and the food contains a good selection of traditional Mexican dishes such as *carne asada* (beef strips marinated in red chile sauce and barbecued) as well as thick-cut steaks and south-of-the-border specialties like *boca del rio*, a strip steak that is split and stuffed with chiles and spices. The all-you-can-eat luncheon buffet and Sunday brunch mix Mexican and gringo food. ~ Avenida López Mateos 1000; 76-49-00. MODERATE.

A haven for vegetarians in Ensenada, **El Mesón Vegetariano**. ◄ HIDDEN This plain little place features East Indian dishes and green salads, along with a few veggie variations on Mexican standbys. A bulletin board here can help you track down Ensenada's low-profile holistic and metaphysical scene. There is a good bakery next door. ~ Avenida Alvarado 377. BUDGET.

The trendiest restaurant in Ensenada at this writing is **La Embotelladora Vieja**, serving seafood and Continental fare in a big converted warehouse that was once a wine-aging room for the Bodegas de Santo Tomás winery next door. The food is first-rate and the atmosphere makes up in country French romanticism for whatever it may lack in the way of quiet intimacy. But the real attraction is the spectacle of all that wine. The walls are literally covered with racks of wine bottles from every vintner in Baja, and the wine list is formidable. It has become a fashionable place to sample Mexican wines and savor Cuban cigars, so diners may wish to steer toward the far end of the nonsmoking section. ~ Avenida Miramar 666; 74-08-07. DELUXE.

While Ensenada boasts more than its share of fine dining, most Mexican food in restaurants is Americanized for the gringo palate. To try authentic local food, stop at one of the roadside **tamal stands** that line Route 1 south of town on the way to the La Bufadora turnoff. Tamales—cakes of corn meal mush that are stuffed, wrapped in corn husks and steamed—come not only in the meat-stuffed variety familiar in the United States but also with an assortment of other fillings ranging from diced shrimp to pineapple. Some vendors may stare dumbfounded when you order, because of the widely held belief that gringos can't eat real Mexican food without getting sick. My experience with roadside stands in Ensenada and most other parts of Baja suggests that this fear is unfounded. ~ Route 1 south. BUDGET.

GROCERIES　**Supermercado Gigante** carries most of the same food items you'd expect to find in a supermarket in the United States. ~ Gastelum 672; 78-26-44. The waterfront **Mercado de Mariscos**—a genuine public fish market, not just another tourist trap—is the place to go for fresh-caught fish, shrimp, squid, octopus, clams and lobsters. ~ North end of Boulevard Costero. For natural foods, organic produce and herbal remedies, try **La Milpa**. ~ Calle 4 1329; 76-10-05.

SHOPPING　Ensenada is the best gift-shopping town north of Los Cabos, thanks to the large numbers of free-spending cruise ship passengers who stroll the sidewalks of Avenida López Mateos. There's a wide selection of merchandise in all price ranges, and although you won't find Third World prices in Ensenada—or anywhere in Baja—there are bargains to be found in items such as leather goods, silver jewelry, Mexican designer fashions and ceramics. Bartering is inappropriate in stores here, although street vendors are willing to negotiate prices, as are merchants at La Bufadora's flea market and Mercado Los Globos.

Silver prices in retail shops are highly competitive and significantly lower than in U.S. jewelry stores. One reliable shop is **Los Castillo**, a family-owned jewelry chain that started in Ensenada in 1969 and has expanded to resort areas throughout Mexico. The Castillos represent many of the finest designers in Taxco, Mexico's premier silversmithing center, with jewelry in both .925 (sterling silver) and .950 purities. They also carry pewter and ceramic items and handcarved furniture. ~ Avenida López Mateos 815, 76-11-87; second location at Avenida López Mateos 656.

The best feature of the **Santa Paula Bazar**, a crowded curio mini-mall in the heart of the tourist zone, is the stained glass and handblown glass of Armando Ozuna, who practices his craft daily in the front display window to the fascination of onlookers. ~ 537 Avenida López Mateos.

There are bargains to be found in Mexican leather goods, including leather jackets, hats, huaraches, handbags, daypacks, belts, boots and even saddles. Many small shops in the cruise-ship shopping zone along Avenida López Mateos carry similar selections at similar prices. You'll find a wider choice of leather clothing and accessories at **Nuevo México Lindo Talabarteria**, a shop known for its handmade saddles. ~ Calle 1 688; 78-13-81.

Many tourist zone shops specialize in contraband—especially Cuban cigars, firecrackers and switchblade knives. All are illegal in the United States; that's the only reason they're sold here. As a practical matter, the risk of being caught at the border with any of these items is low enough to put this kind of casual smuggling in the cheap-thrills category. Mexican vendors mock U.S. laws that let Americans buy all the firearms they want but outlaw cherry bombs.

At La Bufadora, the street that leads to the geyser overlook is lined with curio shops for blocks. The merchandise is similar to that found in many stores downtown, with an emphasis on leather goods; asking prices start higher than downtown but are negotiable. This tourist shopping area has been dubbed the **flea market** by tour guides, and if you ask a taxi driver to take you to the flea market, this is where you'll wind up. ~ Carretera Punta Banda.

Ensenada does have a swap-meet-style flea market, **Mercado Los Globos**. On the east side of town in an area rarely frequented by tourists, the vast eight-block market operates every day but has the most vendors, as well as the biggest crowds, on Saturdays and Sundays. Browsers can spot occasional Mexican collectibles and

◄ *HIDDEN*

THE SIGN OF SILVER

Many street vendors in the tourist zone offer jewelry that they insist is made of sterling silver. Mexican law requires manufacturers to stamp a number—".925" (the percentage of silver in sterling), ".950" or ".999" (pure silver)—into each piece of jewelry, along with a mark showing who made it. If the number and mark aren't there or are illegible, chances are it's *alpaca*. Sometimes called German silver, alpaca is an alloy of copper, nickel and zinc and actually contains no silver.

curiosities scattered among the produce stalls and piles of cheap plastic housewares. ~ Calle 9 east of Avenida Reforma.

South of Ensenada, olive orchards cover thousands of acres. At **roadside stands** along Route 1, farmers' daughters sell olive oil and several varieties of olives in glass jars.

Travelers crossing the peninsula from Ensenada to San Felipe on Route 3 may want to check out two modest shops in **Ejido Héroes de la Independencia** that sell crude coil pottery made by the Paipai Indians. The last remnant of Baja's original inhabitants, the Paipai live in small groups around the site of Misión Santa Catarina, eight kilometers east of the *ejido*, though the mission itself has been abandoned for more than 150 years. ~ Route 3, Km. 92.

NIGHTLIFE   The place to start an evening investigating Ensenada's night spots is **Hussong's Cantina**, the most famous bar in town and the oldest continuously operating bar in the Californias, Alta and Baja. It was built in 1892 by a family of German immigrants, who established a small brewery on the premises and served German beer to local miners, dockworkers and politicians. Today the old bar looks the same, though its trademark beer is brewed in Mazatlán, and tourists pack the place most nights. Mexican bands play traditional Norteño music late into the night. A Hussong's souvenir shop sells an amazing array of T-shirts, baseball caps, ash trays, bumper stickers and other promotional gear printed with the cantina's logo. ~ Avenida Ruiz 113; 78-32-10.

For a less rowdy crowd and a better view, visit the nightclub on the top floor of the **Hotel Villa Marina**, the tallest building in the city. There's live music Thursday through Saturday nights and disco during the week. Cover. ~ Avenida López Mateos at Avenida Ruiz; 78-33-21.

There are a half a dozen or so other big discos downtown. Designed for crowd management during spring break, these places can seem cavernous on many nights. Check out **Bananas,** if only for the disco's spectacular lightshow. ~ Boulevard Costero 277; 78-20-04.

Ensenada's only gay bar is the low-profile **Coyote Club**. Cover. ~ Avenida Costero 1000.

BEACHES & PARKS   The Pacific Ocean beaches of Baja California Norte are most attractive in the summer and early fall, when they present a less crowded alternative to San Diego and L.A. beaches. The water is too cold for comfort in winter and spring, and it is often windy.

PLAYA ROSARITO This is the closest great Mexican beach to the U.S. border, so it is full of funseekers on most weekends. People live in luxury condos along Playa Rosarito and commute to work in San Diego. If peace and quiet is what you want, Rosarito isn't the place to look for it. Surfers say the waves here are awesome. ~ Located 24 kilometers south of Tijuana on Route 1.

▲ **Chuy's Trailer Park** has 26 RV campsites on the beach with full hookups, hot showers and a restaurant; $25 per night. 2-16-08.

PLAYA CANTAMAR 🏃 🏊 🎣 Calmer than Rosarito, this pretty three-mile beach is separated from the highway by a broad field of sand dunes—a favorite weekend playground for noisy ATVers. There are resort hotels but no camping. ~ Located 47 kilometers south of Tijuana on Route 1.

PLAYA MAL PASO 🏃 🏊 🎣 This wide, soft beach runs for almost three miles and is largely undeveloped. It is known for its grunion runs, which draw a small crowd of fishwatchers and curiosity seekers every full-moon and new moon night in spring and summer. Silvery, seven-inch adult fish lay their eggs in the beach sand, somehow timing it so that ten days later they will hatch during a peak high tide. When they do hatch, the surf boils with thousands of baby fish, as locals scurry around catching them in buckets. ~ You can reach this beach through the Mal Paso RV Park, 71 kilometers south of Tijuana on Route 1, or Outdoor Resorts of Baja, one kilometer farther south.

▲ Despite its name, the **Mal Paso RV Park** is rustic enough to suit tent campers better than RVers. Sites are undefined; beach camping is permitted. No hookups, though there are restrooms and cold showers. Sites cost just $4 per night. ~ Route 1 Km. 71, La Misión. In contrast, **Outdoor Resorts of Baja**, a kilometer down the highway on the same beach, has it all: hot showers, laundry room, sauna, swimming pool, hot tub, game room, lighted tennis courts and even a miniature golf course. The 137 sites are on concrete pads and have full hookups, including cable TV. Sites cost $24 to $35 per night, with an extra charge for pets. Reservations are accepted. ~ Route 1 Km. 72; reservations—1177 Broadway, Suite 2, Chula Vista, CA 91911; 619-942-2264, 800-356-2252.

BAHÍA DE TODOS SANTOS 🏃 🏇 🏊 ⛵ 🎣 🚤 🛥️ All the way around the rim of the bay, beaches arc north and south from the Port of Ensenada. The northern reaches, around Las Rosas Resort, are the most attractive segment of the beach, and the southern part around Estero Beach Resort is also good. Closer to the port, the beach is less appealing, its waters clouded and discolored by oil films and muck stirred up from the bay's shallow bottom by ship propellers. Even in its urban sections, though, the beach makes for an interesting walk. ~ Route 1 from Punta San Miguel north of Ensenada to Ejido Chapultepec south of the city.

▲ Ensenada's most centrally located beach campground is **Campo Playa RV Park**, just over the bridge south of downtown on the east side of Boulevard Lázaro Cárdenas; you must walk across this bridge to reach the beach. There are 90 sites, all with concrete pads and hookups, and hot showers. Fees are $16 per night. ~ Boulevard Las Dunas at Calle Diamante; 76-29-18. For about the same price you could camp at the **Estero Beach Resort**, toward the south end of the bay, and enjoy the resort's facilities, including snorkeling, horse, bicycle, sailboard and Jet Ski rentals and tennis courts. There are 60 sites, all with concrete pads and hookups, and hot showers. Fees are $18 per night. ~ Route 1, Km. 10.5; 76-62-30, fax 76-69-25.

PLAYA PUNTA BANDA 🏃🚴🏊🛶🚣🚤🛥 A long, straight, sandy beach runs along the north side of Punta Banda, the narrow peninsula that encloses the Bahía de Todos Santos. Like the peninsula itself, the beach is largely undeveloped. Surf fishing here is said to be the best in the area. ~ Turn west off Route 1, 18 kilometers south of Ensenada.

▲ **La Jolla Beach Camp** is a modest resort for RVers and tenters, with hot showers, a restaurant, a boat ramp and horse rentals. Campsites are on the beach and undefined; $6 per night. **HIDDEN ►** No hookups. ~ Carretera Punta Banda Km. 12.5. Several **ejido camping areas** are located on the Punta Banda road between Km. 2 and Km. 8, offering primitive camping without such niceties as hookups, flush toilets or water. The steep dirt-road descent from the main road to the beach in this area makes these campgrounds all but inaccessible to motor homes but pleasantly secluded for tent and pickup campers. The fee is $1 per night.

▼▼▼▼▼▼▼▼▼▼▼▼
San Felipe Area

One of the most popular destinations in Baja, San Felipe has managed to preserve a "hidden"—if not an undiscovered—feel. Catering primarily to the motor-home and camper crowd, it lacks the big-resort ambience that characterizes other Baja hot spots like Ensenada and Los Cabos. On a remote bay near the northern end of the Sea of Cortez, San Felipe is separated from the heavily populated Pacific Coast by the highest mountains on the Peninsula. To get there, you must cross the Baja's most arid desert; once you arrive, you'll find a friendly little town where English is spoken everywhere and U.S. dollars are the preferred currency. Since the bottom fell out of the local fishing industry, tourism and vacation real estate development account for virtually all economic activity in San Felipe.

Jesuit priests landed on San Felipe's beach in the 18th century and established a small port for the purpose of delivering supplies to the Misión San Pedro Mártir in the forbidding mountains to the west. In 1806, when the mission closed, San Felipe was abandoned.

Drawn by the astonishing abundance of marine life in the northern Sea of Cortez, fishermen gradually migrated to San Felipe's bay and beach to establish a ramshackle village where people had no problem feeding their families but could not export their seafood for cash income because there was no way to carry fresh fish across the vast desert to market.

Prosperity came a step closer in 1952, when Mexico granted the United States the right to put a radar station at the south end of Bahía de San Felipe in exchange for funds to pave the road south from Mexicali. San Felipe was soon exporting huge quantities of shrimp to California and Arizona in refrigerated trucks. Sport fishermen from the United States started coming to San Felipe to catch *totuava*, a challenging 250-pound game fish known to anglos as sea trout. For 15 years, the fishing capital of San Felipe reigned as the most thriving community in the Baja.

Disaster struck in 1967, when a tropical storm totally destroyed San Felipe. While residents were struggling to rebuild, the Mexican government leased fishing rights in the Sea of Cortez to the Japanese fleet. In an operation that was unprecedented in scale, huge factory ships moved in and used long-line drift nets and giant underwater vacuum cleaners to extract most of the marine life from the northern gulf. The Mexican government finally terminated Japan's fishing rights by declaring the area off-limits to all commercial fishing for export. Today, San Felipe's small fishing and shrimping fleet only supplies local restaurants. The *totuava* has been declared an endangered species, and it is against the law to catch one.

San Felipe's economy was rescued from total collapse by RVs. With low prices and miles of undeveloped beaches just a few hours' drive from Phoenix or San Diego, San Felipe has become Mexico's top-ranking destination for trailer, camper and motorhome travelers, as well as dune buggy and all-terrain-vehicle enthusiasts. Though the winter months can be chilly, gringo "snowbirds" outnumber local residents between Christmas and Easter. The gringo presence reaches a frenzied peak during March, when college students from all over the western United States descend on San Felipe for spring break. Since the typical San Felipe visitor is fairly self-sufficient, the restaurant and resort hotel industry has not kept pace with the rise in tourism. Curio shops and liquor stores are plentiful, though.

Getting to San Felipe is half the fun. The distance from Mexicali is 198 kilometers; from Algodones, it's about the same, though unlike the Mexicali highway, the first part of the trip before you join Route 5 is quite slow. As it leaves the Valle de Mexicali agricultural zone, Route 5 crosses a broad green wetland along the west bank of the **Río Hardy**, a short tributary of the Colorado

SIGHTS

River. It forms an estuary, lush with reeds and tall grass and alive with herons, egrets and other wading birds, as it flows alongside the highway for about 12 kilometers before merging with the Colorado River. Most years, the Colorado itself is completely dry, since the water is diverted to irrigate farms on both sides of the border.

The Laguna Salada is so salty that plants cannot grow there.

As it veers away from the river, the road plunges across the heat-shimmering **Laguna Salada**, the largest dry lake bed in Baja. This usually empty "Salt Lake" was part of the Sea of Cortez until 400 years ago, when the buildup of silt on the river delta separated the lake from the gulf. It has taken from then until now for the lake bed to dry out completely. Some areas toward the north end still fill with water in times of heavy rain. In fact, Route 5 is elevated as much as nine feet above the barren, parched desert because even this part of the lake bed can still occasionally flood. Do not stop on the levee or walk or drive on the lake bed: the apparently hard, dry surface can conceal patches of soft mud or quicksand.

Beyond the Laguna Salada, the north end of the Sea of Cortez begins to come into hazy view across the vast, shimmering mud flats of the **Colorado River Delta**. Fifteen miles wide and up to 60 miles long, the flats are so nearly level that normal tides shift the coastline in and out by many miles twice a day. Before the Colorado's flow was completely diverted, the area was a green wetland teeming with life. As the freshwater supply dropped, the marshes' rising salt content killed the plants, leaving only sterile mud flats where seagulls glide in search of clams and crabs.

The highway gradually nears the sea as it runs south across the **Desierto de San Felipe**. In the rain shadow of the high peaks of the Sierra San Pedro Mártir, this is the driest desert in Baja. Most of this area receives between one and two inches of rain per year—though near the mountains there are places where, locals say, rain has never fallen in human memory. The desert is a pale, gravelly, alkaline expanse without the smallest tuft of grass. Not even cactus grows. The only plant life consists of creosote bushes, ocatillos and diminutive, green-barked palo verde trees. With only the tiniest of leaves, these plants do little to relieve the stark, dry look of the landscape—except during late April of some years, when the ocatillos erupt in a spray of flamingo-pink blossoms and the branches of the palo verdes fill to overflowing with yellow flowers.

It is 72 kilometers from the highway junction where Route 3 from Ensenada joins Route 5 to the town of San Felipe. From there, the road angles closer and closer to the sea. The last 15 kilometers before reaching San Felipe run less than a kilometer from the beach. Packed-sand roads provide access to beachfront campgrounds, fish camps and vacation lot developments. Expect a military security checkpoint at the El Dorado Ranch Estates turnoff 11 kilometers north of town.

An improbable four-lane divided boulevard, Calzada Chetumal, whisks you out of the desert and straight into the middle of San Felipe, passing a towering modernist monument and circling a landmark traffic roundabout, known in these parts as a *glorieta*. Despite this grand entrance, the town has only 13,000 residents, and the "downtown" commercial area is only two streets wide and four blocks long. The two main streets are one-way in opposite directions: the beachfront street, called simply Malecón, runs north; one block inland, Avenida Mar de Cortez runs south.

The center of activity is the **malecón**, the sidewalk promenade along the wide, white beach that borders the business district. Young lovers linger on the steps and low walls at the foot of a crude statue that depicts a fisherman dragging a huge *totuava*. Nearby, (normally) gentle waves lick the sand and beachgoers relax in the shade of a few thatch-roofed shelters or pitch their own tents on the sand for relief from the sun's glare. North of the statue, fishermen beach their motorized *pangas*. Beyond the north end of the *malecón*, in a large, bowl-shaped sand lot, lies a jumble of fishing boats wrecked by storms.

San Felipe's best sight is the view from the **Virgin of Guadalupe Shrine**, located on the conical hill above the cliffs at the north end of town. A 120-step climb up the concrete stairway to the squarish, white concrete block shrine is amply rewarded with a spectacular view of San Felipe's mountains, desert, beaches and bay.

To experience the Desierto de San Felipe up close, head north of town on Route 5 for 11 kilometers to a wide road that runs toward the mountains. A sign says "El Dorado Ranch Estates," and there is sometimes an army security checkpoint at the intersection. **El Dorado Ranch Estates** was a scheme hatched in the mid-1980s to attract vacationers to San Felipe. Thousands of lots were given away to gringos in a mail order contest. The giveaway lots were worthless, waterless, arroyo-slashed, rattlesnake-infested land, but for an extra payment owners could trade them in on better lots close to the highway. Today, the "upgrade" subdivision has become a sizeable community of snowbirds in trailers and prefab cottages. As the wide dirt road heads east across pale, sandy ground studded with ocatillo and palo verde, after ten kilometers or so it passes a scattering of survivors living in tents and RVs on the original prize lots.

Beyond the last signs of civilization, the road forks. Turn around here if your vehicle is not suitable for driving in sand. The left fork meanders south along the base of the mountains, passing through several small ranching villages before it deadends. Drivers of fat-tire trucks, Baja bugs, all-terrain vehicles and

dirt bikes who take the right fork will soon find themselves crossing the **Laguna Diablo**, a long, narrow lakebed of dry sand. The
lakebed is normally so hardpacked that smugglers have been
known to use it as an airstrip, and a standard passenger car can
cross it with no problem. But in relatively wet years, it can become the kind of place that even off-roaders must speed across
for fear that if they slow down, they'll sink up to their axles in
the drifting sand. Before taking this route, be sure you have a full
day's supply of water. Before crossing sandy areas, get out and
walk the road to see where the soft and hard parts are. And if
you do get stuck, dig the sand away from the wheels, let half the
air pressure out of each tire and don't slow down until you get
back to the highway. You can pump your tires back to the cor-
rect pressure at the Pemex station in San Felipe.

After the road crosses the first segment of the Laguna Diablo,
a two-track ranch road exits to the left and heads for the base of
10,154-foot **Picacho del Diablo**, the highest mountain on the Baja
peninsula. It is possible to climb to the summit from the trailhead
parking area at road's end, but most hikers content themselves
HIDDEN ► with exploring the lush hidden landscape of **Cañon del Diablo**,
where year-round springs feed pools, waterfalls and streams, creating a long, hidden oasis whose flora ranges from cardón and
barrel cactuses to cedars, oaks and willows. Past the turnoff to
Cañon del Diablo, the road continues across the broader part of
the Laguna Diablo and eventually meets Route 3 about 100 kilometers north of San Felipe on the way to Ensenada.

A less risky side trip from San Felipe is down the narrow, paved
coastal **road to Puertecitos**, 76 kilometers to the south. Though
pitted with potholes and interrupted by *vados*—eight-foot-deep
dips designed to control the course of flash floods after occasional
mountain rainstorms—the road is easily passable by motor homes,
passenger cars and trucks with boats in tow. Rarely out of sight
of the sea, the route takes motorists through a landscape that is
stark, pale, flat and arid. Besides the ocatillos and palo verdes of
the San Felipe area, the vegetation includes occasional giant *cardón* cactuses. An unusual dwarf tree found along this route is the
incense tree or *torote colorado*, whose twigs give off a distinctive
perfume scent when burned like incense. The squat, pinkish tree's
trunk is shaped like an elephant's foot, so some people call it a
kind of elephant tree; however, it belongs to a completely separate genus from the white-barked elephant trees found in the Desierto Central and farther south.

HIDDEN ►   The strange little village of **Puertecitos** is segregated into a
Mexican barrio, where local fishermen and their families live in
small, crude shacks, and a gringo enclave where snowbirds and
expatriates hide out, as far beyond the reach of telephones, TV
ads and the IRS as you can get towing a boat. You'll know this

is no ordinary retirement community as soon as you enter the village, passing the Public Library and U.S. Post Office, twin edifices that appear to be remodeled outhouses, and the sign that reads "Sobriety Checkpoint Ahead." Puertecitos residents have elevated stealing U.S. road signs to an art form, and houses all over town are festooned with notices of nonexistent School X-ings, Mansion Districts, Bus Stops, Unauthorized Areas and Freeway Entrances.

On a rocky beach near the point south of the village are **Puer-tecitos Hot Springs**, a cluster of sulfurous pools, each a different temperature. Bathers here quickly become so relaxed that they don't mind the mineral odor. Admission.

◄ HIDDEN

For most sightseers, including anybody in a rental car, Puertecitos is the end of the trip; return to San Felipe by the same route. If your vehicle has high clearance and four-wheel drive, the rough road that continues south from Puertecitos, known as the **Carretera Gonzaga**, offers an adventurous short cut to points south on the Baja Transpeninsular Highway. The Mexican government has been promising for years to pave this road. It's a notion that looks great on paper—an alternate route to Baja California Sur that would stimulate tourism on the gulf coast and relieve overcrowding at the Tijuana border crossings. But anyone who has driven the road from Puertecitos to Gonzaga knows that it is not likely to become a highway any time soon. Walk each questionable segment before attempting to drive it. In dry weather, most of the route is manageable in a passenger car whose driver has nerves of steel; but a series of steep, rocky grades beginning 27 kilometers south of Puertecitos and continuing for about 20 kilometers makes for a hair-raising trip. The roadbuilding effort so far has consisted of pouring bags of wet cement down the daunting slopes.

The Carretera skirts volcanic coastal mountains on its way to **Bahía San Luís Gonzaga**, as isolated a piece of paradise as you're likely to find in Baja. Long, soft sand beaches along the north part of the bay offer good swimming; fishing is best toward the south end of the bay with its mountainous coastline. Scattered vacation homes have sprung up along the water even in this remote place; their owners get there by boat, not by car.

◄ HIDDEN

From Alfonsina's, a beachfront restaurant and sometime gas station with basic rooms to rent near the north end of Bahía San Luís Gonzaga, the road veers inland, goes 60 kilometers across a plateau and joins The Baja Transpeninsular Highway in the middle of the Desierto Central, halfway between Cataviña and the turnoff to Bahía de los Angeles.

The **Motel El Cortez**, on the beach about five blocks south of the statue at the center of the *malecón*, is ideally located for taking in all the local action. You know, the ATVs and monster trucks that cruise the waterfront from breakfast time to mid-evening. Its

LODGING

78 clean, modern rooms have TV, air conditioning and a pleasantly all-American motel ambience. Facilities include an outdoor pool and a boat ramp. ~ Avenida Mar de Cortez; 7-10-55; reservations: P.O. Box 1227, Calexico, CA 92232. MODERATE.

Rock-bottom lodging can be found at the **Motel El Pescador**, which caters mainly to Mexican workers. The 24 spartan guest rooms are clean and air-conditioned, with tired double beds, private toilets and not much else. Staying here costs about twice as much as camping. Though not on the beach, it's close to everything in town. ~ Avenida Mar de Cortez at Calzada Chetumal; 7-10-44. BUDGET.

The newest resort hotel in town is the two-story, 120-room **Hotel Costa Azul**. Though the rooms are fairly ordinary, the location at the south end of the *malecón* is excellent, and the carefully tended landscaping creates an oasis against San Felipe's stark desert backdrop. There is a heated outdoor pool. ~ Avenida Mar de Cortez at Calle Ensenada; 1-15-48, fax 7-15-49. MODERATE.

The **Club Villa Las Brisas** has 50 suites, each with a fully equipped kitchen, living room, dining room and one or two bedrooms. The suites also have color TVs, air conditioning, and balconies with barbecues and ocean views. The hotel has a laundry room and a small convenience store. ~ Carretera Aeropuerto; 7-11-88. MODERATE.

Hotel & Suites Las Misiones San Felipe offers all-inclusive family plans for two- and three-night stays. Its 20 condo-style suites are modern and bright, and some have kitchenettes. The grounds are landscaped to resemble a desert oasis, complete with palm trees around the three swimming pools, and there are tennis courts. Its location is too far south to walk to town easily. ~ 800-464-4270 in the U.S. MODERATE.

The fanciest address in town is the **San Felipe Marina Resort**. The 58 luxury beachfront suites have sea-view balconies or patios and kitchenettes with microwaves. There are also a master suite and villas that can sleep up to eight; these rent in the ultra-deluxe range. Mexican handicrafts decorate the walls. Facilities include tennis courts and outdoor and indoor heated swimming pools. Despite the resort's name, the planned 100-slip yacht marina is still just a dream. ~ Carretera Aeropuerto Km. 4.5; 7-15-69, 7-14-55. DELUXE.

DINING

San Felipe is a great place to enjoy seafood on the cheap. The *malecón,* the three-block beachfront promenade in the center of town, is lined with small open-air restaurants called *comedores* —**Mariscos Norma's, Tacos y Cockteles Blanca**, and a dozen or so others—that serve fish tacos, shrimp cocktails, steamed clams, seven-seafood chowder and whole fried fish. The decor at these simple eateries is limited to picnic tables or plastic chairs and tables with checkered tablecloths; whatever they may lack in ambience, they recoup with sea views. ~ Malecón. BUDGET.

Located at the end of the *malecón*, **Rosita Restaurant** specializes in fish, lobster and clams—like every other restaurant on the San Felipe waterfront. However, it is just about the only place in town that serves steaks. There is a fine beachfront sea view. Open for breakfast. ~ Malecón. MODERATE.

Larger indoor restaurants are found away from the ocean along the town's main street. **Cachanillas** serves assorted shrimp and fish dishes, chile rellenos and other Mexican standards in a simple, air-conditioned atmosphere. (The same family also runs Cachanillas Taco Stand on the Malecón.) ~ Avenida Mar de Cortez 146; 7-10-39. MODERATE.

Practically next door, **Los Gemelos** is a cool, clean little restaurant with a varied menu of seafood and Mexican fare including pollo en mole—chicken in a delicious chile-and-chocolate sauce. Starting at 7 a.m., the breakfast menu offers a full range of American (bacon and eggs) and Mexican (*chilaquiles* and fruit plates) selections. ~ Avenida Mar de Cortez 136; 7-10-63. MODERATE.

The **Restaurant China Ocean** serves exceptional Chinese stir-fries in a dimly lit Asian atmosphere. Not surprisingly, the best choices on the menu involve shrimp, scallops, squid and other local fruits of the sea. ~ Avenida Mar de Cortez 148; 7-18-66. MODERATE.

The dining room at **San Felipe Marina Resort**, the undisputed best in town, features local seafood dishes such as shrimp in cilantro sauce and corvina in garlic sauce. The dining room with its three-story lofted cedar ceiling commands a panoramic view of the Sea of Cortez. ~ Carretera Aeropuerto Km. 4.5; 7-15-69. MODERATE.

✔ CHECK THESE OUT—UNIQUE DINING

- *Budget:* Feast on fish tacos and steamed clams at **Mariscos Norma's** or one of San Felipe's other beachside *comedores*. *page 112*
- *Moderate:* Crack open a local lobster fresh from the ocean at **Puerto Nuevo**, located between Rosarito and Ensenada. *page 100*
- *Moderate:* Taste succulent seafood and traditional Mexican fare in a historic setting at the **Old Mill Restaurant** in San Quintín. *page 120*
- *Deluxe:* Sup on filet of manta ray and other French delicacies at **El Rey Sol**, in business in Ensenada for more than 50 years. *page 101*

Budget: under $5 Moderate: $5–$10 Deluxe: $10–$18 Ultra-deluxe: over $18

GROCERIES   Like many Baja towns, San Felipe has no public produce market. Though the rich farming valley of Mexicali is just two hours away, the fresh fruits and vegetables to be found in San Felipe are usually disappointing. Look for them, along with assorted packaged foods and canned goods, at the main supermarket, **Abarrotes La Vaquita**, at the north end of the shopping district. ~ Avenida Mar de Cortez 338. You can get catch-of-the-day fish and other fresh seafood for a cookout at **Mariscos Chona**, a fish market located in a residential neighborhood just north of Calzada Chetumal. ~ Avenido Puerto de Guaymas 200; 7-10-19. Near the Restaurant China Ocean, **Panificadora Singapur** sells delicious fresh-baked bread and pastries at very low prices. ~ Avenida Mar de Cortez 122.

SHOPPING   Avenida Mar de Cortez, San Felipe's main commercial street, is lined with souvenir shops. The main stock in trade is T-shirts, bathing suits, sun hats, dark glasses and other assorted beach paraphernalia. Determined shoppers will find better-than-average selections of Mexican arts and crafts at **Curios Mitla** (Avenida Mar de Cortez 100; 7-11-32) and **Curios Roberta** (Avenida Mar de Cortez 222; 7-10-66).

NIGHTLIFE   San Felipe is not a place to go for glamorous nightlife. The after-dark scene is dominated by **Rockodile**—a big, youth-oriented club, built around a volleyball court, that strives for a spring break atmosphere all year. The sound system blares rock and disco and the beer flows freely until the wee hours. ~ Malecón 199; 7-12-19. The next-best bet is the mellower **San Felipe Beachcomber**, a sports bar that transforms itself into a dance hall after the televised games are over. ~ Calzado Chetumal at Malecón; 7-10-44.

BEACHES   **PLAYA LAS ALMEJAS** This eight-mile-long beach north of San Felipe is lined with campgrounds and private-lot developments, which are separated from the beach by steep sand banks in many places. More people seem to choose this beach than anyplace else in the San Felipe area to blast around on ATVs. The name, Spanish for "the clams," refers to the good clamdigging on the vast, wet sand flats that form at low tide as the surf recedes by half a mile or more. ~ The beach runs from Playa Blanca, eight kilometers north of San Felipe, to Campo Los Amigos, 22 kilometers north of town. Any road that does not have a guarded gate or a "members only" sign can provide beach access, though campgrounds may charge you a small day use fee.

▲ A number of large private campgrounds may be found along this beach. Though their main trade is RV travelers, tent campers are welcome at all of them, and after paying the site fee you can leave your car at the campground and pitch your tent right on the beach. Centrally located on the beach, **Pete's El Paraiso Camp** is the largest and has the most amenities, including a restaurant, bar, laundry room and exercise room; $10 per night. ~ Route 5, 13 kilometers north of San Felipe; no phone. Facilities are more limited at **Campo Los Amigos** at the north end of the beach, but they do include hot showers for a small extra charge; $7 per night. ~ Route 5, 22 kilometers north of San Felipe.

PLAYA SAN FELIPE 🏃 🏖 🛶 🚣 🚤 🛶 This beach starts at the hill where the Virgin of Guadalupe Shrine stands at the north end of town and curves around the Bahía de San Felipe, in an arc broken only by the marina, to Punta Estrella at the south end of the bay. The "downtown" part of the beach, along the malecón, is young and lively on winter weekends and frenetic during spring break. Toward the south end of town, the same beach is enjoyed by resort hotel guests. Still farther south, lot developments line the quieter part of the beach; free access is easy through any of several defunct developments that have vanished over the years, leaving landscaped but unpaved boulevards in the sand beyond the ruins of ostentatious entrance gates. ~ Access is from the *malecón* in San Felipe and points south along the road to Puertecitos.

▲ San Felipe has more than a dozen private campgrounds, almost all of them on the beach. Most welcome tenters, though several have only sites with concrete pads—best for motor homes but bad for backpackers' backs. One of the most luxurious is **San Felipe Marina Resort and RV Park**, a 143-site campground with full hookups (including cable TV), a restaurant, a swimming pool and a laundry room; sites are $25 to $35 per night, depending on the season. ~ Carretera Aeropuerto Km. 4.5; 7-14-35. San Felipe's most secluded campground is **Campo Numero Uno**. On a small cove just north of town, it is separated from the main beach by the cliffs below the Virgin of Guadalupe Shrine. There are rest rooms, palapa shelters and not much else at this campground, which is popular with Mexican families. There is a small beach and a gravelly tidal flat where locals gather mussels. Tent and RV sites are $10 to $12 per night. ~ Avenida Mar de Cortes.

◄ HIDDEN

NORTH OF PUERTECITOS 🏃 🏊 🛶 A nameless, almost unbroken 24-mile strand of beach extends from the village of Bahía Santa Maria south almost to Puertecitos. Intermittent beachfront campgrounds and lot developments dot the northern part of the beach. It becomes wilder and harder to reach by road the farther south you go. ~ The north end of the beach is 40 kilometers south of San Felipe on the road to Puertecitos.

▲ There are eight beach campgrounds in the area. All are primitive, lacking the niceties of some of the motor-home camps around San Felipe but ideal for tenters and tailgaters who want to be far away from tourist crowds. **Campo Jacaranda** is among the most basic and affordable—in fact, camping here is free. There are no hookups or other amenities, except outhouses. ~ Located 85 kilometers south of San Felipe; no phone. Octavio's **Campo Playa Escondido** may have the nicest location along this stark stretch of coastline, sharing a pretty, sandy cove with a local fish camp where the fishermen will often take campers out in their *pangas* for a small fee. Sites cost $5 per night, and there are outhouses and cold showers. ~ Located 88 kilometers south of San Felipe.

SOUTH OF PUERTECITOS   There are several beautiful beaches along the rugged four-wheel-drive road that continues south from Puertecitos. Playa La Costilla, 10 kilometers south of the village, is calm and ideal for swimming, with an offshore reef that makes for good snorkeling. Playa Bufeo, 63 kilometers south of Puertecitos, is a wide, sugar-white beach renowned for great surf fishing. Seven miles farther down the road, Playa El Faro also offers excellent swimming and fishing; it is one of the most remote beaches in Baja, and you'll probably have it all to yourself.

▲ There are no established campgrounds south of Puertecitos, but primitive camping is permitted on all beaches.

▼▼▼▼▼▼▼▼▼▼▼▼▼
San Quintín Area

The San Quintín Valley doesn't look much like the land of big cactuses and stark, jagged mountains that the word *Baja* conjures in many travelers' minds. For most of the 196-kilometer trip south from Ensenada, the highway runs through orchards and crop fields on a broad, flat plain inland from the coast. As you drive among vineyards, olive orchards and tomato fields, pause to consider the miracle.

Land reform and irrigation have transformed this region from a landscape so arid that all pre-20th-century attempts to settle it met with failure. Faint outlines of old adobe walls are all that remain of the early missions that first introduced agricultural crops to the area. A cemetery filled with English names and a ruined pier are the only evidence of grandiose gringo land development schemes in the 19th century.

Today, resorts are few and most of the Pacific coast remains wild and windswept. To see the ocean, take your chances on any of the numerous farm roads that turn off to the west from the main highway.

SIGHTS   Kilometer markers on the highway to San Quintín tell how far south of Ensenada you are. **Ejido Uruapan**, an ordinary-looking farm community near kilometer 41, exemplifies the growing presence in Baja of other Pacific Rim powers. The village of 1000 people has a factory that processes sea urchins for export to Japan, where they are used to make sushi. A Japanese company built the plant and runs it under a cooperative agreement with the *ejido*. The strawberry greenhouses are also a Japanese joint venture.

The town of Santo Tomás, 51 kilometers south of Ensenada, is the site of the **Misión Santo Tomás de Aquino**, founded by Dominican priests in 1791. Some of the grapes grown in the valley today, and used in making Ensenada's Bodegas de Santo Tomás varietal wines, are descendants of the Dominican vineyards. Only fragments of melted adobe walls remain of the former mission church, on the east side of the highway.

The ruins of **Misión San Vicente Ferrer**, located 88 kilometers south of Ensenada near the present-day town of San Vicente, date back to 1781, when the Dominicans built it as the headquarters for their northern missions. The sad remains of old adobe walls are all that remain of the fortresslike church. The ruins are half a mile west of Route 1 on an ungraded dirt road.

Got time for an all-day side trip? Here's an easy expedition to one of the most unexpected places in Hidden Baja—the **Sierra San Pedro Mártir**. The sierra are the highest on the Baja Peninsula thanks to a single massive, white granite crag: 10,498-foot **Picacho del Diablo**, the "Devil's Peak," looms at the extreme eastern edge of the sierra. Although it seems to drop straight down on the east side for 9000 feet to the floor of the Desierto de San Felipe, the road up the west side is a beautifully scenic drive up long, gentle grades. As you go south on Route 1, watch for the side road on the left (east) just after kilometer 140 and just before crossing the bridge over the little Río San Telmo. A sign says "SAN TELMO/OBSERVATORIO." This is one of the widest, smoothest unpaved roads in Baja. It's a 200-kilometer round trip from the highway, so it might be wise to gas up at the Pemex in Colonet first.

The road takes you through a progression of contrasting landscapes as it makes its way into the high country. Soon after you pass through San Telmo, a tiny hillside village comprising half a dozen farmers' houses and a white concrete chapel with a lawn where cows graze, fields of hay and wheat give way to juniper, piñon and oak. An hour's drive will take you past a turnoff on the left for a very rough four-wheel-drive road that goes 26 kilometers north to Mike's Sky Rancho, a legendary bed and breakfast for bikers (see "Ensenada Area Lodging"). Immediately after this, another road turns off on the right and plunges down a long hill to **Rancho San José**, also called Meling Ranch, a 10,000-acre working cattle spread that doubles as a guest ranch. Visitors are welcome, though no gas or food is for sale there.

At higher elevations, where the ground is covered with snow (and the road is often closed) in winter, tall pine and fir trees grow, with scattered groves of aspen and a few San Pedro Mártir cypress, a rare species that grows only in these mountains. More

HIDDEN ▶

than 170,000 acres of tall, cool forests and wildflower meadows have been set aside as **Parque Nacional Sierra San Pedro Mártir**, a vast wilderness that is virtually roadless except for this route. One of Mexico's least-known national parks, it receives only an estimated 300 carloads of visitors per year!

After crossing the cattle guard that marks the park entrance, the road winds its way up to the **Observatorio Nacional de Mexico**, set on a ridgeline at 9300 feet above sea level. The observatory is only open on Saturdays from 11 a.m. to 1 p.m., at which time guided tours in Spanish are offered to any sightseers who may show up. Not many do. The rest of the week, the gate two kilometers below the observatory is locked, but hikers can park and walk up to two nearby overlooks for spectacular views of Picacho del Diablo and Cañon del Diablo.

From **Vallecitos**, a parklike meadow six kilometers before the locked gate, the three-story, domed white observatory due north on the ridgeline makes a reliable landmark while exploring the forest of sugar pine, lodgepole pine and white fir that surrounds the meadow. Were it not for the profusion of jays and songbirds, Vallecitos would be absolutely silent—on weekdays, at least.

The mountain range and park were named for the **Misión San Pedro Mártir**, established in 1794 about 18 miles—as the crow flies; more like 30 miles by hiking trail—south of the present-day observatory, in a part of the mountains that remains all but inaccessible to this day. The mission proved to be a hopeless folly for the Dominican priests who came to Christianize the indigenous people of Baja. Even though more Indians lived in these cool, wet, forested mountains teeming with wildlife than in any other part of the peninsula, it was so hard to bring in supplies from either coast that the mission was shut down after only 12 years. Today, you have to be an amateur archaeologist to spot the melted adobe ruins, which have fared worse than most others because of the higher rainfall.

Back on Route 1, at kilometer 169 you'll come to an unpaved road to the left (east) that leads eight miles to the village of Santo Domingo, site of the ruins of **Misión Santo Domingo**. One of the first missions in northern Baja, it was established by Dominican priests in 1775 and operated for 64 years. Though deteriorated beyond recognition, the church's three-foot-thick adobe walls are still visible after two centuries. The ruins are located in a pasture just west of the village school.

San Quintín and its adjacent southern "suburb," Lázaro Cárdenas, form a community of 25,000 at the southern end of Baja's Pacific agricultural plain. San Quintín dates back to 1884, when Mexican President Porfirio Díaz granted vast land concessions covering most of Baja California Norte to a New York-based corporation with plans to sell the land to expatriate U.S. wheat farmers and make flour for export. The company built a flour mill and port facility along the shore of San Quintín's sheltered estuary, but the few pioneers who bought farms in the area retreated northward as drought destroyed their crops year after year. The next time a wet year came along, the New York company seized the opportunity to sell San Quintín—land, town, port and mill—to a British investment group, which brought settlers from England and built a larger mill, shipping docks and a customs house. They even started construction of a railroad line to San Diego. But the wheat farmers fared no better than their predecessors. Drought returned, and the last of the colonists left San Quintín by 1900.

Remnants of the failed enterprise can still be seen. A wide gravel road to the right (west) one kilometer south of Colonia Lázaro Cárdenas leads to **Puerto San Quintín** on the grassy shores of the sheltered estuary. The old grist mill has been extensively restored and is now the site of the Old Mill Restaurant. The British shipping pier is about a mile down the coast, behind the Muelle Viejo Motel, and still farther along is a graveyard known as the Old English Cemetery, although today few English names are to be found on the headstones and wooden crosses there. Irrigation has transformed the arid fields that defeated American and British farmers into some of the richest vegetable farmland in Baja. Once again, the Valle de San Quintín is occupied by newcomers from a distant land—this time Mixtec Indians from the poor state of Oaxaca in southeastern Mexico. They struggle as stoop laborers to support families on Mexican minimum wage in the agri-industrial farmlands that fill the valley today.

The **Old Mill Motel** offers 34 units, including simply furnished sleeping rooms, studios with kitchenettes and two-bedroom suites with fireplaces. The bayside location is exceptional for birdwatching and fishing. The restaurant here serves the best food between Ensenada and San Quintín; it also has the most popular gringo fishermen's bar on this part of the coast. Rowdiness can last late into the night. If you can't, ask for a unit as far away from the restaurant and bar as possible. No phones. ~ Located about 8 kilometers south of San Quintín; Reservations: 11217 Adriatic Place, San Diego, CA 92126; 619-428-2779, 800-479-7962, fax 619-271-0952 in the U.S. BUDGET.

LODGING

Rancho Sereno Bed & Breakfast has just three guest units on the shady, wooded grounds adjacent to the headquarters of a working ranch. Each unit is individually decorated, and the largest has a king-size bed and a fireplace. There is electricity for limited hours, no air-conditioning, TV or phones. Reservations are essential. ~ Located 2.5 kilometers west of Route 1 south of San Quintín; 909-982-7087 in the U.S. MODERATE.

The **Hotel La Pinta**, at the north end of Playa Santa María, would be a fairly conventional budget motel in many parts of America except for its location. Most of the sprawling one-story complex's 58 rooms look out on Bahía San Quintín, and it's the only hotel in sight on the gentle, grassy shoreline. Most guests come here for the fishing, which is said to be exceptional. No phones or air-conditioning. ~ Route 1, Km. 16 south of San Quintín; 5-28-78. MODERATE.

Rancho San José (Meling Ranch) is a guest facility and working cattle ranch high in the Sierra San Pedro Mártir, near the park boundary. The ranch has a spectacular hill country setting and a remarkable history. It was founded in 1899 by Harry and Ella Johnson, who bought a franchise from the Mexican government giving them dominion over a vast expanse of the sierra. It succeeded where other Baja ventures of that era because Johnson discovered a deposit of gold on his land and made a quarter of a million dollars from his mine before 1911, when the ranch was destroyed and Johnson's family was slaughtered while he was on a business trip to the United States. His only surviving daughter, Alberta, married Norwegian expatriate Salve Meling, who rebuilt the ranch in the 1920s. The Melings acquired a reputation for hosting travelers in the Sierra San Pedro Mártir, and their ranch became a popular celebrity retreat in the 1950s. The late Alberta Meling was the first woman to drive the newly paved Baja Highway in 1973, arriving in Cabo San Lucas on her 90th birthday.

The ranch's ten guest rooms are rustic. Deer hunters in autumn are the primary clientele; spring and summer adventurers wishing to explore the 10,000-acre ranch and the wilderness of the Sierra San Pedro Mártir are more than welcome. The ranch has no phones but does have an airstrip for fly-in guests and a swimming pool. ~ Reservations: Rancho Meling, Apartado Postal 1326, Ensenada, or Meling Fishing and Hunting Services, 1777 Knapp Drive, Vista, CA 92804. MODERATE.

DINING

HIDDEN ▶

The **Old Mill Restaurant** is one of the Baja Highway's pleasurable surprises. Set on the grassy shore of Bahía San Quintín, it stands on the site of an old flour mill built by an anglo land development company as part of an overly optimistic plan to transform the sunbaked coastal plain into the breadbasket of the Californias. The original mill has been expanded by disassembling a former fish cannery, shipping it from northern California and rebuilding it plank by plank. The house specialty is lobster. Dozens of them crawl, huddle and clack their claws in a large aquarium tank in the front room, unwittingly waiting to be boiled at your pleasure. (You can also order fish.) A guitarist sings ballads from the dinner hour on, the sunset view is exquisite, and gringo fishermen swap yarns up and down the restaurant's central bar late into the evening. ~ South of San Quintín. MODERATE.

The commercial strip of San Quintín and Ejido Lázaro Cárdenas runs along both sides of the highway for ten kilometers. The restaurants and *comedores* along this busy stretch of road cater more to truck drivers than to gringo tourists. They serve spicy Mexican food and seafood at low prices. A cut above average, **El Alteño** serves plentiful food in a simply furnished concrete block building, with live music while you eat. It is located near the town movie theater. Closed in summer. ~ Route 1, Km. 189. BUDGET.

Another hole-in-the-wall eatery worth looking into, **La Bota** serves American-style steaks and baked potatoes to a mainly Mexican clientele. It is located near the Pemex station at the south end of town. ~ Route 1, Km. 189. BUDGET.

GROCERIES

Very basic provisions are available at dozens of tiny, family-run grocery stores along the highway in San Quintín and Lázaro Cárdenas. You can get cornmeal, wheat flour, canned goods, Coca-Cola and candy; don't expect much else. Vegetable sellers wander up and down the long commercial strip with boxes of tomatoes and whatever other fruits or vegetables are currently being harvested in the valley.

BEACHES & PARKS

PARQUE NACIONAL SIERRA SAN PEDRO MÁRTIR 🚶 🚲 🐎
Picacho del Diablo, the highest mountain peak in Baja, presides over the vast, pine-clad sierra. The climate is alpine and cool. The wildlife is abundant. The only access for passenger cars is the unpaved road that runs from Route 1 to the park entrance, a distance of 79 kilometers, and continues through the park to the Mexican National Observatory. ~ Carretera San Telmo-Observatorio.

▲ There is a small, privately run campground within the national park. Facilities are minimal and the setting is beautiful. Sites cost $10 per night.

PLAYA SAN RAMÓN 🚶 🎣 🏄 This popular surfers' beach spans 12 miles of the Pacific coast west of San Quintín. It is wide and fringed with sand dunes, and the flats at low tide are a good place to dig for Pismo clams. People fish from the shore near the rocky point at the southern end of the beach. ~ Turn west off Route 1 two kilometers south of Colonia Vicente Guerrero and continue on the unpaved road for four miles to the dunes; walk to the beach from there.

▲ There are no camping areas right on the beach—the soft sand makes vehicle travel treacherous. On the road to the beach, **Mesón Don Pepe RV Park** has 50 campsites with concrete pads and full hookups, as well as a tent area. The restrooms have hot showers. Fees are $4 for tents, $8 for motor homes. ~ Colonia Vicente Guerrero; 6-22-16. Nearby on the same road, the larger **Posada Don Diego RV Park** has similar facilities plus a volleyball court. The 100-site campground caters to caravans and seems deserted when they leave. Sites cost $10 per night. ~ Colonia Vicente Guerrero; 6-21-81.

PUERTO SAN QUINTÍN 🏃 🐟 There's no beach on the inner bay, which was once the port for American and British wheat-farming colonies, but the grassy banks are fine for strolling and fishing. ~ Turn west off the main highway four kilometers south of the army base at Lázaro Cárdenas and follow the unpaved road for six kilometers to the shore.

▲ You can camp near the shore of Bahía San Quintín at the **Old Mill RV Park**, an attractively landscaped park that has 24 tent and RV sites and a clean, central bathhouse. Fees are $11 per night for tents (no hookups) and $16.50 for RVs (full hookups). ~ Puerto San Quintín Road; no local phone. U.S. reservations: Viva Mexico, 619-479-3476, 800-330-7799, fax 619-691-0855.

PLAYA DE OESTE MEDANO 🏃 🏊 🐟 This long, lonely strand runs along the Pacific side of the narrow spit of land protecting Bahía Falsa and Bahía Quintín. There are two popular surfing areas: the north end offers a long, rolling break, while the southern tip, known as Cabo San Quintín, has a wicked point break. Surfers usually have the place to themselves; wind and heavy surf discourage sunbathers and casual swimmers. ~ Follow the unpaved road west from Lázaro Cárdenas to the shore, a distance of about 12 kilometers, and then continue south along the beach. Beware of sand traps.

▲ There are no facilities for campers. Nobody is likely to stop you if you want to pitch a tent, but if you spend the night out here, alone with the banshee wind and smashing waves, you'll know why the early settlers chose a more sheltered location on the other side of the bay.

PLAYA SANTA MARÍA 🏃 🐠 🏊 🚤 🐟 Another surfers' secret, this wide white beach stretches for miles along the coastline of the Bahía Santa María. While the northern part of the beach is best for surfing, the whole bayshore is a good place to fish the surf for corbina or dig for large Pismo clams. Toward the south, Playa Santa María blends seamlessly into Playa Pabellón—the distinction between the two beaches seems to depend on which road you take to get there—forming a continuous ten-mile strand that ranks as one of the most beautiful Pacific beaches in Baja. ~ Thirteen kilometers south of the bridge that separates San Quintín and Lázaro Cárdenas, turn off Route 1 at the sign for La Pinta Hotel. Go past the hotel and the end of the pavement, six kilometers to the beach.

▲ There is a decrepit excuse for a campground at the **Cielito Lindo Motel and RV Park**, located where the road stops at the north end of the beach. There are no hookups or designated campsites, and the restrooms leave much to be desired; this discourages the RV crowd and suits surfers just fine. Sites cost $5 per night.

PLAYA PABELLÓN 🏃 ⛵ 🎣 Backed by low sand dunes, this lonely beach continues south along the shore of Bahía Santa María. Fishermen beach their pangas here between dawn and dusk forays out onto the bay. The water is good for swimming in the summer and fall, and there's interesting beachcombing all year. Huge clamshells lie strewn in the sand, along with occasional pieces of driftwood, packaging debris printed in Japanese, and other mysterious objects that have floated across the Pacific on ocean currents.

▲ A large sign at the entrance to **El Pabellón RV Park** warns, "No Racing Motor Cycle or etc. in Camp Ground"—that's how flat and open this sandy park at the dunes' edge is. The local ejido that owns it has planted rows of casuarina trees to protect campers from the constant winds of winter and spring. The entrance road is landscaped with bright flowering bushes, and there is a central restroom with hot showers and flush toilets. Other than that, you're on your own; there are no hookups or clearly defined campsites. Fees are just $5 per night. ~ Watch for the sign and turn right off Route 1, 28 kilometers south of San Quintín. The campground is about two kilometers off the main road.

▼▼▼▼▼▼▼▼▼▼▼▼▼▼

Outdoor Adventures

FISHING

ENSENADA The waters around Ensenada are famed for California yellowtail. Other game fish include white sea bass, albacore, bonito and barracuda. Fishing charter offices are located near the fish market, and you can save money by joining a group charter with any of several outfitters, such as **Gordo's Sport Fishing** (Paseo Costero at Avenida Gastelum) and the **Ensenada Clipper Fleet** (Paseo Costero at Avenida Gastelum; 78-21-85).

SAN FELIPE Barracuda, rockfish and yellowtail are among the fish commonly found in San Felipe waters. Bonefish also run here in the summer months. For charters, contact **Alex Sport Fishing**. ~ Malecón 241; 7-10-52. The sand flats at low tide offer excellent clamming.

SAN QUINTÍN Tuna is the catch of choice along this part of the coast. Boat charters can be arranged at the fishing supply store at the **Old Mill Motel and RV Park**. ~ Puerto San Quintín; 77-76-91, fax 77-76-93, or 800-995-8482 in the U.S.

SURFING & WIND-SURFING

ENSENADA The beaches around **Rosarito** have been attracting hordes of surfers since the Beach Boys were kids. But the pros say the greatest surfing in the Ensenada area is to be found at

Islas de Todos Santos, a pair of islands six and a half miles off-shore at the mouth of Bahía de Todos Santos. Waves here can reach a height of 30 feet. The beach on the ocean side of the south island catches the waves in a long, rolling break that is a surfer's dream, and the accelerated swells that speed through the narrow passage between the south and north islands are a superthrill. You'll find current surf information and boards for sale (but not for rent) at **Tony's Surf Shop**. ~ Boulevard Juárez 312; 72-11-92.

SAN QUINTÍN Those who have discovered the well-hidden beach at the north end of **Playa de Oeste Medano** call it one of the best surfing spots on the Pacific coast. If you don't have a dune buggy, you'll have to carry your board for about a mile, skirting a dormant volcano cone, to get there. Farther south and easier to reach, Playa Santa María is a favorite surfer hangout.

SAILING & PARA-SAILING

ENSENADA The place to arrange for a bird's-eye view of Ensenada is **Baja Para-Sail**, located near the tourist office on the waterfront. ~ Paseo Costero 609; 8-18-79.

SAN FELIPE Parasailing can be arranged through **Rainbow Aquatic Sports**. This enterprise also rents Yamaha Wave Runners —sort of like motorcycles that run on water—and offers discounts to senior citizens. ~ Malecón Sur 210; 7-19-40.

KAYAKING

ENSENADA The **Islas de Todos Santos**, at the mouth of the Bahía de Todos Santos, are a six-and-a-half-mile paddle from Punta Bandas. Visitors to the islands will find soaring cliffs and sun-soaked beaches, harbor seals sea lions and abundant bird life. Kayak trips to the area, including transportation and kayaks, can be arranged through **Southwest Sea Kayaking** in San Diego. ~ 619-222-3616 in the U.S.

SAN FELIPE Kayakers head for the remote **Bahía de San Luís Gonzaga**, about 70 kilometers south of Puertecitos on a rugged four-wheel-drive road. The bay makes a good jumping-off point for exploration of the **Islas Encantadas**, six small islands with seabird rookeries at the mouth of the bay. One of Baja's more ambitious kayak challenges is the 75-mile trip along the rugged, deserted coast from Bahía de San Luís Gonzaga south to Bahía de los Angeles. Rental kayaks are hard to find in the San Felipe/Puertecitos area; most adventurers bring their own.

WHALE-WATCHING & BOAT TOURS

ENSENADA During the winter months, whalewatching excursions to the Islas de Todos Santos can be arranged through the **Museo de Ciencias de Ensenada**. ~ Avenida Obregón 1463; 78-71-92.

TENNIS

ENSENADA A number of resorts in the Rosarito and Ensenada area have tennis courts for guest use, but only the **Baja Beach**

and Tennis Club is open to the general public. Court fees are expensive. ~ Route 1, Km. 16 south of Ensenada; U.S. reservations and information, 619-283-8519.

SAN FELIPE Riding all-terrain vehicles (ATVs)—those big-tired little vehicles like four-wheeled motorcycles—on beaches, desert roads and the main street of town is a favorite San Felipe sport. Even though it's called "off-roading," you'll want to stay *on* the roads in the Baja backcountry, which can be as hazardous as it is fragile. You can rent an all-terrain vehicle at **C.J. ATV Rentals** (Avenida Mar de Cortez) or **ATVs San Felipe** (Calzada Chetumal at Avenida Mar de Cortez).

OFF-ROADING

ENSENADA Riding horses on the beach is a popular activity in Rosarito. Every day, cowboys bring strings of rental horses to the beach to wait for customers, especially in the area of the Rosarito Beach Hotel.

RIDING STABLES

SAN FELIPE The ultimate hike in the area is an ascent of 10,154-foot **Picacho del Diablo**, the Baja's highest peak. The 11-mile trail goes along the floor of **Cañon del Diablo** most of the way, through vegetation that changes gradually from desert to the lushness of a tropical oasis as it passes waterfalls and bathing pools. The last part, beyond the backpackers' campground at the upper end of the canyon, is steep and challenging, climbing 4000 feet in less than two miles. The round trip takes four days. Shorter treks into Cañon del Diablo are also rewarding.

HIKING

SAN QUINTÍN The **Parque Nacional San Pedro Mártir** offers some of the finest hiking on the Baja peninsula. A trail up the gentler western slope of Picacho del Diablo to the summit starts from the end of a two-track road that branches off the main park road at Vallecitos and continues southeast for about eight miles. The ten-mile round trip can be completed in a (long) day. Another

✔ **CHECK THESE OUT—UNIQUE OUTDOOR ADVENTURES**

- Surf the Islas de Todos Santos at the mouth of Ensenada's bay, where waves can break 30 feet high. *page 123*
- Kayak to the Islas Encantadas in the Bahía de San Luís Gonzaga, one of the most isolated bays on the Sea of Cortez. *page 124*
- Ride a horse along Rosarito Beach, where other diversions range from parasails to wave runners. *page 125*
- Hike the lush Cañon del Diablo in the Sierra San Pedro Mártir (reaching the trailhead is half the adventure). *page 125*

trail that starts near the astronomers' residences below the Mexican National Observatory gate leads to a stand of shimmering aspen trees and a viewpoint overlooking Cañon del Diablo. It's a four-mile round trip to the overlook. For a longer trek, a right fork in the trail at the aspen grove continues to the rim of Cañon del Diablo.

▼▼▼▼▼▼▼▼▼▼▼▼

Transportation

AIR

ENSENADA Ensenada has no regularly scheduled passenger flights at this writing. The city's **Aeropuerto el Cipres** (6-63-03) has accommodated commercial air service from U.S. cities in the past, and charter flights from the U.S. land there from time to time.

SAN FELIPE Air L.A. (800-010-0413) in Mexico flies commuter planes in to **San Felipe International Airport** from Los Angeles four times a week. There is no other regularly scheduled passenger service.

BUS

ENSENADA **Autotransportes de Baja California** (ABC) and **Tres Estrellas de Oro** operate frequent first-class bus service up and down the Baja peninsula, stopping in Ensenada at the bus terminal at Calle 1 and Avenida Riveroll. ABC also runs buses between Ensenada and San Felipe. **Transportes Norte de Sonora** runs daily buses between Ensenada and both Tecate and Mexicali.

SAN FELIPE **Autotransportes de Baja California** operates daily bus service to and from both Ensenada and Mexicali. San Felipe's bus terminal is at Avenida Manzanillo and Avenida Mar de Caribe; 7-15-16.

BOAT

Ensenada is a major port of call for **Royal Caribbean** and several other cruise ship companies that sail from San Pedro Docks in Los Angeles. Royal Caribbean's *Viking Serenade* takes three- and four-day cruises to Ensenada with intermediate ports of call at Catalina Island and San Diego. ~ 1050 Caribbean Way, Miami, FL 33132; 800-327-6700, or contact your local travel agent.

CAR

Route 1, the Carretera Transpeninsular or Baja Highway, runs from Tijuana to Ensenada, a distance of 190 kilometers. On this segment of the route, you have two choices—the *carretera libre* (free highway), which makes its slow way through the busiest part of Rosarito, or the fast, four-lane *carretera cuota* (toll highway), which covers the distance in no time. From Ensenada, if you continue south on Route 1, you will reach San Quintín in another 196 kilometers.

Route 3 crosses the peninsula from Ensenada to San Felipe, a distance of 250 kilometers. San Felipe can also be reached via **Route 5** from Mexicali, a distance of 184 kilometers. Both routes are well-maintained, paved two-lane highways.

ENSENADA Hertz has an office in the Bahía Mall at Avenida Riveroll and Calle 2; 8-37-76, or 800-654-3001 in the U.S. **Ensenada Rent-Car** is located at Avenida Alvarado and Avenida López Mateos; 8-18-96. Rental rates run considerably higher in Ensenada than in Tijuana. Vendors around the Plaza Cívica have motor scooters for rent.

CAR RENTALS

SAN FELIPE **El Dorado Travel Center** rents cars. ~ Mar Caribe 395; 7-12-78. All-terrain vehicles are available from ATV's **San Felipe** ~ Calzada Chetumal and Mar de Cortez; and from **C.J. ATV Rentals.** ~ Avenida Mar de Cortez.

ENSENADA Ensenada has many independent taxis. It is not customary to hail taxis when they are moving; instead, you board them at any of the many taxi stands, called *sitios*, all along Avenida López Mateos and Avenida Benito Juárez, as well as elsewhere around the downtown area and in front of the larger hotels.

PUBLIC TRANSIT

Several private companies provide inexpensive bus service along main avenues in Ensenada. Minibuses serve nearby villages and rural areas from a station on Calle 4 between Avenidas Macheros and Riveroll.

SAN FELIPE Taxis are not plentiful in San Felipe, perhaps because almost all visitors arrive in their own vehicles. The central taxi stand is on Avenida Mar de Cortez, or you can call for a cab at 7-12-92. There are no public buses here.

▼▼▼▼▼▼▼▼▼▼▼▼▼▼▼▼▼▼▼▼▼▼▼
Addresses & Phone Numbers

Ambulance: Ensenada—78-14-00
Hospital: San Felipe—7-10-06 or 7-15-44
Police: Rosarito—dial 060; Ensenada—76-24-21 or dial 134; San Felipe—7-13-50 or 7-10-21
Green Angels: 76-46-75
Secretaría de Turismo del Estado de Baja California Norte: Rosarito: 2-02-00; Ensenada: Avenida López Mateos 1250-13B; 72-30-22; San Felipe: Avenida Mar de Cortez at Calle Manzanillo; 7-11-55
Comité de Turismo y Convenciones de Rosarito: 2-03-96
Comité de Turismo y Convenciones de Ensenada: 78-24-11

SIX

Central Baja

A vulture perches motionless atop a thirty-foot cactus spire, tiny eyes peering through the sun's glare at the motor homes, Baja bugs and eighteen-wheelers that speed along the narrow strand of two-lane blacktop. A wild burro loiters in the shade of a stone grotto where painted symbols mark the spot of an ancient shamanic ritual; the thousand-year-old magic lingers. A whirlwind sweeps across a sand flat, exposing the million-year-old fossil of a sea snail as large as a dog. Baja's vast, surprisingly green central desert reveals the wonders of life spanning the centuries in such abundance that it is doubly remarkable that almost no human beings live there today.

The population of Baja lives along the border and the coasts. In the central section of the peninsula, however, both the Pacific and Sea of Cortez shores are mostly uninhabitable, and nearly unreachable, because of steep cliffs that plunge from jagged mountain ridges into the watery depths. The Baja Highway heads straight down the peninsula's centerline in a two-stage crossing of North America's wildest desert. For the adventurous, this 200-mile stretch of empty highway is the heart and soul of the Baja. It's like Alaska with 100-degree heat, or like the loneliest road in Nevada but with fewer people. It's one of the last great North American wildernesses.

Before the 1974 completion of the Baja Highway, the vast desert formed an all but impassable barrier between the relatively modern north, with its factories, agribusiness and weekend beach-party towns, and the southeast coast with its easygoing tropical ambience and centuries of colonial history. Today, motorists can cross this vast desert in an easy 50-mile-an-hour day—or take their time and experience the natural wonders of environments that are unique on earth.

Between the fanciful landscapes of the Desierto Central and the stark vastness of the Desierto Vizcaíno, travelers can detour to the coast and visit two remote oases that couldn't be more different—Bahía de los Angeles, a mecca for sport fishermen and kayakers on the shore of an idyllic, island-studded bay, and Guerrero Negro, a wind-blasted salt company town with cheap motels, good and not-so-good restaurants, and, in the winter, more whales than anyplace else on the continent. It is also the only place covered in this chapter that has TVs or phone service.

Travelers with tough vehicles can bounce farther off the highway on unpaved back roads to explore vanished desert settlements—old mine camps and 18th-century Spanish colonial mission churches; two of the most remote are still used today. Still longer backcountry trips lead to Baja's most remote beaches. Finally, there are the islands, large and small, that lie off both coasts. As uninhabitable as the desert, some harbor huge seabird colonies and elephant seal rookeries, while others boast world-class surfing beaches and scuba-diving sites.

▼▼▼▼▼▼▼▼▼▼▼▼
Desierto Central

The journey south on the Baja Highway changes character suddenly and dramatically as you leave the coastal plain and plunge into the Desierto Central, a bone-dry, spiny wonderland whose diversity of drought-resistant vegetation makes it the most magical desert landscape in North America. Here you can wander among spirelike cardones, surreal cirios, squat and twisted elephant trees, giant century plants, tree-like yuccas and a myriad of other exotic subtropical flora. Even if you never leave your vehicle, the half-day drive through this uninhabitable wonderland is an experience you'll never forget. Bring plenty of water.

SIGHTS

The Baja Highway turns away from the Pacific coast, winding through volcanic hills and down the side of a canyon to reach **El Rosario**, a tiny town that boasts a famous café, the last Pemex station before the desert, and not much else. The pavement ended at El Rosario for many years before 1974, when the Mexican government, flush with oil revenues, undertook the monumental project of paving the road all the way to the tip of Baja. Today, El Rosario marks the point where the coastal plain gives way to deep desert.

The highway takes a sharp left turn in the center of town. To see the hidden sights of El Rosario, at the left turn in the highway turn right instead. Take the next left and ford the Rio del Rosario (an arroyo that normally contains little or no water); crude road signs mark the 16-kilometer route to **Punta Baja**, a long, rocky spit of land reaching out into the Pacific. The rugged beaches there are used by the fishermen of the tiny village of **Agua Blanca** but rarely seen by travelers.

◄ HIDDEN

Along the way, about two and a half kilometers from the highway on a bluff above the arroyo, sections of adobe wall still stand from **Misión Nuestra Señora del Rosario de Abajo**, built in 1802 to replace an earlier mission whose spring had run dry. Only the sketchy outlines of walls remain of the older mission—**Misión Nuestra Señora del Rosario Viñadaco**, the first Dominican mission in California, built in 1774—just off the main highway near the

Motel Sinai. The mission at El Rosario closed in 1832; diseases imported by the Spanish had so devastated the local Cochimí population that there were too few converts to work the fields.

HIDDEN ▶ Fishermen at Agua Blanca can often be hired to take visitors to **Isla San Jerónimo,** ten miles offshore to the south. The barren island has a small fishing camp and an old lighthouse, as well as the wreck of a large tuna-fishing boat. Other wrecks lie just offshore; they're hard to dive because of choking seaweed. A sizable sea lion colony inhabits the south end of the island. Other wildlife includes a strange legless lizard found only on Isla San Jerónimo.

Leaving El Rosario, the highway soon narrows as it begins a gradual, winding ascent through volcanic hills and mesas. This is mining country. The area no longer produces copper, but semiprecious stones such as turquoise, onyx, hematite, azurite and malachite are mined here. The adobe monoliths visible a short distance west of the highway on a side road from the tiny village of El Progreso, 63 kilometers south of El Rosario, were part of HIDDEN ▶ the two-foot-thick walls of **Misión San Fernando Velicata.** The mission was built in 1769 by Padre Junipero Serra to minister to the Guiricata Indians. It operated for 49 years but, like most Spanish colonial missions in Baja, was abandoned after epidemics wiped out the indigenous population.

Just beyond El Progreso, an unpaved road turns south to the small village of **Santa Catarina.** The road is well used but has steep grades and should be traveled only in a high-clearance vehicle beyond Santa Catarina village. Fifty-six kilometers from the highway is an area where fossilized ammonites—giant snail-shaped sea creatures—are found. Another 11 kilometers on the same road HIDDEN ▶ brings you to **Puerto Catarina.** Scattered ruins mark the site of an old shipping port built for exporting onyx from the quarries at El Marmol during the early years of this century. The makeshift shacks of a fish camp are all that lies at the end of the road today.

HIDDEN ▶ **El Marmol** is an abandoned onyx quarry 16 kilometers from the highway on an unpaved road that exits to the east near tiny San Augustín, 85 kilometers south of El Rosario. This is an interesting and easy side trip that mineral buffs should not bypass. From 1900 to 1958, the quarry produced some of North America's finest, most delicately hued onyx, also called travertine. Cre- HIDDEN ▶ ated by mineral deposits from a fuming spring called **El Volcán,** a hot two-mile hike beyond the quarry, the onyx at El Marmol is translucent and striated in green, ochre and umber. Easier to work than marble, yet able to take a high polish and resist staining, the stone was quarried in huge blocks at El Marmol, then freighted by wagon more than 50 miles across the desert to Puerto Catarina and shipped to the United States, where it was used for

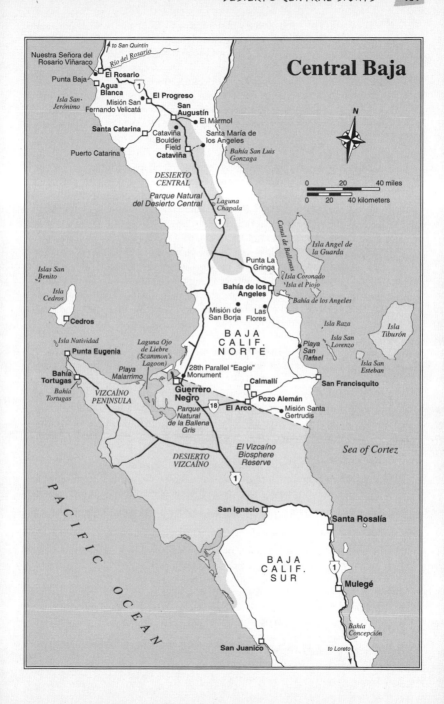

Central Baja

to San Quintín

Nuestra Señora del
Rosario Viñaraco

Río del Rosario

El Rosario

Punta Baja

Agua
Blanca

El Progreso

1

San
Augustín

Isla San
Jerónimo

Misión San
Fernando Velicatá

El Mármol

Santa Catarina

Cataviña
Boulder
Field
Cataviña

Santa María de
los Angeles

Puerto Catarina

Bahía San Luis
Gonzaga

DESIERTO
CENTRAL

Parque Natural
del Desierto Central

Laguna
Chapala

1

N

0   20   40 miles

0   20   40 kilometers

Islas San
Benito

Isla
Cedros

Canal de Ballenas

Isla Angel de
la Guarda

Punta La
Gringa

Isla Coronado
Isla el Piojo

Cedros

Bahía de los
Angeles

Bahía de los Angeles

Isla Natividad

Punta Eugenia

Laguna Ojo
de Liebre
(Scammon's
Lagoon)

Misión de
San Borja

Las
Flores

Isla Raza

Isla San
Lorenzo

Isla
Tiburón

Bahía
Tortugas

Playa
Malarrimo

B A J A
C A L I F.
N O R T E

Playa
San
Rafael

Isla San
Esteban

Bahía
Tortugas

VIZCAÍNO
PENINSULA

28th Parallel "Eagle"
Monument

Calmallí

San Francisquito

Guerrero
Negro

Pozo Alemán

18   El Arco

Misión Santa
Gertrudis

Parque
Natural
de la Ballena
Gris

El Vizcaíno
Biosphere
Reserve

Sea of Cortez

DESIERTO
VIZCAÍNO

1

San Ignacio

Santa Rosalía

P A C I F I C   O C E A N

B A J A
C A L I F.
S U R

1

Mulegé

Bahía
Concepción

San Juanico

to Loreto

statuary, doorknobs, tabletops, and floor and wall facings. At its peak, El Marmol was a thriving company town inhabited by hundreds of Mexican workers and their families as well as two generations of gringo owners. With the development of modern plastics, demand for onyx declined until the stuff was not worth hauling to the coast. The quarry was abandoned and the town gradually died. Visitors can see what's left of a one-room schoolhouse and a jail, both built of massive blocks of onyx. The quarry is intermittently mined on a small scale by men from a nearby *ejido*, who sell the onyx to factories in Tijuana that make it into curio items such as chess sets and elephant statuettes.

The **Cataviña Boulder Field** marks the northern extent of Parque Natural de Desierto Central, a hundred-mile-long scenic area protected from development by Mexican law. The park flanks the highway for about six miles on each side, with frequent parking areas and a number of unpaved roads that provide backcountry access to mines and ranches beyond the park boundaries. The drive through the park presents the most spectacular desert scenery to be found anywhere along the Baja Highway, and the boulder field is even more spectacular than the rest. The area is strewn for miles with round white boulders the size of houses, and studded with majestic *cardón* cactuses that tower above the giant rocks.

The town of **Cataviña** has only about ten buildings and a population of a few dozen hardy souls, but it is the only oasis with any kind of travelers' amenities—namely a campground, a motel, a couple of restaurants and the only Pemex station—on this long desert crossing. With a scenic location and interesting cave paintings nearby, Cataviña is the obvious base camp for anyone wishing to take time to explore the Parque Natural del Desierto Central.

The ruins of **Santa María de los Angeles Cabujacaamag**, the last Jesuit mission on the Baja Peninsula, located 29 kilometers east of town on a road so sandy and rutted that even four-wheel-

---

✔ **CHECK THESE OUT—UNIQUE SIGHTS**

- Imagine yourself on another planet amid the otherworldly "boojum tree" forests of the **Parque Natural de Desierto Central**. *page 134*
- Take an adventurous backroad trip to **Misión de San Borja**, the first well-preserved Spanish mission on the way south. *page 137*
- Ply the waters of **Scammon's Lagoon** between December and March for closeup views of thousands of gray whales. *page 143*
- Venture beyond the ghost town of El Arco to reach **Bahía San Francisquito**, one of the Baja's most secluded beaches. *page 147*

drive vehicles have a hard time getting there. Dirt bikers sometimes rise to the challenge. The mission was built in 1767 and used
for only two years before jurisdiction over the northern Baja missions was transferred to the Dominican Order, which chose to
abandon this remote site.

Sixty kilometers south of Cataviña, the Baja Highway crosses
Laguna Chapala, a normally dry lake bed that marks the mid-
point of the Desierto Central crossing. Rare rainstorms briefly fill
this "lake," which has no outlet, and then evaporate, leaving deposits of salt and minerals. A short distance beyond Laguna Chapala is one of the most impressive stands of *cardón* cactus in Baja.

The **Motel Sinai** on the east edge of El Rosario offers the best accommodations in the area—a dozen remarkably plain cinderblock
motel units with double beds and satellite TV, designed more for
truck drivers than gringo tourists. The motel also operates a walled
30-unit RV park—$12 per night with restrooms, showers and a
laundry room but no hookups. ~ Route 1, Km. 56, El Rosario.
BUDGET.

In Cataviña, the 28-room **Hotel La Pinta Cataviña**—the largest building in town—is typical of the La Pinta chain of motels
found up and down the peninsula. It has pleasant though plain
air-conditioned rooms, an outdoor swimming pool and tennis
courts. A noisy electrical generator runs from 6 p.m. to midnight.
~ Route 1, Km. 174, Cataviña. MODERATE.

Rancho Santa Ynez, three-fourths of a mile off the highway,
offers very simple hostel-style dormitory accommodations. This
is a favorite dirt bikers' haunt, though it's hard to see the advantage over camping out. ~ Route 1, Km. 176, Cataviña. BUDGET.

LODGING

Mama Espinosa's in El Rosario has been a Baja Highway landmark for almost 50 years. Until 1974, the pavement ended right
in front of this plain little restaurant, making it the natural ren-
dezvous and departure point for innumerable expeditions into
the desert wilderness. Breakfast here is inexpensive and good, and
the lobster burritos—a surprise reminder that the little desert village of El Rosario is only seven miles from the Pacific coast—are
among central Baja's best roadside attractions. T-shirts and car-
toon placemats perpetuate Mama Espinosa's mystique, though
there's little competition in sight. The centerpiece of the simple
decor is a collection of fossilized ammonites—giant snails that
lived during the dinosaur era and reached almost two feet in diameter. They were found by fishermen on a remote part of the
coast about 40 miles south of El Rosario. ~ Route 1, Km. 55, El
Rosario. BUDGET.

The restaurant at the **Hotel La Pinta Cataviña** offers a predictable menu of Mexican and American dishes, including a taco-

DINING

and-enchilada combination plate just like you'd expect to find in a typical Mexican restaurant in the U.S. The restaurant is cool, clean, cheerful and, unlike other Cataviña eateries, open from around noon to well after dark. ~ Route 1, Km. 174, Cataviña. MODERATE.

Near Cataviña, **Rancho Santa Ynez** serves breakfasts of huevos rancheros con chorizo (fried eggs smothered with chile sauce, with spicy, crumbly Mexican sausage on the side) and, in the afternoon, taco-and-enchilada dinners. (Mexicans are accustomed to eating the main meal of the day during afternoon siesta; don't count on finding this place open during the gringo dinner hour.) The ambience is simple, the menu limited and the prices very reasonable. ~ Route 1, Km. 176, Cataviña. BUDGET.

GROCERIES   In El Rosario, near Mama Espinoza's and the Pemex station, there is a fairly complete food store, called **Supermercado**.

Cataviña has a small grocery store attached to a palm-thatched *comedor* called **La Enramada**.

BEACHES & PARKS

PLAYA DEL ROSARIO 🚶 🏊 Sunbathers may be disappointed by this remote, stony beach, but beachcombers are likely to love it. The beach lies at the edge of a fossil-rich expanse of petrified forest, and the surf continually exposes fragments of fossilized dinosaur bone and petrified wood. The road from the highway to the beach passes through the heart of the petrified forest, where broken stone trunks of prehistoric palms and tropical evergreens litter the sunbaked terrain. Fossil remains of duckbilled dinosaurs known as hadrosaurs have been found in this area, along with prehistoric crocodiles, some of the oldest evidence of mammal life and a unique "missing link" between dinosaurs and modern birds. ~ Turn right where the main highway turns left in El Rosario. Take another right at the first fork, then keep right at each subsequent fork in the road. It's seven and a half kilometers to the beach.

PARQUE NATURAL DE DESIERTO CENTRAL 🚶 🚲 On a series of mesas stretching for a hundred miles down the middle of the peninsula, some of the world's most fantastic desert forests grow. Towering *cardón* cactuses, blue palms, squat elephant trees and tapered, slender cirios cover the slopes of the mesas, and everywhere is a profusion of prickly pear, barrel cactus, candelaria, ocotillo, cholla, velvet cactus, galloping cactus and agave. Ravens, hawks and vultures perch atop the cactuses, and woodpecker holes in the trunks of the big *cardones* make nests for many kinds of desert songbirds. Ancient Indian rock art is found several places in the park. The area is protected by stringent environmental laws intended to make it eligible for UNESCO Biosphere Reserve status,

Mystery of the Ancient Artists

The Cataviña area is where the greatest concentration of **Indian cave paintings** are found. The geometric patterns measure from about 12 to 18 inches in size, made with mineral hues—mainly black, white, various shades of red, and sometimes ochre. Several "schools" of rock art are found in central Baja, apparently painted by different groups of the same ancient race. Farther south, in the vicinities of San Ignacio and Mulegé, the sites are less numerous but far more elaborate, depicting human and animal figures in huge murals. The largest known site, hard-to-reach Gardner Cave in the rugged Sierra San Francisco, contains a mural more than 500 feet wide and 30 feet high. These mysterious paintings date back as much as 1500 years. At many sites, several layers of newer motifs have been painted over older ones, suggesting that the paintings were made over a span of centuries.

The meaning of the images is not known; they may have had shamanic or other ritual significance. More puzzling is the question of who painted them. The Cochimí people, who lived in the area when the first Spanish explorers and missionaries arrived, had no evident artistic tradition and disavowed any knowledge of the paintings' origins. Anthropologists attribute them to an ancient race known only as "the Painters," about which nothing at all is known.

The most extensive painted-cave sites can only be reached by a long four-wheel-drive trip. Some paintings, however, are close to the highway. Look for good examples in a small grotto among the largest boulders on the skyline about half a mile north of the highway near kilometer marker 171. Another site is 400 meters up the trail from the rest area located one and a half kilometers north of the Hotel La Pinta Cataviña. Small roadside signs that say "Pinturas Rupestres" mark other painting sites.

but don't expect park rangers or entrance gates, much less a visitor center. The area has been preserved in its natural state, and the only amenities are roadside pull-outs where you can park and stroll among the cactuses. ~ Route 1 runs through the center of the park from the Cataviña Boulder Field, 75 kilometers south of El Rosario, to the turnoff for Bahía de Los Angeles.

▲ The village of Cataviña, the only human settlement within the natural park, has two campgrounds. The *ejido*-run **Cataviña Trailer Park** has 67 tent and RV sites, some with electricity, and restrooms with hot showers. Sites cost $9 per night. There is also an informal camping area—little more than a big graded parking lot—behind the Rancho Santa Ynez restaurant south of Cataviña. There are no amenities except restrooms; bring your own drinking water. Sites cost $2 per night. Side roads provide boundless camping opportunities for tent and small-truck campers.

▼▼▼▼▼▼▼▼▼▼▼▼▼▼
Bahía de los Angeles

Near the southern edge of the Parque Natural de Desierto Central, a paved road branches off the Baja Highway and heads for the Sea of Cortez coast, an hour's drive away, to dead-end at Bahía de los Angeles —the Bay of Angels. Named after the bay, the town, with its seasonal population of about 1300, is one of the most remote coastal settlements of any size on the Baja. Isolated on both sides by inaccessible coastlines where volcanic cliffs plunge straight down into the sea depths, Bahía de los Angeles is certainly the most out-of-the-way place in Baja that you can reach by paved road.

On first impression, the gringo fishing village of Bahía de los Angeles is an unappealing little place. Since there is no simple way to dispose of such items as defunct washing machines and broken sofas, over the last 50 years the main street has become lined with discarded furniture and appliances, creating the ambience of a Goodwill store in paradise. Most residents live in rows of mobile homes and bungalows radiating inland from the beach. The rumble of the gasoline-powered generator that supplies the only electricity carries from one end of town to the other. (After ten at night the power plant runs a smaller generator.) The water supply comes from an artesian well in the mountains thirty miles away and flows through the small blue pipe that runs beside the road into town. The water fills a community tank, where town residents wait in line to replenish their household water supplies. There isn't a telephone within a hundred miles.

It's not the town's character that lures so many snowbirds from the United States to Bahía de los Angeles each winter. It's the bay, one of the most magnificent spots on the Sea of Cortez. Sport fishermen from California started colonizing Bahía de los Angeles in the 1940s, when the only way to get there was by private plane. Today, while the area continues to attract anglers, a new breed of sea kayakers and whale and dolphin watchers is infiltrating this Hemingwayesque community with eco-consciousness notions.

All the Spanish colonial mission ruins north of the Baja California Sur state line have been abandoned for so long that little is left to see—except Misión San Francisco de Borja Adac, commonly known as **Misión de San Borja**. Natural springs—one hot, one cold—created an oasis in the mountains that made it an Indian population center and an obvious place for missionary work. The solid stone church, built by Dominicans in 1801, replaced a Jesuit mission established on the site in 1762. Although the church was abandoned by the missionaries in 1818, ranchers who came to graze cattle in the high mountain meadows preserved it and their families continue to worship there to this day. The hot and cold springs still flow a short walk from the church. Fragments of an old aqueduct stand amid the ragged remnants of orchards. A cowbell clangs in place of the original church bells, and a cemetery bears witness to the generations who have inhabited this isolated place. A few still do, though the condition of the road that takes you there shows infrequent use. To reach the mission from the paved road in to Bahía de Los Angeles, you need a high-clearance vehicle. Follow the narrow, unpaved road that turns off to the south 22 kilometers from town (or 45 from the Baja Highway). Then it's 26 kilometers of slow, careful driving to the old mission.

Bahía de los Angeles—the town—is not a sightly place. A few minutes' drive in either direction, though, the pavement ends and you have your choice of great beach hideaways. An adventuresome driver in a rugged vehicle can continue around the bay to spots where no human has left a footprint in years.

The **Museo de Naturaleza y Cultura**, a block west of the main road near the center of town, packs an extraordinary hodgepodge of area artifacts into its cramped quarters. There are whale skeletons, Seri Indian tools carved from turtle shells, fossils of prehistoric horses, and exhibits on 19th-century gold mining around Bahía de los Angeles. Open for about two hours most afternoons. ~ Bahía de los Angeles.

Bahía de los Angeles—the bay—conceals a mostly submerged mountain range whose peaks form a protective chain of islands along the mouth of the bay. These islands provide safe haven for more than 500 species of fish by making the bay too treacherous for the big industrial fishing ships that have devastated the fish population in other parts of the Sea of Cortez. Further protected from storms and surf by Isla Angel de la Guarda, the largest of all the islands off the Baja coast, the bay first offered a safe harbor to sailing ships in 1746.

Some of the islands across the mouth of the bay show massive, rocky ridgelines; others are round, barren rocks so caked with guano that they look like snowcapped mountaintops rising pure white out of the turquoise bay a few miles offshore. **Isla Coronado**, the northernmost island, is four-and-a-half miles long and has more land area than the other 14 islands combined. Because the longest distance between any two islands is two miles, Bahía de los Angeles is an ideal spot for sea kayaking. Ospreys inhabit Isla Coronado and other islands, and there is a large pelican colony on Isla el Piojo.

On the eastern skyline, an entire mountain range looms above the water, giving Bahía de los Angeles more the feel of a large lake than a sea harbor. The mountains are on **Isla Angel de la Guarda** —Guardian Angel Island—and rise more than 1300 feet above sea level. Between Bahía de los Angeles and Isla Angel de la Guarda lies the **Canal de Ballenas**. The deep, calm channel with its abundant marine life is a favorite rest stop in the winter months for no less than five species of whales—including blue whales, the largest animal species that has ever lived on earth. Dolphins, too, are often spotted cruising the channel in pods of as many as a hundred.

In the last decades of the 19th century, long before the present-day town of Bahía de los Angeles was born, the mountains that surround the bay saw a brief flurry of gold, silver and copper mining. Remnants from this era offer the best excuses for landlubber adventuring in the area. The ghostly old mine camp of **Las Flores** dates back to the 1890s, when nearby Mina San Juan produced more than $2 million worth of silver. To get there, follow the only road south from Bahía de los Angeles for 16 kilometers, bearing right at the fork where the south shore road turns off to the left. A three-foot-thick stone vault where silver ingots were stored marks the site of the old refinery. Ore was brought down from the mine in two miniature trains linked by a pulley cable, then lowered in buckets over impassable cliffs from one train to the next. (One of the little locomotives that pulled the ore trains to and from

◆◆

✔ CHECK THESE OUT—UNIQUE LODGING

- *Budget:* Book a room at the plain and simple **Vera Cruz Motel** in Bahía Tortugas—the only lodging on the lonely Vizcaíno Peninsula. *page 148*
- *Budget:* Breathe in the fresh ocean air from your simple, stone-walled palapa at **Gecko Camp**, on the south shore of Bahía de los Angeles. *page 139*
- *Budget:* Enjoy the ceiling fans and hot showers at Guerrero Negro's **Motel El Morro**, a welcome find after a long desert drive. *page 143*
- *Moderate:* Spend a night in the heart of the Desierto Central's boulder field and cactus forest at **Hotel La Pinta Cataviña**. *page 133*

Budget: under $35   Moderate: $35–$70   Deluxe: $70–$105   Ultra-deluxe: over $105

the mines can be seen outside the Museo de Naturaleza y Cultura in Bahía de los Angeles.) Ruined buildings, machinery and heaps of reddish mine waste are scattered across the abandoned town.

The road continues past Las Flores, paralleling the coastline from afar for 130 kilometers to the still more remote fish camp of San Francisquito. Travelers on this adventurous backroad route can take a different route upon leaving San Francisquito and drive 72 kilometers to rejoin the Baja Highway south of Guerrero Negro. The rough trip requires a sturdy high-clearance vehicle, and extra cans of gasoline may be a fine idea. For more on the trip, see the Desierto Vizcaíno section in this chapter.

LODGING

RV sites outnumber motel rooms by at least fifty to one in Bahía de los Angeles. The best accommodations are at the **Motel Villa Vitta,** a modern 30-room place with air-conditioning, a swimming pool and a jacuzzi. No phone or TV, but there is electricity most of the day, thanks to the noisy generator nearby. On the main road in the center of town, the Villa Vita has access to the beach and boat ramp a block away. The motel also has a large RV park with hookups ($12 per night). ~ Bahía de los Angeles; 760-741-9583 in the U.S. BUDGET TO MODERATE.

The original tourist facility in Bahía de los Angeles, **Casa Díaz** has 15 spacious though spartan stone cabanas with simple furnishings, private baths, solar-heated showers and a beachfront location. There is also a handful of run-down RV campsites on the premises. ~ Bahía de los Angeles. Reservations: Apdo. Postal 579, Ensenada, BC. BUDGET.

Somewhere between a campground and a cabana complex, **Gecko Camp** has ten stone-walled palapas. Unfurnished except for crude tables, they are nonetheless cozy and private, and each one has the beach and bay right out the front door. Bring your own lantern, hammocks, bedding and kitchen gear, and you can easily go native for the season here at $10 per night. The central restrooms have solar-heated showers. ~ Six kilometers south of Bahía de los Angeles (keep left at the fork). BUDGET.

DINING

The best restaurant in Bahía de los Angeles is **Guillermo's,** located near the center of town in the white building at the big RV park of the same name. Fresh seafood fills the menu, with several shrimp choices, lobster *estilo Puerto Nuevo,* and catch-of-the-day fish dishes. Sea bass, when available, is a specialty. Diners on the outdoor terrace overlook the bay from the cool comfort of palapa sunshades. ~ Bahía de los Angeles. MODERATE.

Two blocks north of Guillermo's on the town's main street, **Las Hamacas** serves seafood at slightly lower prices, along with standard Mexican dishes. Especially popular for breakfast, the restaurant features both gringo fare (eggs, bacon, pancakes) and

Mexican favorites such as *chilaquiles*—tortilla pieces and chicken scrambled in a creamy red chile sauce—and tropical fruit salad. This place, too, has a great bay view. ~ Bahía de los Angeles. BUDGET TO MODERATE.

GROCERIES   Fish and other fruits of the sea are abundant. Fresh produce is virtually nonexistent, but you can get such staples as macaroni and cheese, canned peas and Pan Bimbo (Mexico's answer to Wonder Bread) at several small stores in Bahía de los Angeles. The main food store in town is located on the main street just south of the **Motel Villa Vitta**. You'll also find groceries, along with fishing supplies and general-store goods, at **Guillermo's** and **Casa Diaz**.

NIGHTLIFE   Get enough sportsmen together, add booze, and there's bound to be after-hours action even in the most out-of-the-way places. The boys swap fishing stories late into the evening around the bar at **Guillermo's**, and the restaurant's atmospherically lighted patio is as romantic a waterfront setting as you could want. There's another gringo bar, without the sea view, up the street at **Motel Villa Vitta**.

BEACHES & PARKS   **BAHÍA DE LOS ANGELES BEACHES** 🏄 🏖 🚤 🛥 ⚓ Ten miles of unbroken beach line the western shore of Bahía de los Angeles from the rocky outcropping of Punta La Gringa in the north to the Estero de la Mona wetlands at the south end of the bay. Windsurfers and kayakers head for the north beaches, best for launching. Sun worshippers find blissful seclusion at both ends, as far as possible from the center of town, where the beach feels practically urban; with several boat ramps, it's the hub for sport fishing on the bay. ~ Unpaved roads, wide and well-graded though steep in places, run north and south from town for the length of the beach.

▲ Free RV and tent camping is allowed all along the north beach from town to Punta la Gringa—first-come, first-served, no hookups, no restrooms. In town, the large RV and tent campgrounds at Guillermo's, the Motel Villa Vitta and Casa Diaz all have hookups, at $10 to $12 per night. Six kilometers south of town, Gecko Camp has tent and RV sites without hookups for as little as $5 per night.

PARQUE NACIONAL ISLA ANGEL DE LA GUARDA 🥾 🏖 🚤 ⚓ The largest island off the Baja coast, Isla Angel de la Guarda was once part of the peninsula but broke away a million years ago. Because there is no fresh water, the island has never been inhabited by humans. Pristine but not very inviting, its steep slopes grow the same vegetation as the mountains west of Bahía de los Angeles —*cardones*, agave, elephant trees and boojum trees. There are sea caves on the exposed eastern coast and a sea lion colony on a small cay off the northern tip, and the mountains host an abundance of bird life along with some rare lizard species. ~ Located seven to ten miles off the coast, east of Bahía de los Angeles. By asking at Guillermo's or any fishing shop, you can often locate a fishing guide to take you to the island. It is also possible—though strenuous and potentially hazardous—to get there by sea kayak.

▲ Camping is allowed. The best campsites are at the northern and southern tips of the island.

MID-RIFT ISLANDS WILDLIFE SANCTUARY 🕴 🛶 🚤 🛥 Isla Raza is off-limits to humans in March and April, when elegant terns, royal terns and rare Heerman's gulls numbering in the hundreds of thousands make their nests there. Guides operate tours from Bahía de los Angeles to view the bird colonies at Mid-rift Islands from a distance during nesting season. At other times of year, you can visit the island and ponder the mysterious mounds of rock that cover its surface. There are more than a thousand of these *"monumentos"* on the island, neatly piled to heights of five feet. Perhaps built by Seri Indians, egg gatherers or convicts at hard labor, their origin and purpose has been forgotten. To the south, Isla San Lorenzo and smaller neighboring islands host the world's largest brown pelican colony. ~ Southeast of Bahía de los Angeles, a chain of 45 large and small islands parallels the coast at a distance of about ten miles. Getting there by sea kayak is possible, though risky.

▲ Camping is permitted on Isla San Lorenzo and Isla Esteban.

Following the Baja Highway south for 133 kilometers past the Bahía de los Angeles turnoff, motorists cross the state line between Baja

▼▼▼▼▼▼▼▼▼▼▼▼▼▼
Guerrero Negro Area

California and Baja California Sur, where a monument with an eagle statue commemorates the opening of the highway in 1974. A few miles down the road, near the turnoff to Guerrero Negro, there is often an army check point—the only one you're likely to encounter in laid-back Baja California Sur.

With a population of more than 7000, Guerrero Negro is the first large town south of San Quintín. The people of the town work for Exportada de Sal, S.A. de C.V., the world's largest salt producer, which ships out 6.5 million tons of salt each year—more than 35,000,000 pounds of the stuff each day! The operation gathers salt from evaporating ponds that cover more than 300 square miles near the shore of the extremely saline lagoon south of town, and takes it by truck and ferry to its port on Isla Cedros for shipment to the United States, Canada and Japan. Until recently, the company was under American ownership and could not sell salt within Mexico because of trade restrictions; when the Japanese-based multinational Mitsubishi Corporation bought the salt works, it immediately gave 51 percent ownership to the Mexican government and received in return the right to sell salt to Mexicans —a profitable deal because it meant a dramatic reduction in shipping costs.

Despite its size, this company town has fewer lodging and restaurant options than little Bahía de los Angeles, but it has more stores selling groceries and basic necessities. Guerrero Negro is more than just a pit stop between the Desierto Central and Desierto Vizcaíno, however. From December through March, salt-encrusted Laguna Ojo de Liebre south of town is one of the best whalewatching spots in North America—the calving ground for thousands of gray whales. The weather is windy and often chilly in winter; if you're looking for sunny tropical beaches, this is not the place. Wildlife watchers, however, will rate it as a high point of their Baja expedition. Even when the whales are gone, the abundance of bird life on this lagoon is beyond belief.

SIGHTS

The **Monumento Aguila**, a dramatic bronze sculpture of a Mexican eagle that greets travelers at the state line as they approach Guerrero Negro, is oddly appropriate: sea eagles, or ospreys, are so abundant in the area that they nest atop many of the power poles along Guerrero Negro's streets. Crossing the state line takes you from the Pacific time zone to the Mountain time zone. Set your clock forward an hour when heading south, and back on the return trip.

There is nothing approximating a tourist sight in Guerrero Negro itself. Drive the length of the main street to Guerrero Negro's salt company and Pemex station, then turn right and continue past the traffic *glorieta* to take the road to the **old salt port**. The smooth, wide unpaved road runs north for ten kilometers along the top of a levee, through coastal wetlands teeming with herons, egrets, and other wading birds. The site of the old salt-shipping facility overlooks Laguna Guerrero Negro. The lagoon and later the town were named for the S.S. *Black Warrior*, an American ship that was overloaded with whale oil in 1858. Its sails could not move the overweight ship, which foundered on the sand bar at the mouth of the bay. The wreck was visible for many years. In the 20th century, the salt company found that the same sand bar limited the size of the ships that could use their salt port and moved the port offshore to Isla Cedros after a few years. Ruined walls of huge warehouses and loading docks remain, providing pelican perches and osprey nesting places. Whales often congregate around the mouth of the lagoon; they're sometimes visible through binoculars from the parking area above the salt port. Whalewatching boats sometimes depart from here, too.

South of town, Laguna Ojo de Liebre—also called Scammon's Lagoon—is a more popular whalewatchers' destination. The road to **Parque Natural de la Ballena Gris** turns off the main highway 10 kilometers south of town and runs for 24 kilometers west to the shoreline. It is unpaved but wide and smooth. Other roads in the area are marked off-limits to unauthorized vehicles. Heed the signs: monster salt trucks that seem the size of cruise ships, twice the width of a semi truck and rolling on tires ten feet in diameter, careen down these roads at high speed, and woe be unto the mere passenger car or motor home that gets in the way. The park is situated along a windy, soggy coastline green with creeping plants, close to the mouth of the narrow, salt-crusted estuary where the whales go to give birth to their calves. Whalewatching boats leave frequently from the park dock in season. When the whales are gone, the park is closed.

LODGING

The **Hotel La Pinta**, seven kilometers out of town near the state line, offers the nicest lodging in the Guerrero Negro area. The 27 guest rooms are modern, spacious and bright, with hot water, satellite TV, air conditioning and a swimming pool. ~ Route 1, Km. 128; 800-336-5454 in the U.S. MODERATE.

On the road that leads into town from the highway, the **Motel El Morro** has 32 clean, spare and spacious rooms with ceiling fans, private baths and hot showers. ~ Boulevard Zapata (Apdo. Postal 144), Guerrero Negro; 7-04-14. BUDGET.

Room rates are even more affordable at nearby **Motel Las Dunas**. At under $20 a night, you wouldn't expect anything special here, and you'd be right. Each of the 12 clean, modest rooms has a private bath with shower, a double bed and not much else. There is also an RV park on the premises. ~ Boulevard Zapata, Guerrero Negro; 7-00-57. BUDGET.

The **Malarrimo Motel** is a recent addition to the legendary restaurant of the same name. Four guest units with private baths are situated in two duplexes. The walls seem to be made of plywood, but comfortable beds, hot showers and cheerful decor make for a welcoming stopover between two vast expanses of desert. Behind the motel and restaurant is an RV campground with hookups for 12 rigs ($12 per night). The sites are paved or graveled, making for uncomfortable tent camping. The only alternative for tent campers is the windblown coastal campground at Parque Natural de Ballena Gris. ~ Boulevard Zapata, Guerrero Negro; 7-02-50, fax 7-00-20. BUDGET.

Motels get smaller and cheaper the farther west you go on Boulevard Zapata, closer to the salt company headquarters. Places such as the **Motel Gámez** near city hall cater to transient workers, not tourists, and offer the bare minimum in comfort—mattresses on concrete pedestals in cramped, colorless quarters—but if you're looking for a roof over your head, a little privacy and a shower that's solar-heated if you're lucky, all for the same price as a campsite, this 12-room hotel will fill the bill. ~ Boulevard Zapata, Guerrero Negro.

DINING

One of the culinary highlights of driving the Baja Highway is the **Restaurant-Bar Malarrimo**, the finest dining between Ensenada and La Paz. It is the principal attraction at the little tourist center of the same name at the east end of Guerrero Negro's main street. Seafood is prepared with a flair that is part Continental, part California nouveau. Besides the lobster, shrimp and catch of the day typical of Baja seafood restaurants, the menu features big Pismo clams, abalone and a rich *marisco* soup. The wine cellar is the best in the Baja backcountry. Soft lighting, heavy, rustic chairs and tables, and real cloth tablecloths help make for a little splurge of luxury to celebrate achieving the Baja Highway's halfway point. ~ Boulevard Zapata, Guerrero Negro; 7-02-50. MODERATE TO DELUXE.

The other contender for tourist business is the **Baja Sur Restaurant**, at the hotel of the same name. The seafood fare tries to rival the Malarrimo but does not quite succeed. Shrimp in garlic sauce, lobster *estilo Puerto Nuevo* and sea bass steaks are featured. The ambience is supplied by a TV set in one corner of the dining room. ~ Boulevard Zapata, Guerrero Negro; 7-02-50. MODERATE.

Most other restaurants in town seem aimed at a local trade more than tourists. Wood paneling—a nice touch in a town that otherwise seems built entirely of concrete blocks—creates a homelike atmosphere at **El Fogón de Sal**, on the north side of the street

✔ **CHECK THESE OUT—UNIQUE DINING**

- *Budget:* Don't expect to find restaurants in the remote coastal village of Bahía Tortugas; instead, feast on fresh fish tacos from the **comedores**. *page 148*

- *Budget:* Visit El Rosario's **Mama Espinosa's**—giant fossil snails set the ambience at this Baja landmark. *page 133*

- *Moderate:* Dine on sea bass and lobster under palm-thatched canopies on a bayfront patio at **Guillermo's** in Bahía de los Angeles. *page 139*

- *Moderate to deluxe:* Experience the finest seafood dining between Ensenada and La Paz at the **Restaurant-Bar Malarrimo** in Guerrero Negro. *page 144*

Budget: under $5   Moderate: $5–$10   Deluxe: $10–$18   Ultra-deluxe: over $18

midway through town. The food is typically Mexican; sizzling rolled fish tacos are a specialty. ~ Boulevard Zapata, Guerrero Negro. BUDGET.

The little **Restaurant Lupita**, located near the Supermercado la Ballena in the center of town, appeals to Mexican tastes with plates of spicy fish and shrimp tacos served in very simple surroundings. It's a popular place for Mexican-style breakfasts. ~ Boulevard Zapata, Guerrero Negro. BUDGET.

During the afternoon, dozens of open-air *comedores* open up along the main street to serve salt company workers on their midday siesta breaks. The food—fish tacos, *birria* (goat), tamales, *carne asada* and other Mexican favorites—is as good as you'll find in Guerrero Negro's budget-priced restaurants, and prices are so low that you can fill a picnic basket to the brim for a few dollars.

Restaurants in Guerrero Negro provide soy sauce on the table instead of salt: until recently, the town's huge Japanese-owned salt-mining operation was forbidden to sell its product in Mexico. All the salt was exported, while Japanese soy sauce was imported for local consumption. The practice has persisted; most likely, by the time they get off work, local people don't want to look at any more salt.

GROCERIES The **Supermercado la Ballena** has as good a selection of nonperishable foodstuffs as you'll find in central Baja. You'll find such convenient on-the-road fare as pop-top fruit juices, packaged cookies, dried fish and that ubiquitous backcountry staple, canned peas. ~ Boulevard Zapata, Guerrero Negro.

NIGHTLIFE Gringo travelers congregate after dark in the **Restaurant-Bar Malarrimo**. ~ Boulevard Zapata, Guerrero Negro. Look for the local version of disco action late into the night at **Mario's Restaurant-Bar**, at the Motel El Morro on the road into town.

BEACHES & PARKS **PARQUE NATURAL DE LA BALLENA GRIS** ⊸ This coastal park provides access to Laguna Ojo de Liebre near the narrow, salty estuary where the whales calve. In the winter, when 18,000 to 20,000 whales gather in the lagoon, the park's dock is busy with low, open, motorized boats that take sightseers out among the whales. There is also an observation tower where visitors can often view the whales from shore through binoculars. Open December through March only. ~ Turn west off the main highway at the big hand-lettered sign 10 kilometers south of town; follow the wide, unpaved road for 24 kilometers to the park.

▲ A vaguely defined row of tent and RV sites without hookups lines the lagoon shore north of the boat dock. Camping costs $12 per night. Tenters may find camping uncomfortable on this chilly, windy stretch of coastline.

▼▼▼▼▼▼▼▼▼▼▼▼▼▼
Desierto Vizcaíno

South of the salty oasis of Guerrero Negro lies the widest and wildest part of Baja—the Vizcaíno Desert. From the Pacific coast to the Sea of Cortez, a distance of 140 miles as the crow flies, stretches the Vizcaíno Biosphere Reserve. No road signs mark the reserve's boundaries, but it is the largest protected habitat area in Mexico. Reserves like this are created around the world under the UNESCO "Man and the Biosphere" program. A "core area" is protected by regulations more stringent than those that apply to federally designated wilderness areas in the United States; commercial and industrial exploitation is banned in adjacent populated areas but local people are permitted to use the natural resources. In the case of the Vizcaíno Biosphere Reserve, the human population is found almost entirely in fishing camps along the Pacific coast, as a jagged range of extinct volcanoes makes the Sea of Cortez coast inaccessible by both land and sea.

Motorists on the Baja Highway cross the center of the Vizcaíno Desert on the 140-kilometer journey from Guerrero Negro to San Ignacio. Compared to the cactus wonderland of the Desierto Central, this stretch of desert is bleak. Giant *cardón* cactuses, many of them thickened, crippled or scarred by brutal sandstorms, stand sentinel over the landscape, alongside the woody gray skeletons of *cardones* from centuries past. The climate is too dry for decay, and there is no one around to break them up for firewood. Many of the smaller cactuses are colorless and nasty—galloping cactus, which creeps along the ground as it grows to form impassable thickets, and jumping cholla, whose stiff, sharp spines grip anyone who brushes against it so tight that removing them may require pliers. Dust devils scour the glaring desert and send writhing white plumes of sand a hundred feet or more in the air.

Adventurous travelers who are not deterred by this howling wilderness can explore westward from the main highway and discover some of the most remote coastline in Baja.

SIGHTS

HIDDEN ▶

From Route 1, motorists with rugged vehicles or dirt bikes will find an intriguing side trip 29 kilometers south of Guerrero Negro (near kilometer marker 154), where another major road turns off to the east and goes to a cluster of old mining towns—**El Arco**, **Pozo Alemán** and **Calmallí**. The three old towns were booming gold camps in the 1920s, with a population numbering in the thousands. Officially designated Route 18, the road was once paved but has deteriorated so badly that high clearance and tough tires are advisable, and a four-wheel-drive vehicle is a big help in certain patches. It is 42 kilometers to El Arco; the former boom town has a tiny population and a well-kept church that serves the area's scattered ranches. Beyond El Arco, the "pavement" ends and four-wheel drive is advisable. Four kilometers farther on, at

Pozo Alemán, little is visible but stone foundations and the old well for which the town was named. There, a left fork goes nine kilometers north to Calmallí, where tumbledown buildings and the strewn wreckage of mining equipment are mute reminders that it was once the site of the richest mine in the district.

A sharp right turn where the pavement ends at El Arco puts you on the road to **Misión Santa Gertrudis**, one of the best-preserved and least visited Spanish colonial missions in central Baja. The road is wide and well maintained, but may require high clearance. Founded in 1752, the mission thrived despite its remote location because a freshwater spring irrigated its fields, orchards and vineyards. It produced the finest wine on the peninsula for many years, exporting it in stone vessels for lack of wood. In its heyday, the mission supported a community of 1500 Cochimí Indians. Although the missionaries abandoned it in 1822, a handful of Indians remained to keep the fields productive, and local fruit and vegetable farmers have maintained the church ever since. One unique feature of the old adobe church is its bell tower, built not on top of the church but 50 yards away. A small museum in the church displays Cochimí Indian artifacts. Pilgrims from all over the Baja trek to this church to observe the Fiesta de Santa Gertrudis on November 16.

◄ *HIDDEN*

If you continue straight instead of turning left at the Pozo Alemán fork, a long, desolate road continues northeast for 74 very slow kilometers, with fantastic scenic vistas overlooking vast expanses of *cardón* forest. The road goes to the isolated fishing camp of **San Francisquito**—a secluded beach on the Sea of Cortez with a few very basic palapas that can be rented if anybody is around to rent them from. It is on a small cove with good fishing for sea bass and barracuda. West of San Francisquito, a rough four-wheel-drive road runs northward to Bahía de los Angeles. This 130-kilometer trek approaches the sea at an even more remote beach, **Playa San Rafael**, then winds among volcanic peaks of over 3000 feet before descending into Bahía de los Angeles. Those who take on the challenge of this wild backcountry drive may want to carry extra fuel; gasoline is sometimes sold from drums at San Francisquito, but you can't count on it.

◄ *HIDDEN*

◄ *HIDDEN*

Back on the Baja Highway, another long side trip leads to Bahía Tortugas, on the tip of the Vizcaíno Peninsula. This road turns off Route 1 to the west, 71 kilometers south of Guerrero Negro. The first 26 kilometers are paved; the remaining 122 kilometers to the Pacific are not. They're sometimes badly washboarded but good enough to accommodate all passenger vehicles, including motor homes.

Staying on the main road, you cross a barren coastal plain and salt flats en route to **Bahía Tortugas**, the largest town on the Vizcaíno Peninsula, with a population of about 3000. Fishing for lobster and abalone is the main business here. Tourism has become a factor in the local economy, with a small but steady stream of gringo visitors arriving by boat and RV in roughly equal numbers. There are exceptionally fine beaches along the bay south of town —a good spot to dig for Pismo clams—and a few miles north, near the small village of Punta Eugenia.

Isla Cedro, the largest island off Baja's Pacific coast, lies 12 miles north of Punta Eugenia, the tip of the Vizcaíno Peninsula. The 12.5-mile-long, almost beachless island comprises two mountain peaks rising 3950 and 3488 feet above sea level; a broad saddle between them is sliced by the sheer cliffs of a deep, narrow canyon called the Gran Cañon. The north slopes of both mountains are covered by a "cloud forest" of evergreens that stand as much as 40 to 50 feet tall. Clumps of ball moss cling to the trees and obtain their moisture from the thick sea fog that often shrouds the island. Isla Cedro ("Cedar Island") refers to the juniper trees that grow here. The forest also contains two unique tree species, the Cedros Island pine and the Cedros Island oak, and provides habitat for a rare subspecies of mule deer and several unique rodent and lizard species. Pueblo de Cedros, on the east side of the island, has been a fishing village for centuries, ever since Cochimí Indians lived on the island. They were the only native people to hunt gray whale, killing the great beasts with spears.

Exportación de Sal moved its shipping port to Isla Cedros in 1967, and today the prosperous Pueblo de Cedros has a population of more than 3000—about half that of Guerrero Negro. As in Guerrero Negro, almost everybody on the island works for the salt company. Aside from the town, the island is undeveloped, and the northern half is practically inaccessible by land.

LODGING   The only accommodation on the Vizcaíno Peninsula, the very basic **Vera Cruz Motel**, has twin beds, baths with solar-heated showers, and nothing else. ~ Bahía Tortugas. BUDGET.

Several Isla Cedros residents offer simple rooms for rent in their homes or adjacent guest cottages. Availability depends on the presence or absence of transient dock workers. Watch for "se renta" signs. ~ Isla Cedros. BUDGET.

DINING   Several *comedores* along the main road in Bahía Tortugas offer fish tacos. For a full Mexican dinner, try the no-frills restaurant at the **Vera Cruz Motel**. ~ Bahía Tortugas. BUDGET.

GROCERIES   If you're heading for the Vizcaíno Peninsula, stock up on food before leaving Guerrero Negro. Groceries are scarce in these parts.

BEACHES & PARKS   **PLAYA MALARRIMO** 🏃 Along the way to Bahía Tortugas, a turnoff goes north to one of the most interesting out-of-the-way beaches on the Pacific coast—if you're equipped to get there. The side trip to Playa Malarrimo requires four-wheel drive to cross rocky areas and deep sand drifts. This hard-to-reach beach near the mouth of Scammon's Lagoon has a reputation for some of the best beachcombing in the world. Ocean currents from the North Pacific swirl into the north coast of the Vizcaíno Peninsula, depositing Japanese floats, huge logs from British Columbia and plastic containers from many lands along the powdery beach. There are no travelers' facilities of any kind, and you can spend days at Playa Malarrimo without seeing another human being. ~ The road, marked with a small sign that says "Malarrimo," turns off from the route to Bahía Tortugas about 80 kilometers from the Baja Highway. It's another 42 kilometers to the beach.

▲ There are no restrictions on camping at Playa Malarrimo. Fierce winds can make the experience less than idyllic, though.

▼▼▼▼▼▼▼▼▼▼▼▼▼
Outdoor Adventures

BAHÍA DE LOS ANGELES Although old-timers will tell you that fishing in the Bahía de los Angeles is not what it used to be, it's still the top sportfishing center on the Sea of Cortez. Especially during the summer months, the catch includes sea bass, dorado (mahi mahi), tuna, halibut and grouper, as well as many exotic species of tropical fish (including triggerfish, considered a delicacy in these parts). Yellowtails run during the winter months. Fishing guides and limited fishing supplies are available at Guillermo's and Casa Díaz. Fishing is said to be better farther south at the remote outpost of Bahía San Francisquito.

FISHING

EL ROSARIO AREA There's good diving on the reef of the south end of **Isla San Geronimo**, off Punta Baja near El Rosario, though sea lions can be possessive about the area. They are unaccustomed to human visitors, whose presence may set off a din of barking. **Arecife Sacramento**, a reef a few miles south of the island, lies so close to the surface that it can only be dived on a calm day when swells are less than two feet. Its top is a forest of surf grass—a slender, waving seaweed that grows up to 12 feet tall here and harbors an amazing array of underwater life, including huge lobsters, giant sea bass and benign horn sharks. Several ships have wrecked here, including the reef's namesake, the paddlewheel steamer *Sacramento*, which went down in 1872 with a fortune in silver and gold. Another good shipwreck dive on the reef is the *Goodwill*, a luxury yacht that sank in 1969.

DIVING

BAHÍA DE LOS ANGELES Isla Coronado is the most popular diving area (scuba divers prefer the east coast, snorkelers the west coast around little Isla Mitlan), though the whole rock reef where the bay plunges into the Canal de Ballenas is scuba-suitable. Bring your own air—there is no longer a dive shop in town.

VIZCAÍNO PENINSULA The **Islas San Benito**, a cluster of three tiny islands 16 miles northwest of Isla Cedros, has been the ruin of tuna boats, industrial fishing ships and even an oil tanker. Several of the wrecks make great dives. The waters around these islands also boast a junglelike kelp forest and rock reefs teeming with fish, supporting some divers' claim that the San Benitos offer the best scuba diving in Baja. Guides on Isla Cedros take divers and nature lovers out to these remote islands, which also have a large elephant seal colony The main limitation is air, since the passenger planes that fly from Guerrero Negro to Isla Cedros won't carry many scuba tanks, and once there, there's no place to refill them.

SURFING & WIND-SURFING

EL ROSARIO AREA **Punta Baja**, on the coast a few miles west of El Rosario, is a surfers' secret with a long right-point break.

BAHÍA DE LOS ANGELES Windsurfing is becoming popular here because the protected waters develop little chop in the wind. The prevailing wind is out of the north, enabling windsurfers to sail seven miles from **Punta La Gringa**, north of town, through the cluster of islands in the middle of the bay before landing on the far shore.

VIZCAÍNO PENINSULA Five miles offshore from Bahía Tortugas, **Isla Natividad** offers great surfing summer and winter. The break on the east side of the island is known for big, long tubes and lots of them. Locals in Bahía Tortugas and Punta Eugenia take surfers across to the island, a 45-minute trip each way, and **Scorpio Surfing Tours** leads trips to the island from July through September. ~ P.O. Box 4184, Chula Vista, CA 91909; 619-425-8154.

KAYAKING **BAHÍA DE LOS ANGELES** Seri Indians routinely crossed the Sea of Cortez by canoe just south of here. By following the coast of

---

✔ **CHECK THESE OUT—UNIQUE OUTDOOR ADVENTURES**

- Scuba in the surf grass with horn sharks and giant lobsters on Sacramento Reef off Punta Baja near El Rosario. *page 149*
- Discover why Isla Natividad is one of the great secret surfers' beaches of the Pacific coast. *page 150*
- Paddle a sea kayak from island to island across the turquoise waters of Bahía de los Angeles. *page 150*
- Hike the mountain peaks, grand canyon and evergreen forest of Isla Cedros, the big island off the tip of the Vizcaíno Peninsula. *page 152*

giant Isla Tiburón on the mainland side, then hopping through the Mid-Rift Islands, they could make the crossing without ever being more than seven miles from shore. Modern kayakers have made the crossing, too, but it's not an adventure to be taken lightly. Most kayakers restrict their island-hopping to stepping-stone expeditions across the mouth of the bay, where the longest distance between islands is two miles. **Guillermo's** has a few rental kayaks.

GUERRERO NEGRO AREA   Formerly a favorite kayaking spot, Scammon's Lagoon and nearby waters are now off-limits to kayaks and other private boats during whale season. Access to Scammon's Lagoon is difficult at other times of year, when the road to Parque Nacional de Ballena Gris is closed, but kayaking on Laguna Guerrero Negro offers solitude and fine birdwatching. There are no kayak rentals in town.

BAHÍA DE LOS ANGELES   While several species of whales are commonly spotted in the Canal de Ballenas between the bay and Isla Angel de la Guarda during the winter months, their appearance is unpredictable enough that local guides offer boat trips for birdwatching instead of whalewatching. Whether you take one of these jaunts or paddle your own kayak among the islands, you stand a fair chance of encountering a Minke, gray or blue whale in the bay.

WHALE-WATCHING & BOAT TOURS

GUERRERO NEGRO AREA   Scammon's Lagoon is the largest of three gray-whale calving grounds along the Pacific coast of Baja. The whales come because the shallow lagoon has a high salt content, making for more buoyancy and easier births. The whales were all but exterminated in the 1850s, and only in the 1990s has their population returned to pre-whaling levels—18,000 to 20,000 according to recent counts. From December through March, guides take whalewatchers out in large motorized *pangas* from the dock at **Parque Nacional de Ballena Gris** south of Guerrero Negro. Reservations are not necessary; departures are intermittent through midafternoon. The boats are prohibited by international treaty from approaching within 100 yards of a whale, but it's okay if the whale approaches the boat. Since gray whales often seem as curious about humans as we are about them, close encounters with the great beasts are more likely than not. Whalewatching expeditions to the mouth of Laguna Guerrero Negro, offered by guides who advertise their services at restaurants in Guerrero Negro, depart from the **Old Salt Port** north of town.

VIZCAÍNO PENINSULA   Guides from Bahía Tortugas and Punta Eugenia are often available to take nature lovers by boat to the **Islas San Benito** to see the elephant seals and large colonies of sea birds.

HIKING   **DESIERTO CENTRAL**   The area around Cataviña invites short hikes in the marvelous cactus forest and boulder fields. There are few visible trails, and the baking midday heat makes it advisable to limit hiking to the early morning and dusk. Follow arroyos to avoid getting lost. Most examples of rock art seem to be found near arroyos, too.

BAHÍA DE LOS ANGELES   The **Mina Santa Marta**, an abandoned mine from the 1880s, makes for the most spectacular hiking or backpacking trip in the area. From the public dump two miles south of town, the bed of a former railway runs six steep miles up the canyon to the mine site. Hikers can also follow the old narrow-gauge railroad bed partway up to **Mina San Juan** from the ghost town of Las Flores.

VIZCAÍNO PENINSULA   Hikers will find challenging trails on **Isla Cedros**. A five-mile ascent from Pueblo de Cedros to the 3950-foot summit of Pico Cedros earns you a spectacular view of the nearby Islas de San Benito, Isla Natividad, the Vizcaíno Peninsula and the distant shore of Scammon's Lagoon. From the summit, the trail descends the north side of the mountain and splits. The right fork goes down into the Gran Cañon and eventually to a secluded beach at the canyon mouth, seven miles from the mountain summit. The left fork follows the canyon rim for several miles before veering into the heart of the forest. The total distance from the summit is eight miles.

▼▼▼▼▼▼▼▼▼▼▼
Transportation

There is no commercial air service to El Rosario, Cataviña or Bahía de Los Angeles, though the latter has a good airstrip to accommodate the numerous private pilots who fly in.

AIR

Aerolineas California Pacificos has flights from Guerrero Negro to Isla Cedros every weekday morning, returning the same afternoon. Since the old DC-3s are provided mainly for the convenience of salt company workers assigned to Isla Cedros, the prices are surprisingly reasonable—a fraction of what fishermen charge to take you to the island by boat from the much closer Bahía Tortugas. The same airline has flights between Guerrero Negro and Bahía Tortugas three times a week. There is no other regular air service to or from Guerrero Negro.

BUS   Autotransportes de Baja California operates four first-class buses daily from Tijuana and one from Mexicali, stopping in Guerrero Negro on their way south to La Paz and Los Cabos.

A first-class bus runs from the Tijuana terminal to Bahía de los Angeles once a week, leaving at 6 a.m. on Saturday and returning on Sunday.

El Rosario, Cataviña and the Parque Natural Desierto Central are along **Route 1,** and Guerrero Negro is just a short distance off the main highway. Bahía de los Angeles is 67 kilometers off the Baja Highway on a paved road that, confusingly, is also designated as Route 1. The unpaved road from the main highway east to remote Bahía San Francisquito is designated as **Route 18,** while the road west to the tip of the Vizcaíno Peninsula has no route number but is referred to as the **Carretera Bahía Tortugas.**

▼▼▼▼▼▼▼▼▼▼▼▼▼▼▼▼▼▼▼▼▼▼

Addresses & Phone Numbers

Policia, Guerrero Negro: 7-02-22
IMSS Hospital y Clínica: 7-04-33
Secretaría de Turismo de Bahía de los Angeles: Avenida López
    Mateos 1250, Ensenada; 50-32-06

SEVEN

Southern Baja

Imagine impossibly brilliant turquoise water—so still that each dip of your paddle leaves concentric ripples as your kayak glides along the surface of Bahía Concepción, so clear that you can see triggerfish darting below. Feel the thrill as curious dolphins surround you. On the distant shore, white sand beaches lined with palm trees and giant cactus provide the kind of camping spots that daydreams are made of.

If any one part of the peninsula represents the spirit of "hidden" Baja, this is it. In this chapter, you'll discover many of the best places on the peninsula for kayaking, sport fishing and whalewatching, as well as the best-preserved old Spanish colonial mission churches, ancient Indian rock art and unexpectedly verdant canyons hidden deep in the mountains.

It's not that the towns of Southern Baja are off the beaten path—all of them lie along the Baja Highway. But they seem seem lost in time: the colonial outposts of past centuries live on as havens for gringos and Mexicans alike who choose to be refugees from civilization. At San Ignacio, Mulegé and Loreto you'll find 18th-century missions that did not return to dust, like the forlorn ruins of the north, but lived on thanks to the farm families who have cultivated the fields and orchards for many generations. These towns share a tropical, easygoing hammock-between-palm-trees feel that Los Cabos must once have had. Then there's Santa Rosalía, a unique old French colonial mining town that has survived both the departure of the French and the closing of the mine.

When it comes to great beaches, this area is hard to beat. Bahía Concepción, between Mulegé and Loreto, is so idyllic that many people camp along its beaches for months at a time, creating a do-it-yourself resort atmosphere with separate beaches for different camping styles, from full-hookup motor homes with boats in tow to four-wheel-drive tailgaters in search of utter solitude.

Two decades ago, the government agency that created Cancún and Los Cabos proclaimed its intention to create another mega-resort along the beaches south of

Loreto, but dropped the project when hotel chains proved skeptical about investing there. Today, though the picture-perfect little resort area has fewer than 300 hotel rooms, it boasts the region's only international airport—with three planes a day—and the only golf course between Tijuana and Los Cabos.

This sandy stretch of low-rent paradise has avoided Los Cabos–style resort crowds and preserved its unique character because it is so hard to get to. You can get to Santa Rosalía by ferry from the Mexican mainland, or to Loreto by plane direct from Los Angeles, but there is no place to rent a car for hundreds of miles. This leaves the magnificent seascapes exclusively to the modest flow of tourists who come by motor home, van, camper truck, car or motorcycle. Many are in a hurry to reach La Paz or Los Cabos when they first discover this area and resolve to linger here on their trip back north. A growing number return year after year for longer stays.

San Ignacio Area

From its location on the map—in the middle of the Desierto Vizcaíno, separated from the Pacific coast by vast salt flats and from the Sea of Cortez by the Tres Vírgenes volcano field—travelers might expect San Ignacio to be another of those forlorn desert outposts that punctuate Central Baja's long, empty highway stretches. Those who take the winding, two-kilometer road that descends into town from the Baja Highway are in for a pleasant surprise. San Ignacio is a lush little desert oasis and the first town on the southward trip down the Baja Peninsula that feels like Old Mexico.

What maps do not reveal is that San Ignacio is set in a broad valley flanked on both sides by sheer volcanic cliffs and filled with date palm trees. Although the spring-fed Río de San Ignacio, which parallels the highway just north of town, doesn't go anywhere—its water normally evaporates in the desert sun long before reaching the Bahía de San Ignacio—it provides a reliable water source for the palm trees, as well as the oranges, pomegranates, grapes and corn grown on compact farms surrounding the town.

The palms were planted by Franciscan missionaries, who founded Misión San Ignacio Kadakaamán on the site in 1728. Thanks to the reliable water supply and rich soil, the mission grew to become the largest on the Baja Peninsula, ministering to more than 5000 Cochimí Indians. Since 1840, when the mission was abandoned, the palm trees have grown wild to dominate the town's skyline and colonize the river valley as far as the eye can see. Today, San Ignacio is a farming and ranching center with a population of 4000, including many fair-skinned descendants of German sailors who were stranded in nearby Santa Rosalía by a naval embargo during World War I.

In the summer of 1997, tinder-dry palm trees caught fire and set buildings ablaze throughout the north side of town. Townspeople and tourists rallied to fight the fire, stopping it just short of the church. Although the adjoining museum was damaged, the old mission survived the flames intact.

San Ignacio is the point of departure for two adventures into the Baja backcountry. Both are usually undertaken with guides from San Ignacio. Some of Baja's most magnificent Indian rock painting caves are found in the rugged canyonlands to the north; the most pristine—and controversial—of Baja's gray whale calving areas is Laguna San Ignacio, to the west. During the winter, some guides offer multi-day tours that include visits to both the caves and the lagoon.

SIGHTS

The tallest building in town, **Misión San Ignacio** has the most ornate exterior of any Baja mission church; it recalls the great architecture of old Spain on a small scale. The timeworn, four-foot-thick volcanic stone walls were erected at the direction of Jesuit missionaries in 1728; Dominicans extensively renovated the church in 1786, adding false columns, biblical statuary, Moorish-style roof ornaments, and elaborate stonework around the windows and doorways. The church is open to the public in the daytime and early evening. A smaller structure beside the church houses a collection of Indian pictographs found on rocks nearby. The museum was closed because of fire damage in 1997, but it's expected to reopen soon. ~ San Ignacio.

Across the street from the church is a **zócalo**, or town plaza, as shady and inviting as any in the tropics of mainland Mexico. Giant old Indian laurel trees form a sheltering canopy over the plaza. A handful of small stores and restaurants—pretty much all there is to the town—stands across the street from the south side of the plaza. ~ San Ignacio.

Several of the most spectacular Indian cave-painting sites in Baja are found in the **Sierra de San Francisco**, due north of San Ignacio. Rising to 5200 feet above sea level, the steep, barren mountains conceal deep, palm-lined canyons that were home to a mysterious Indian race from about A.D. 500 to 1500. Unlike the rock art farther north around Cataviña, the murals in this region depict humans and animals—deer, mountain lions, birds and even whales. The sites are under the protection of Mexico's Instituto Nacional de Antropología e Historia and can only be visited with a licensed guide.

HIDDEN ▶

The most frequently visited rock art site in the San Ignacio Area, **Cueva Palmarito** is reached by a five-mile hike or mule ride from Rancho Santa Marta. The spectacular mural covers a cliff face 150 feet long and 60 feet high, sheltered by a rock overhang. Guided tours can be arranged leaving from San Ignacio, or motorists with high-clearance vehicles can make the two-hour drive to the ranch and obtain a guide there. To reach the ranch, drive

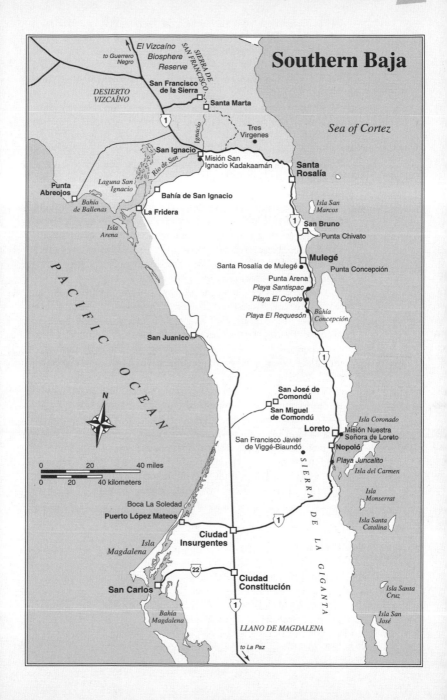

Southern Baja

to Guerrero Negro

El Vizcaíno Biosphere Reserve

DESIERTO VIZCAÍNO

SIERRA DE SAN FRANCISCO

San Francisco de la Sierra

Santa Marta

Tres Virgenes

Sea of Cortez

San Ignacio

Misión San Ignacio Kadakaamán

Santa Rosalía

Punta Abreojos

Laguna San Ignacio

Bahía de San Ignacio

Bahía de Ballenas

La Fridera

Isla San Marcos

Isla Arena

San Bruno

Punta Chivato

PACIFIC OCEAN

Mulegé

Santa Rosalía de Mulegé

Punta Concepción

Punta Arena

Playa Santispac

Playa El Coyote

Playa El Requesón

Bahía Concepción

San Juanico

N

San José de Comondú

San Miguel de Comondú

Loreto

Isla Coronado

Misión Nuestra Señora de Loreto

San Francisco Javier de Viggé-Biaundó

Nopoló

Playa Juncalito

Isla del Carmen

0   20   40 miles

0   20   40 kilometers

SIERRA DE LA GIGANTA

Isla Monserrat

Isla Santa Catalina

Boca La Soledad

Puerto López Mateos

Ciudad Insurgentes

Isla Magdalena

Isla Santa Cruz

22

San Carlos

Ciudad Constitución

Bahía Magdalena

1

LLANO DE MAGDALENA

Isla San José

to La Paz

14 kilometers east from San Ignacio on the Baja Highway and turn off to the north on the marked Santa Marta road. This narrow, rocky road winds higher and higher into the mountains, affording spectacular views of the Vizcaíno Desert and the canyons of the Sierra de San Francisco, for 29 kilometers to dead-end at Rancho Santa Marta.

An even more challenging rock art expedition takes travelers up the west side of the sierra to the remote village of **San Francisco de la Sierra**, where guides are available for the three-day round **HIDDEN ▶** trip by burro to **Gardner Cave**, also known as Cueva Pintada. Considered the finest known example of Baja rock art, this mural beneath the volcanic cliffs of Arroyo San Pablo measures 30 feet high and more than 500 feet long, with layer upon layer of images of men, women and wildlife. The cave was named for mystery novelist Erle Stanley Gardner, who devoted his later years to exploring the Baja backcountry and who wrote books and magazine articles about his discoveries—including Gardner Cave, which he found in 1962. To reach San Francisco de la Sierra, go 45 kilometers northwest from San Ignacio on the Baja Highway and turn east on the unpaved road near kilometer marker 118; a small sign reads "Pinturas Rupestres." The road serves several area ranches; it is wide and well-graded, and passenger cars should have no problem, though motor homes may find some switchbacks difficult to negotiate. It is 37 kilometers from the highway turnoff to the village. Visitors who aren't up to the long burro trek to Gardner Cave can see a more modest mural just off the road, two and **HIDDEN ▶** a half miles below San Francisco de la Sierra. The site, **Cueva de Ratón**, is similar in character to that at Gardner Cave but only about 30 feet long. A guide is required, and local police patrol the area to stop trespassers.

HIDDEN ▶   **Laguna San Ignacio** lies 67 kilometers west of the town of San Ignacio on a well-maintained—though unnervingly narrow—unpaved road that is usually suitable for passenger cars. It's the only one of Baja's three gray-whale calving areas (the others are

▸▸

✔ CHECK THESE OUT—UNIQUE SIGHTS

Scammon's Lagoon and Bahía Magdalena) that remains untouched by development. The road leads past several tiny fish camps to Punta Yuca, a muddy, rocky point near the mouth of the 17-mile-long lagoon. This vantage lets whalewatchers view the great beasts from shore much closer than at Scammon's Lagoon or Bahía Magdalena. Guides at the fish camps of La Laguna and La Fridera offer whalewatching boat trips during the winter months.

Continuing west from San Ignacio toward Santa Rosalía, the Baja Highway skirts the base of the 6300-foot **Volcanes Tres Vírgenes.** These barren peaks, their steep slopes splashed with colorful red and black hues, are Baja's only active volcanoes. Major volcanic activity occurred here as recently as the 1850s, and contemporary hikers sometimes report fumes in or near the southernmost of the three craters.

San Ignacio has just two hotels. The better one is **Hotel La Pinta,** **LODGING** similar in style, decor and amenities to the other properties in this ubiquitous Baja motel chain. On the way into town from the main highway, it has bright, air-conditioned rooms, a swimming pool and a game room. ~ San Ignacio; phone/fax 4-03-00. MODERATE.

The other lodging choice is **La Posada San Ignacio,** a no-frills budget motel on a back street two blocks southeast of the *zócalo.* The plain, utilitarian rooms are kept spotless by the friendly German-Mexican managers, who also guide cave-painting tours. ~ San Ignacio; 4-03-13. BUDGET.

The largest and best equipped of several campgrounds in San Ignacio is **El Padrino RV Park,** set among palm trees just south of Hotel La Pinta. Seven of the 38 campsites have full hookups, and the restrooms have hot showers and flush toilets—luxuries that other campgrounds in the area lack! There's even a swimming pool. ~ San Ignacio; phone/fax 4-00-89. BUDGET.

Lonchería Chalita, a casual dining room with singing birds in an **DINING** old home on the west side of the *zócalo,* has *comida corrida* dinner specials that change daily, as well as local favorites like *chiles rellenos* (stuffed chile peppers) and *pescado al mojo de ajo* (fish in garlic sauce). ~ San Ignacio; 4-00-82. BUDGET.

Farther up the same street, **Restaurant-Bar Rene,** a thatch-roofed open-air eatery by a small pond, serves American-style breakfasts and simple seafood dinners such as *calamar* (squid) and *camarones empanizados* (breaded shrimp). ~ San Ignacio; 4-02-56. BUDGET.

Located in the Hotel La Pinta, **Las Cazuelas** is clean, classy and tourist-oriented. The traditional Mexican fare emphasizes regional specialties from the mainland, such as *pollo en mole* (chicken in a chocolate-and-chile sauce), as well as shrimp and lobster selections. ~ San Ignacio; 4-03-00. MODERATE.

Restaurant-Bar Flojo, the plain-looking restaurant in El Padrino RV Park, specializes in surprisingly low-priced lobster tails and other seafood offerings, as well as heaping burrito plates. ~ San Ignacio; 4-00-89. BUDGET.

On the main highway near the San Ignacio turnoff, Restaurant Quichili serves fresh seafood dishes as well as Mexican-style beefsteaks. The decor is minimal, the service is cheerful, and the cleanliness is striking. ~ Route 1, Km. 3.

GROCERIES There is a Conasupo—a government-run convenience store that sells milk, eggs, tortillas and other staples—at the intersection where the road to San Ignacio leaves the main highway.

SHOPPING San Ignacio is the home of a unique homebrewed liqueur called Damiana, known throughout Baja California Sur as a potent aphrodisiac. It is usually available in the little general store on the south side of the *zócalo*.

▼▼▼▼▼▼▼▼▼▼▼▼▼▼▼
Santa Rosalía Area

Baja Highway travelers (and travel writers) generally don't pay much attention to Santa Rosalía, a workingman's town with no beach to speak of and fewer recreational facilities than auto parts stores. The rare visitor who takes time to stroll around may find a rude charm there; the town's character is absolutely unique.

Santa Rosalía is the seaport for all the towns covered in this chapter. It lies directly across the 100-mile-wide Sea of Cortez from Guaymas, western Mexico's largest port city. Car ferries connect Santa Rosalía with the mainland and bring in cowboy clothing, hardware, kitchen utensils, magazines and all the other merchandise on display in the shops—much of it otherwise unavailable between Ensenada and La Paz. This connection with mainland Mexico sustains a population of 14,000, making Santa Rosalía the region's largest town, even though the copper mine that was the original reason for its existence shut down in 1985.

Santa Rosalía was founded in 1885 by the Rothschild family's Paris-based mining corporation, Compania de Boleo. A German shipping company, Casa Moeller, sold the House of Rothschild its rights to mine copper there but retained the exclusive right to transport ore from the mine. The French copper mine grew into a huge operation with nearly 400 miles of tunnels, a large smelter with fuming smokestacks, and a work force of thousands—mainly Yaqui Indians from mainland Sonora and Japanese and Chinese immigrants managed by colonialist French overseers. The cultural mix was further complicated during World War I, when the United States Navy impounded the German ships used to transfer the ore, stranding hundreds of German sailors in Santa Rosalía. Many married local women and settled down in Santa Rosalía and nearby San Ignacio, where their descendants still live.

Most of the French population left with the closing of the mine, but the names of the town's two residential districts—Mesa Francesa and Mesa Mexicana, situated on opposite sides of the canyon and downtown area—recall the segregation that divided the town in earlier times.

Motor homes have problems negotiating the narrow streets and tight corners in town. The best plan is to park in the vicinity of Parque Morelos, at the east end of town just off the highway, and walk.

SIGHTS

The best-known landmark in the city of wood is a unique latter-day "mission church" made of cast iron. The **Iglesia Santa Bárbara** was designed and built by architect Alexandre Gustave Eiffel for the 1889 Paris World Exposition. Eiffel (who built the Eiffel Tower for the same fair) unveiled his prefab design as a prototype for churches to be erected by Catholic missionaries in French colonies around the globe. The design won praise and awards, but enthusiasm for the concept waned after the exposition, and the disassembled pieces of the church ended up in a storage warehouse in Brussels, where officials of Santa Rosalía's mining company discovered it. They shipped the pieces around Cape Horn to Santa Rosalía, to be assembled in 1897 a block south of the town plaza. Painted battleship gray, the church's exterior is plain and simple. Inside, it is more ornate and traditional, and the stained-glass windows cast a heavenly glow. ~ Avenida Alvaro Obregón at Calle Altamirano.

The town's paved and rather plain *zócalo*, **Plaza Benito Juárez**, is located two blocks south of the Eiffel church, bounded by Calles Altamirano and Plaza and Avenidas Constitución and Carranza. Facing the *zócalo*, the block-long, many-windowed **Palacio Municipal** is one of the town's most elaborate examples of French colonial architecture. ~ Avenida Carranza.

Relics of Santa Rosalía's mining days are scattered around town. Historic photos are on display in the **Biblioteca Mahatma**

"LA CIUDAD DE MADERA"

Copper from the mine and smelter at Santa Rosalía was shipped up the Pacific coast to refineries in Oregon and British Columbia; the same ships brought back lumber. Santa Rosalía's French colonial style wood-frame houses and public buildings, now preserved under historic district regulations, are unique in Baja, giving the town its nickname—"the city of wood."

Gandhi—the only public library between Ensenada and La Paz—near the east end of Santa Rosalía. ~ Avenida Constitución at Calle Playa.

An old **locomotive** that hauled ore from the copper mine to the smelter stands in front of the Hotel Frances, on the mesa north of town. ~ Calle Jean-Michel Cousteau.

Santa Rosalía's harbor lies to the east, beyond Route 1. The wide **Andador Costero** (coast walkway) runs south from the ferry dock at the harbor entrance. The most peaceful place in the bustling town, the walkway affords fine views of the harbor and Isla Tortugas, a dome-shaped, uninhabited island about 15 miles offshore.

HIDDEN ▶ Southeast of Santa Rosalía, and only four miles offshore, **Isla San Marcos** is an away-from-it-all possibility for fishing, hiking and primitive camping. The mountainous island has a large seal colony off the northern tip, and a mining camp and active gypsum mine near the south end. It is within kayaking distance from San Bruno, 29 kilometers south of Santa Rosalía. A free boat takes mine workers to Santa Rosalía on Friday mornings at 6 a.m. and returns to the island around 10:30 a.m.; visitors are welcome to ride along, though a week is a long time to wait for the next boat to leave the island.

LODGING Several small, very inexpensive hotels downtown cater mainly to Mexican travelers coming or going on the ferry. A good choice is the **Casa de Huéspedes Olvera**. Its 11 rooms are clean, carpeted and cooled by ceiling fans. Most have shared baths. ~ Avenida Venustiano Carranza at Calle 1; 2-00-57. BUDGET.

Another good bet for rock-bottom budget lodging is **Hotel Blanco y Negro**, hidden away on a side street at the south end

---

✔ CHECK THESE OUT—UNIQUE LODGING

- *Budget:* Spend a night at the **Hotel Frances**, a hilltop hotel left over from French colonial days in Santa Rosalía. *page 163*
- *Budget:* Check into **Las Trojes Bed and Breakfast Hotel**, former wooden granaries brought from Michoacán and converted into bed-and-breakfast lodgings in Loreto. *page 172*
- *Moderate:* Stay at Mulegé's best beachfront resort, **Hotel Serenidad**, and hear about the time it was seized by local "revolutionaries." *page 166*
- *Ultra-deluxe:* Bask *au naturel* at **Eden Loreto Resort**, an all-inclusive getaway at the would-be mega-resort of Nopoló. *page 173*

Budget: under $35   Moderate: $35–$70   Deluxe: $70–$105   Ultra-deluxe: over $105

of Calle 3 (a one-way street running the wrong way; take Calle 4 to get there). This 19th-century wooden building has nine rooms ranging from singles with shared bath to larger, two- and three-bed rooms with private baths and local TV. ~ Avenida Sebastian at Calle 3; 2-00-80. BUDGET.

Once the finest lodging in town, the **Hotel Frances** was built by the mining company on a hilltop above town in 1886 to accommodate business visitors. It closed down along with the copper mine in 1985 but continued to operate as a restaurant. A national historic monument, the hotel reopened recently after a complete interior renovation. Its 17 guest rooms have air conditioning, local TV and touches of ersatz elegance. There's a swimming pool and a shaded patio. The second-floor balcony has a view of the town and the old copper smelter. ~ Calle Jean-Michel Cousteau; phone/fax 2-02-52. BUDGET.

A mile south of Santa Rosalía on Route 1, **Hotel El Morro** has 24 modern, spacious rooms with air conditioning and TV. The Spanish-style white stucco hotel overlooks the Sea of Cortez, and some rooms have patios with sea views. The hotel has a swimming pool. ~ Route 1 south; phone/fax 2-04-14. BUDGET.

Although there are no beachfront resort accommodations in Santa Rosalía, there's a well-hidden one midway between Santa Rosalía and Mulegé. **Hotel Punta Chivato** overlooks miles of deserted beaches on the Canal San Carlos from its solitary vantage on a rocky point. Its 28 rooms have fireplaces and two double beds apiece. There's a swimming pool and a sundeck suspended over the cliff, and mountain bikes, sea kayaks and a volleyball court are available for guests' use. Beachcombers will find seashells as well as tide pools teeming with life; snorkelers can explore the rock reef just offshore. To get there, turn east off Route 1 at kilometer 156 and follow the graded dirt road for 20 kilometers to the hotel. The hotel has its own airstrip for fly-in guests, and an RV campground. ~ Punta Chivato; 3-01-88; fax 2-03-95. MODERATE.

Café Tokyo is one of the better eateries in downtown Santa Rosalía. It is run by a Japanese-Mexican family whose ancestors came to work in the mine generations ago. Despite the name, and the Japanese sign painted on the front window, the fare is thoroughly Mexican, as are most of the patrons. Specialties include enchiladas and seafood cocktails. ~ Avenida Alvaro Obregón 15. BUDGET.

DINING

Near the park at the east end of town, **Tercos Pollito** serves rotisserie-roasted whole chickens, which you can eat there or take out. The small, no-frills restaurant also serves a tasty seafood soup. ~ Avenida Alvaro Obregón at Calle 1; 2-02-28. BUDGET.

Restaurante Selene, south of the ferry dock, has sea views and nicely presented lobster dinners, as well as traditional Mexican food. Service can be on the slow side, but air conditioning makes it one of the more comfortable places in town to wait. ~ Route 1 south; 2-06-85. MODERATE.

GROCERIES   Founded by the mining company nearly a century ago, the **Panadería El Boleo** still makes French pastries and baguettes as well as traditional Mexican *bolillo* rolls and sweet rolls. It has a reputation among Baja buffs as the best bakery on the peninsula. For the widest selection, stop by before 10 a.m. Later in the day, you may find only *bolillos*. ~ Avenida Alvaro Obregón at Calle 3.

BEACHES & PARKS   **PUNTA CHIVATO** 🏃 🏊 🛶 A series of white beaches parallels the rough dirt road to Hotel Punta Chivato for about ten miles. The first, Playa La Palmita, is accessible by passenger car; others, farther from the main road, may require four-wheel drive because of sandy road conditions. Playa El Chivato, near the hotel, is among the prettiest spots on the Sea of Cortez. They're all good spots for collecting seashells. ~ The road to Punta Chivato turns off to the east at Kilometer 156, about 42 kilometers south of Santa Rosalía.

▲ The beachfront campground at Punta Chivato, operated by the hotel, has palapas, outhouses and unheated showers, but no hookups. Sites cost $5 per night.

▼▼▼▼▼▼▼▼▼
Mulegé Area

During the winter, gringos make up the majority of the population in Mulegé. Stores in the little town of 6000 are geared to the needs of snowbirds. The Río Mulegé, also known as the Río Santa Rosalía, flows along the south edge of town from springs in the mountains to the west. It is lined with shady RV campgrounds and North American–style bungalows dripping with bougainvillea and greenery.

The river—one of the few freshwater streams in Baja that flows year-round—supports the effulgent vegetation that gives Mulegé its tropical feel. It's easy to believe you're in steamy southern Mexico. In reality, Mulegé lies almost 400 miles north of the Tropic of Cancer, at about the same latitude as Corpus Christi, Texas, or Palm Beach, Florida.

Mulegé was founded as a Jesuit mission in 1705. The original church was destroyed in 1770 by a tropical storm—one of several that have flattened this palm-thatched town over the centuries— but not before a new stone church had been built to replace it. Mulegé grew to become one of the largest settlements in Baja in the early 19th century. Its fortunes waned when a much larger shipping port was built to the north, at Santa Rosalía. The missionaries' date palm plantations and fruit orchards had fallen into neglect by the 1930s, when farmers banded together to work them as an ejido.

The opening of the Baja Highway transformed Mulegé's economy from agriculture to tourism practically overnight. Since then, land title complications have been a frequent source of friction between local *ejidatarios* and newcomers. In 1996, a group of peasant activists seized the Hotel Serenidad, the largest hotel in town. The group evicted the guests and held the hotel for a year while the *ejido* and the municipal government fought in court over who owned the land on which it stands. More than a thousand other pending land title disputes still hinder development in the Mulegé area.

Santa Rosalía de Mulegé was built between 1754 and 1766. The stone church was designed in an "L" shape, with the architectural simplicity and grace characteristic of southern Baja missions. The mission was abandoned in 1828, but the church has been restored several times and is still used for worship. Inside the dimly lit church are an 18th-century bell and a statue of Santa Rosalía. The church stands on a mound overlooking the town and the river. To get there from town, follow Calle Zaragoza as it goes under the main highway and crosses the river, then turn right and follow the river road for a quarter-mile.

SIGHTS

Mulegé was captured for a single day by U.S. forces during the Mexican War.

The **Museo Mulegé** displays items from the original mission, as well as Indian artifacts, antique diving gear and a presentation on mining in the region. The museum is housed in an old territorial prison that was in use until 1975. It was known as the *cárcel sin cerraduras*—prison without locks—because inmates were free to leave during daylight hours to work on local farms: Mulegé's remote location was enough to preclude escape. Many local residents today are descendants of convicts from the mainland who were sent to Mulegé's prison. ~ Calle Cananea.

Mulegé's major attraction, **Bahía Concepción**, lies south of town. Thirty miles long and only three miles wide at the mouth, sheltered by a mountainous peninsula, the crystal-clear, turquoise bay with its multitude of beaches stands out as the most idyllic seashore in all of Baja and a world-class sea-kayaking mecca. All the beaches on the west side of the bay are easily accessible from the main highway, and all have campgrounds—some luxurious and others fairly primitive. At the bay's south end, a dirt road leaves Highway 1 and curves around the shore, where the beach is strewn with seashells and locals dig for the huge chocolate clams served in local restaurants. Continuing up the rugged, undeveloped eastern shore, the road gradually deteriorates into a four-wheel-drive track, passing many small beach areas on its way to the lighthouse at Punta Concepción.

Two of the best-known and most-studied Indian rock art sites in Baja are near Mulegé, and either one can be seen on a one-day HIDDEN ► guided tour. The murals at **Gruta San Borjitas** are unusual in that many of the large human figures depicted there are shown shot with arrows. These images, also found at other sites around Mulegé, are virtually the only evidence suggesting warfare among the Indian people of Baja. Some of the figures have male genitalia, not found in rock art elsewhere, and petroglyph drawings of female sex organs cover the side walls of the cave. Northwest of Mulegé, Gruta San Borjitas is reached by a 52-kilometer drive—the last 30 kilometers on a ranch road requiring four-wheel drive—followed by a two-hour mule ride.

HIDDEN ► **Cañon La Trinidad** is closer to Mulegé. You can drive an ordinary passenger car to Rancho La Trinidad, where guides charge less than those in Mulegé. To get there, turn west from the Baja Highway on the road by the ice plant one kilometer north of the Mulegé turnoff. The network of back roads can be confusing; follow signs for San Estanislao until you spot the sign for Rancho La Trinidad. From there, it's a half-mile on foot to the canyon and the first murals—an adventurous hike that involves fording the river and scaling a 12-foot cliff. The murals, like those at Gruta San Borjitas, contain an image of a man shot with arrows and several drawings of genitalia, as well as the "Trinidad deer," cited in anthropology texts as the epitome of Baja rock art. Two other, lesser sites farther up the canyon can be reached by fording the river several times and swimming a quarter of a mile up a narrow slot canyon. The cool, clear spring water there is the beginning of the Río Mulegé, though it flows underground for several miles below the end of the canyon.

LODGING The Mulegé area caters much more to campers than to the resort trade. The closest thing to a luxury hotel is the **Hotel Serenidad**, located on the beach four kilometers south of town. The hotel fell into disrepair in 1996, when local *ejido* activists seized it in connection with a land dispute and closed it down for a year; since reopening it has been undergoing a slow, room-by-room renovation. The 48 guest rooms and two-bedroom cottages are air-conditioned and have fireplaces. Facilities include a swimming pool, tennis court, boat ramp and runway for private planes. ~ Route 1 south; 3-05-30, fax 3-03-11. MODERATE.

At the highway exit for Mulegé, the **Motel Siesta** offers five new, American-style motel rooms with air conditioning. Although it may lack the Margaritaville ambience typical of most Mulegé hotels, it's the only place in town that has hot water all day. ~ Route 1; 3-05-55. BUDGET.

In town, the **Hotel Suites Rosita** has eight huge, air-conditioned, haphazardly furnished two-bedroom suites, each with a separate living room and kitchenette. It's ideal for budget-minded families and groups. ~ Calle Madero 2; 3-02-70. BUDGET.

The recently upgraded **Hotel Hacienda** offers a choice of 18 comfortably furnished rooms, some with air conditioning and the rest with ceiling fans, around a swimming pool and tropical courtyard landscaped with palms and banana trees. The central lounge area is a restored ballroom with a large fireplace for chilly winter evenings. The bar here is Mulegé's favorite party spot, so earplugs are a must for guests who retire early. ~ Calle Madero 1; 3-00-21. BUDGET.

The lowest-cost accommodations in Mulegé—even cheaper than most campsites—are at several guesthouses along Calles Moctezuma and Madero. **Casa de Huéspedes Manuelita** has eight small rooms with private baths, spartan furnishings, sagging beds and table fans. Campers can take a shower here for less than $2. ~ Calle Moctezuma; 3-01-75. BUDGET. **Casa de Huéspedes Canett** has similar amenities, and the bells from the church across the street are guaranteed to wake you up at 6 a.m. sharp. Calle Madero; 3-02-72. BUDGET.

DINING

There are no upscale restaurants in Mulegé, but you'll find an abundance of great Mexican food served in simple surroundings at very reasonable prices. Try **Restaurant El Candil**, a longtime favorite that has been run by the same family for nearly four decades, near the triangular town plaza. The specialty is a heaping combination plate of *chiles rellenos* and tacos served with beans, rice and tortillas. ~ Calle Zaragoza. BUDGET.

Los Equipales Restaurante, an upstairs eatery with cooling breezes and a view that takes in most of the town, has a wide selection of Mexican regional specialties, including big beef and

---

✔ **CHECK THESE OUT—UNIQUE DINING**

- *Budget:* Warm up after whalewatching with a plate of fish tacos at **Restaurant Ballena Gris** in the hidden fishing village of Puerto López Matéos. *page 177*
- *Budget:* Enjoy a bowl of "seven seas soup" full of lobster, crab, fish, shrimp and clams at the open-air **Café La Almeja**, on the beach in Mulegé. *page 168*
- *Budget:* Don't expect sushi or tempura at **Café Tokyo**, just great Mexican food prepared by a Japanese-Mexican family that has operated this Santa Rosalía restaurant for generations. *page 163*
- *Moderate to deluxe:* Savor a steak or try the chocolate clams in chipotle sauce at **El Nido**, Loreto's finest restaurant. *page 173*

Budget: under $5   Moderate: $5–$10   Deluxe: $10–$18   Ultra-deluxe: over $18

chicken burritos and tangy *cocteles de almejas* (clam cocktails). ~ Calle Moctezuma; 3-03-30. BUDGET.

Some of the tastiest food in town can be found at its numerous hole-in-the-wall *comedores*. Near the turnoff from the Baja Highway, **Taquería Doney's** serves good *carne asada* (barbecued beef) tacos and *mulitas* (open-face tacos), as well as some of the tastiest guacamole on the planet. ~ Calle Moctezuma. BUDGET.

On Playa El Sombrerito, the little beach at the end of Calle Morelos where the river meets the sea, you will find **Café La Almeja**, a large open-air palapa that serves a range of seafood dishes including fish tacos, chocolate clams and the house specialty, *sopa de siete mares* (seven seas soup)—a rich stew of just about every kind of seafood that can be found in the Sea of Cortez. ~ Calle Morelos. BUDGET.

GROCERIES   Campers can stock up at any of several grocery stores in Mulegé, including **Mercado El Pinguino** near Motel Siesta on the way into town from the highway, **Casa Yee** on Calle Madero, and Saul's Tienda at the end of **Calle Madero** on the way to Playa El Sombrerito. The only bakery around—and it's a good one—is at **Villa María Isabel**, an RV park on the south side of the river about two kilometers from town. Oaxacan Indian vendors make the rounds of Bahía Concepción beaches most days, selling whatever fresh produce is currently being harvested in the Llano de Magdalena agricultural region.

NIGHTLIFE   What little evening entertainment Mulegé has to offer can be found at the patio bar of the **Hotel Hacienda**, especially on Sunday nights—the hotel's weekly pig roast draws big crowds. ~ Calle Madero 1; 3-00-21. There's also a pig roast on Saturday nights at the **Hotel Serenidad**. ~ Route 1 south; 3-01-11.

BEACHES & PARKS   **PLAYA PUNTA ARENA** 🏃 ⚓ 🛶 🚣 🛥️ ⛵ This is the northernmost of several beaches separated by rocky points along the western shore of Bahía Concepción. Together they make up Baja's most beautiful seashore. Fishermen's shacks, some of them occupied by gringos, line part of the south-facing beach. ~ Turn east off the Baja Highway at Km. 119 south of Mulegé and follow the good unpaved road for three kilometers to the beach.

▲ There is informal camping along the beach. Facilities are limited to outhouses and a few palapas; no hookups. Primitive campsites cost $3 per night; sites with palapas cost $5.

PLAYA SANTISPAC 🏃 ⚓ 🛶 🚣 🛥️ ⛵ A popular spot for self-contained motor-home, van and truck campers, this pretty, sheltered cove can be crowded during the winter season. Besides camping facilities, there are two small beachfront restaurants. ~ Just off Route 1 at Km. 114.

▲ Campsites with palapas cost $4 to $5 per night, with an additional $1 charge for using the outhouses and cold showers. There is a sewage dumping station, but no hookups.

PLAYA LOS COCOS 🏃 🏊 🎣 ⚓ 🚤 ⛵ A forest of palm trees and soft, sugary white sand give this beach a tropical-paradise feel. Fishermen's shacks—some inhabited by gringos, as evidenced by stolen road-sign decor and a Texas state flag or two —occupy the north end of the beach; the rest is camperland. ~ Located off Route 1 at Km. 111.

▲ Campsites cost $4 per night. There are no hookups or shade palapas, though there is a dump station. There are outhouses. No drinking water.

PLAYA EL BURRO 🏃 🏊 🎣 ⚓ 🚤 ⛵ This curved beach on a calm, sheltered cove is one of the most peaceful spots on the west side of the bay. Except when large RV caravans pull in, most campers here are long-term snowbirds who return year after year. It's an appealing spot for tent camping. Across the highway from the beach is an arroyo where examples of Indian rock art can be found. ~ Located off Route 1 at Km. 109.

▲ Campsites cost $4 per night. There are shade palapas and outhouses, but no drinking water.

PLAYA EL COYOTE 🏃 🏊 🎣 ⚓ 🚤 ⛵ Facilities at this beach have gradually been upgraded year after year as increasing numbers of snowbirds have made their winter homes here. El Coyote shares the same protected cove with Playa El Burro, just on the other side of a small, rocky point. Isla Bargo, a small L-shaped island less than a quarter-mile offshore, also has a secluded beach. ~ Located off Route 1 at Km. 108.

▲ Tent and RV sites cost $5. There are palapas, outhouses, showers and drinking water.

PLAYA BUENAVENTURA 🏃 🏊 🎣 ⚓ 🚤 ⛵ The most-developed beach on Bahía Concepción, this beach has a big RV park complete with a restaurant and bar, a convenience store, a boat ramp and restrooms with showers and flush toilets. Although the exposed location makes it less appealing for swimming than most of the other beaches, there is a remarkable abundance of bird life along the beach, from sandpipers to great blue herons and pelicans. ~ Located off Route 1 at Km. 94.

▲ Campsites with shade palapas cost $5 per night; no hookups. Thatch-roofed camping cabins furnished with cots can be rented for $15.

PLAYA EL REQUESON 🏃 🏊 🎣 ⚓ 🚤 ⛵ This popular beach is unique because of the long, sandy spit that projects out to a small offshore island at low tide, submerging as the tide rises. Locals come here to dig for dark brown, hamburger-sized chocolate clams in the shallow flats along the sand bar. ~ Located off Route 1 at Km. 92.

▲ Campsites cost $3. There are outhouses but no other facilities.

PLAYA ARMENTA 🏃 🛶 🦅 🚣 🏄 ⛵ The funkiest of the east-shore sites, this *ejido*-run camping beach is a graceful crescent of white sand around a turquoise cove flanked by steep, rocky hills where vultures perch on tall cactuses. It's generally the least crowded of the beaches accessible from the highway. The shallow cove is ideal for swimming, and a short hike takes you to hilltops with excellent views of the bay. ~ Located off Route 1 at Km. 91.

▲ Campsites cost $3. There are tattered shade palapas and fairly rank outhouses. You can rent the "honeymoon cottage"— an unfurnished palm-thatch cabin on a hilltop past the south end of the beach—for $10 per night.

▼▼▼▼▼▼▼▼▼▼
Loreto Area

The oldest settlement on the Baja Peninsula, Loreto dates back to 1697, when Jesuit missionary Madre Juan María Salvatierra chose it as the site of the first mission in California. Misión Nuestra Señora de Loreto was the headquarters from which all other missionary expeditions in Baja and Alta California were sent forth. Loreto served as the capital of California through the entire Spanish colonial era. In 1829, a few years after Mexico gained its independence from Spain, the town was so devastated by a hurricane that the Mexican government ordered it abandoned and moved the capital to La Paz, bringing Loreto's rich history to an abrupt end.

In the years after the U.S. Civil War, the forgotten ghost town was resettled by a handful of immigrant gringos whose descendants, Mexican families with anglo surnames, make up a significant part of the population today. Fishing was the only occupation in town, and residents lived at the subsistence level for generations until, in the the 1950s, improved shipping methods made a small commercial fishing industry possible.

Loreto languished as little more than a fish camp amid the ruins of bygone grandeur until the 1970s, when the laid-back little town was selected by FONATUR, Mexico's tourism development agency, as the site of a planned mega-resort project similar to Los Cabos. Using proceeds from Mexico's booming national oil company, the government sponsored the construction of an 18-hole championship golf course, a professional tennis complex and a modern airport capable of landing jetliners. Resort hotel chains proved reluctant to make large-scale investments in the Loreto area, though, and eventually the government directed its tourism infrastructure funds elsewhere.

Today, Loreto seems undiscovered—a laid-back, palm-shrouded old town with cobbled streets, flanked by an estuary where herons wade in search of prey as cattle graze along the grassy banks. Fishing pangas line the stony seashore, and squadrons of pelicans patrol the waterfront in impressive numbers. Loreto's modern beach resorts—two of them, at last count—are discreetly tucked away five miles to the south.

SIGHTS

Inscribed in stone above the entrance to **Misión Nuestra Señora de Loreto**, the words "CABEZA Y MADRE DE LAS MISIONES DE BAJA Y ALTA CALIFORNIA" ("head and mother of the missions of Lower and Upper California") and the date "25 OCT 1697" reveal the antiquity of Loreto's church and its importance in colonial times. Although the architecture is less impressive than that of the mission churches at San Ignacio and San Javier, Loreto's church is famous for the wooden figure known as the Virgen de Loreto, widely believed to possess miraculous healing powers. ~ Calle Salvatierra.

An old burro trail runs from the abandoned pier on the south shore of Isla del Carmen up the side of a 1600-foot volcano whose crater is filled with salt—a spectacular four-mile (one-way) day hike.

On the west side of the church stands the **Museo de las Misiones**. Operated by the Mexican Instituto Nacional de Antropología e Historia, the museum contains antique weaponry, artifacts from missions throughout Baja and exhibits about ranching and agriculture, all arranged chronologically to present a 300-year history of Baja. Oddly, no mention is made of the Indians who constituted most of the population of the mission settlements. Admission. ~ Calle Salvatierra.

◄ HIDDEN

Isla del Carmen, a long, mountainous island, lies about ten miles southeast of Loreto. Pangas can be rented to take groups to the island, which is a popular whale watching, fishing and diving area. Now uninhabited, Isla del Carmen was once the site of a mining operation that produced 80 million pounds of salt a year.

◄ HIDDEN

A popular day trip from Loreto is through the rugged Sierra de la Giganta to **San Javier**, site of Baja's most beautiful mission church. Though rough and steep in spots, the road is passable by passenger cars. It turns off the main highway at Km. 118, two kilometers south of Loreto, and goes 37 kilometers into the mountains, climbing to 1700 feet above sea level. Though this remote mountain village has few year-round residents, its general store serves numerous ranches in the area. The mission, **San Francisco Javier de Viggo-Biaundo**, was first established in 1720, and the present stone church dates back to 1744. It is still in use and contains an ornate altar that was carried by burro from Mexico City, as well as several 18th-century religious paintings.

◄ HIDDEN

Beyond San Javier, the road gets even steeper as it continues for another 42 kilometers and descends into a canyon and the twin villages of **San José de Comondú** and **San Miguel de Comondú**. These villages were established in the early 1700s as farms growing food for the mission at San Javier, since the canyon has a reliable year-round water supply. A mission church was later built at Comondú; it no longer exists, but other buildings survive from the original mission complex. The orange groves, vineyards, date palms and fig trees planted by the missionaries still provide a livelihood for residents.

LODGING In Loreto's downtown area, the **Hotel Plaza Loreto** is a two-story white stucco building surrounding a traditional tiled Spanish courtyard with palm trees. The 24 newly remodeled rooms have dark, heavy furnishings and ceiling fans. The location, across the street from the old mission church, adds to the colonial ambience. ~ Avenida Hidalgo 2; 5-02-80, fax 5-08-55. MODERATE.

The most unique accommodations in Loreto are at **Las Trojes Bed and Breakfast Hotel**, located on the beach just north of La Pinta Hotel. During the late 1980s, the owner, Augustin Salvat, located several ancient *trojes* (hutlike hand-hewn wooden granaries, built without nails in a style dating back to the 10th century) in the highlands of Michoacán. His crew of Tarascan Indians disassembled them, brought them by truck and ferry to Loreto and reassembled them along the waterfront. Now renovated as guest cabañas, the eight *trojes* have comfortable furnishings, private baths and air conditioning or ceiling fans. ~ Boulevard López Mateos; 5-06-77, fax 5-02-77. BUDGET.

Travelers in search of a cheap place to sleep may wish to head for the **Motel Salvatierra**, centrally located on Loreto's main street. The rooms, though frayed around the edges, are clean and air-conditioned, with modern private bathrooms. The motel is within easy walking distance of the bus station and eight blocks from the waterfront. ~ Calle Salvatierra 125; 5-00-21. BUDGET.

Even more affordable, the **Hotel San Martin** has small, sparsely furnished rooms a block from the water. The mattresses are thin and sagging, the bathrooms are the size of small closets, the water is rarely more than lukewarm, and the rates for a private room are the same as you'd expect to pay for dorm accommodations in a youth hostel. The young, international backpacker set that gravitates to this place provides an exuberant atmosphere. ~ Avenida Juárez at Calle David; 5-04-42. BUDGET.

In a quiet setting near the waterfront at the south end of town, **Villas de Loreto** is a cluster of homelike, thatch-roofed cabanas and duplexes and adjacent RV park surrounded by large palm trees. The eight guest units are spacious, with tile floors, modern furnishings and kitchenettes; some have sea views. There's a swimming pool and a cobblestone courtyard. A short trail leads to a rocky beach where fishermen park their pangas and pelicans abound. Avenida Antonio Mijares, Colonia Zaragoza; phone/fax 5-05-86. MODERATE.

Loreto's luxury resort accommodations are located eight kilometers south of town in the beachfront Zona Turística de Nopoló. The only hotel on the beach was built by Mexico's now-bankrupt El Presidente chain. It changed hands several times before being bought in 1995 by the Diamond resort group, which reincarnated it as the **Eden Loreto Resort,** an adults-only hedonist playground with private nude and prude beaches and a huge clothing-optional jacuzzi. The all-inclusive rate includes lodging, meals at the hotel's two restaurants, unlimited alcoholic beverages at the disco and poolside bar, and the use of nonmotorized sports equipment including kayaks, sailboards and sailboats. Also included are unlimited greens fees at the nearby Campo de Golf Loreto and use of the courts at the John McEnroe Tennis Center. The 250 spacious, contemporary rooms and suites are air-conditioned, with shaded patios or balconies and satellite TV. ~ Boulevard Misión de Loreto, Nopoló; 3-07-00, fax 3-03-77, or 800-282-3336 in the U.S. ULTRA-DELUXE.

DINING

On your right at the first *glorieta* as you drive into Loreto from the main highway is **El Nido,** by some accounts the finest restaurant in the area. This upscale steak house, part of a Baja chain with other locations in Rosarito and La Paz, specializes in American-style T-bone and porterhouse steaks grilled over mesquite and served with soup, salad and a baked potato. The menu also features tempting seafood options such as chocolate clams in chipotle (smoked jalapeño) sauce with melted ranch cheese. ~ Avenida Salvatierra; 5-02-84. MODERATE TO DELUXE.

The favorite gringo hangout for long, lazy breakfasts, **Café Olé** has good coffee and American-style bacon and eggs or huevos rancheros. Later in the day they serve burgers, fries, burritos and fresh fish filets. You order at the counter, then dine at one of the sidewalk tables. Calle Madero 14; 5-04-96. BUDGET.

One of "downtown" Loreto's better restaurants is **La Terraza.** Upstairs from Café Olé, La Terraza's panoramic windows command the best view in town of Mission Nuestra Señora de Loreto, with the brooding mass of the Sierra La Giganta in the background. The menu presents a range of steak and seafood choices; you might start with the *sopa de mariscos* (lobster, crab, shrimp, fish and clam soup) and follow it with a filet mignon smothered in mushroom sauce or spicy Tampiqueña salsa. ~ Calle Madero 16; 5-04-96. MODERATE.

McLulu's, a four-table taco stand between the mission and the *malecón*, serves the kind of tacos that show you what you're missing at larger restaurants. Besides the fish and shrimp tacos typical of Baja, proprietress Lourdes "Lulu" Armendáriz serves Mexican favorites like chorizo (spicy sausage), picadillo (minced beef) and machaca (beef jerky cooked soft in a piquant sauce). ~ Paseo Hidalgo. BUDGET.

Located at the south end of the *malecón*, **Carmen's** offers glass-enclosed, air-conditioned comfort along with thatch-roofed tropical ambience and a waterfront view. Owned by a northern Californian, the restaurant features gringo-style chicken and beef as well as seafood dishes and Mexican combination plates. ~ Boulevard Costero López Mateos; 5-05-77. MODERATE.

GROCERIES   The largest of several grocery stores in town, the **Supermercado** located at Calle Salvatierra and Calle Independencia west of the town plaza has a good stock of canned foods for campers, as well as limited supplies of fresh produce.

NIGHTLIFE   Loreto is a very quiet place after dark. You'll find live Mexican dance music at **Mike's Bar** (Calle Hidalgo at Calle Madero) and disco at **La Revolución** on the *malecón*. Otherwise, nightlife is pretty much limited to the bars and clubs in several of the larger hotels, including **La Negrita** at Las Trojes (Boulevard López Mateos; 5-06-77), **El Campanario** in the Hotel Plaza Loreto (Avenida Hidalgo 2; 5-02-80) and the **Bar Amber** in the Eden Loreto Resort (Nopoló; 3-07-00).

**BEACHES
& PARKS**   **PLAYA NOPOLÓ** Loreto's resort area has the largest sandy beach on this part of the coast. The stretch fronting the Eden Resort property has been widened and enhanced with loads of sand trucked in from elsewhere. Hikers who go any distance from the hotel find less impressive strands interrupted occasionally by patches of mangroves. A secluded beach area near the resort is designated clothing-optional. Camping is not permitted. ~ Eight kilometers south of Loreto, just off Route 1.

PLAYAS JUNCALITO, TRIPUI AND LIGUI Camping is permitted on three sandy patches along the mostly rocky coastline south of Loreto. The numerous small islands offshore present good fishing and snorkeling opportunities. There is a good boat ramp at the Puerto Escondido vacation home area adjoining Tripui Beach. ~ Located from 23 kilometers to 36 kilometers south of Loreto, the beaches are reached by three marked, unpaved roads that turn off the main highway and go about a mile before reaching the seashore.

▲ Camping is free at Juncalito Beach and Playa Ligui, both favorites among tent campers and tailgaters and not easily accessible by motor homes; no hookups or other facilities. The only option for big rigs is the Tripui RV Park, which has rest rooms with hot showers, a laundry room and a swimming pool. There are a restaurant and a general store at the RV park. The 50 camp sites range from $15 to $18 per night, depending on location.

Ecotourism is coming slowly to Bahía Mag-
delena, the southernmost of Baja's whale
wintering areas. It is the hardest such area
to reach from the United States; although it is the closest whalewatching spot to Los Cabos, this hasn't brought much tourism.
Instead, the limited development along the bay shore has focused
on shipping produce from the irrigated farmlands of the Llano
de Magdalena and phosphate mining for agricultural fertilizer.

Bahía Magdalena Area

Though its ragged, mangrove-choked shoreline has invited little in the way of permanent settlement, Bahía Magdalena has had
a long history of transient visitors. Sea captain Sebastián Vizcaíno
and missionary Clemente Guillén explored the bay shore in colonial times, but each found that the lack of fresh water made it un-
suitable for a town or mission site. American whaling ships out of
San Francisco frequented the bay in the 19th century and, between
1836 and 1846, wiped out the gray-whale population, which has
taken 140 years to recover from near-extinction. The U.S. Navy
seized Bahía Magdalena during the Mexican War and, though
forced to relinquish the bay at the war's end, later established a
naval base there under a treaty with the Mexican government.
During the same period, several American-owned companies tried
to establish agricultural colonies on the Llano de Magdalena, but
all failed. U.S. interests were driven from the area after the Mexican Revolution, but settlement by Mexican nationals did not begin
until the mid-1930s, when ejidos were established on the Llano
de Magdalena.

Today, there are two small seaports in the Bahía Magdalena
area—Puerto López Mateos and Puerto San Carlos. Both can be
reached from the Baja Highway on good paved roads. Guides in
both towns offer whalewatching trips during the winter months.
Puerto López Mateos offers better vantage points for whalewatching from shore but lacks even the minimal food and lodging available in Puerto San Carlos.

While Bahía Magdalena does not lure many motorists off the
main highway, it has long been a popular haunt for gringo yachts-
men. Sheltered from high seas by a hundred miles of barrier islands, the bay is considered to be the finest natural harbor on the
Pacific coast between San Francisco and Acapulco.

Motorists traveling south from Loreto soon leave the coastal Sierra de la Giganta and head out onto the **Llano de Magdalena**.
Llano means "plain," and this prairie is so flat and featureless
that beyond Ciudad Insurgentes, the Baja Highway runs due south
without a single hill or curve for almost 80 kilometers. A vast
aquifer beneath the plain provides well water for irrigation on a
grand scale. The components for chemical fertilizer are found in

SIGHTS

the desert nearby in seemingly limitless quantities. Cotton, oranges, grapefruits, alfalfa and garbanzo beans are among the main crops. The agricultural *ejidos* of the Llano de Magdalena have proven so successful that it is now the fastest-growing area of Baja California Sur, boasting a larger population than Los Cabos.

Ciudad Insurgentes, the smaller of the two main commercial centers on the Llano de Magdalena, is home to about 15,000 people. Just over an hour's drive from Loreto, it is a clean, modern town with little of interest to travelers beyond the necessities—gas, groceries, telephones and auto repair shops. Here a good paved road turns off to the west and goes 37 kilometers to Puerto López Mateos.

HIDDEN ▶

A mere fishing village with a population of 2000 and no gas station, **Puerto López Mateos** is situated at the north end of Bahía Magdalena. The bay narrows into a channel less than a mile wide between the mainland shore and the sandy barrier island, Isla Magdalena. In the winter, the narrow channel brings large numbers of whales close enough to shore to offer great views through binoculars from the town dock.

HIDDEN ▶

An even better whalewatching vantage point is **Playa El Faro**, three kilometers to the north on the unpaved road from town. Pangas launch from Playa El Faro during whale season to take whalewatching groups to Boca la Soledad, where the greatest concentration of whales is found. This gap between barrier islands provides the only access from the bay to the open ocean for 50 miles.

Back on the Baja Highway, 26 kilometers south of Ciudad Insurgentes is **Ciudad Constitución**, the second-largest city in Baja California Sur. The commercial zone lies along the highway, which becomes the impressively wide, palm-lined Boulevard Olachea as it passes through the city, and along Avenida Juárez one block to the east. Banks, car dealerships and a large municipal performing-arts theater reflect the prosperity of this booming agricultural center of 60,000. There is nothing to offer sightseers, though, unless you count as a point of interest the only stoplights between Ensenada and La Paz—a distance of more than 1100 kilometers.

HIDDEN ▶

At Ciudad Constitución, paved Route 22 turns off to the west and continues for 58 kilometers to **Puerto San Carlos**, the main shipping port for the Llano de Magdalena. Truckloads of cotton clatter through the dusty streets when a ship is in port. At other times, things couldn't be much quieter in this backwater town of 4000 people. A sandy beach runs north of town between the road and the bay. The whalewatching from shore is less than awesome, but plenty of local boatmen stand by to take visitors on whale-watching excursions south to Punta Entrada or birding trips along the mangrove canals to the north.

Protecting Bahía Magdalena from the open sea, 70-mile-long **Isla Magdalena** consists mainly of sand dunes tufted with grass; a broad stretch of sandy beach runs along the ocean side for the island's entire length. More ships have wrecked along this shore than anyplace else in Baja, and the remains of several are still visible. The island, which is uninhabited, can be reached by kayak or panga from either Puerto López Mateos or Puerto San Carlos.

◄ *HIDDEN*

There are no real hotels in Puerto López Mateos, though a few residents put out signs offering simple bed-and-breakfast accommodations during whalewatching season.

LODGING

You'll find numerous lodging options in Ciudad Constitución, including the **Hotel Maribel**, with 20 modern, comfortable, air-conditioned rooms with telephones and Spanish-only TV. ~ Calle Guadalupe Victoria 156, Ciudad Constitución; 2-01-55. BUDGET.

The **Hotel El Conquistador** also offers all the comforts of a contemporary motor inn; its 24 rooms have dark wood colonial-style furnishings, dim lighting, hot water, air conditioning and TV. Calle Nicolas Bravo 161, Ciudad Constitución; 2-17-31. BUDGET.

Puerto San Carlos has three good, basic motels. The newest and most comfortable (despite its dubious name), the **Hotel Alcatraz** has 18 cheerful, spacious rooms with ceiling fans and TV. ~ Calle La Paz, Puerto San Carlos; 6-00-17. BUDGET.

The **Hotel Palmar**, also clean and newish, has 12 plain, utilitarian guest rooms with ceiling fans. Calle La Paz, Puerto San Carlos; 6-00-35. BUDGET.

The oldest and least expensive lodging in town is the **Motel Las Brisas,** where eight spartan rooms with table fans surround a gardenless courtyard whose walls are muraled with paintings of gray whales. ~ Calle Madero, Puerto San Carlos; 6-01-52. BUDGET.

In Puerto López Mateos, the **Restaurant Ballena Gris** serves tacos and other simple fare during whalewatching season. ~ Puerto López Mateos. BUDGET.

DINING

You'll find good seafood in Ciudad Constitución at the **Marlín Sonriente**, a pleasant, air-conditioned restaurant near the Hotel El Conquistador. ~ Avenida Juárez at Calle Hidalgo, Ciudad Constitución. BUDGET TO MODERATE.

Low-priced Chinese food is served nearby at **Restaurant-Bar Calafia,** a dimly lit place favored by locals. ~ Calle Nicolas Bravo at Boulevard Olachea, Ciudad Constitución; 2-07-33. BUDGET.

Also in Ciudad Constitución, you can buy whole roasted chickens at **Super Pollo** to eat on the cramped, unpretentious premises or take out. ~ Route 1 north, Ciudad Constitución. BUDGET.

You'll find one of the best selections of fresh produce on the Baja Highway at Ciudad Constitución's **Mercado Central**, a public

GROCERIES

market with nearly a hundred vendors. Prices are good, and bargaining is expected. ~ Avenida Juárez between Calles Nicolas Bravo and Hidalgo, Ciudad Constitución.

BEACHES & PARKS

PLAYA EL FARO ⚓ The only beach with facilities on Bahía Magdalena, Playa El Faro has restrooms and a food stand. Besides being the departure point for whalewatching boats, it's a good spot for viewing whales from shore. The beach itself is not great —an intermittently sandy and sometimes soggy area flanked by low stands of mangroves. Other beaches, deserted and undeveloped, lie farther along the main dirt road north of Puerto López Mateos. The best beaches in the area, however, are on the ocean side of the barrier islands that shelter the bay. They can only be reached by boat, and local *pangueros* can be hired to take you there. ~ Three kilometers north of Puerto López Mateos.

▲ Free tent and RV camping is permitted on Playa El Faro.

▼▼▼▼▼▼▼▼▼▼▼▼▼▼
Outdoor Adventures

The Sea of Cortez coast south of Santa Rosalía, and especially the Loreto area, is considered one of North America's top sportfishing areas.

FISHING Although large-scale commercial fishing has depleted the area in the past, the government has enacted regulations placing the area off-limits to drift-netters and other big fishing boats, and the game fish populations are on the rebound. Yellowtail is the catch of choice during the winter and spring months. Marlin, sailfish and dorado (mahimahi) arrive in the summer; cabrillo and snapper are abundant year-round. Roosterfish, the challenging (though not especially edible) fighting fish prized by Los Cabos fishermen, are found in the spring as far north as Mulegé, and record-size specimens have been hooked in Loreto.

SANTA ROSALÍA There is good deep-sea fishing in the waters east of Isla Santa Inez, and an abundance of smaller fish species in the channel between the Baja Peninsula and the island. Although the town has no fishing-charter reservation service, charter operators can often be found at **Marina Santa Rosalía.** ~ 2-00-11. Anglers can fish for yellowtail from shore at Punta Santa Inez and Punta Chivato.

MULEGÉ In fall and early winter you can fish from shore for snook, yellowtail and roosterfish at the mouth of the estuary where the Río Mulegé flows into the sea. Anglers with boats head for the open sea off the outer shore of the Concepción Peninsula in search of big game fish including tuna, marlin and dorado. Few fishing charters are available in Mulegé.

LORETO The water off the coast of Isla del Carmen is the top fishing area. Shore fishing is said to be incredible off the island's northern tip, though getting there may cost as much as chartering a boat for deep-sea fishing. Charters can be arranged through

Alfredo's Sportfishing ~ Boulevard Mateos at Calle Juárez; 5-01-65 or **Arturo's Fishing Fleet** ~ Calle Juárez at Callejón 2; 5-04-09.

DIVING

MULEGÉ The best diving is in the plankton-rich waters off Isla Santa Inez, swarming with colorful tropical fish. Snorkeling and scuba trips to the island can be arranged through **Mulegé Divers.** ~ Calle General Martínez; 3-00-59.

LORETO The waters off Nopoló and Puerto Escondido are ideal for snorkeling. Scuba enthusiasts head for the rock reefs of the outer islands—Isla del Carmen, Isla Coronada and Isla Danzante —where big fish abound. Snorkel and scuba gear can be rented at **Deportes Blazer.** ~ Paseo Hidalgo 24; 5-09-11.

KAYAKING

MULEGÉ Kayaking has become the most popular sport by far in the Mulegé area. Novices can practice paddling up and down the Río Mulegé before embarking on a fantastic journey across the (usually) smooth, crystalline waters of Bahía Concepción. **Baja Tropicales** rents lots of kayaks—reservations should be made well in advance—and organizes English-language guided all-day tours of the bay. ~ Hotel Las Casitas, Calle Madero 50; 3-00-19.

LORETO The 84-mile trip from Mulegé to Loreto takes about a week and is one of the ultimate wilderness sea-kayaking adventures. The route follows a steep, rocky coastline that is unapproachable by land, with occasional, usually rocky landings suitable for camping. Tamer Loreto sea-kayaking possibilities include excursions to Isla Coronada and Isla del Carmen, ten miles offshore. Open-top kayaks are for rent in Loreto at **Deportes Blazer.** ~ Paseo Hidalgo 24; 5-00-06.

BAHÍA MAGDALENA Sea kayaking is permitted in Bahía Magdalena outside of whalewatching season, though as yet no kayak rentals are available in the area.

◆◆

✔ CHECK THESE OUT—UNIQUE OUTDOOR ADVENTURES

- Paddle a sea kayak across the aquamarine waters of Bahía Concepción, one of the most idyllic kayaking spots on the planet. *page 179*
- Take a whalewatching tour on Bahía Magdalena; you'll also see abundant bird life and a barrier island that has seen more shipwrecks than any other place on the Baja coast. *page 180*
- Ride a mule into the backcountry to see the spectacular ancient rock art in Cueva Palmarito near San Ignacio. *page 180*
- Hike to the 6300-foot summit of Volcanes Tres Vírgenes, a cluster of massive, dormant volcanoes between San Ignacio and Santa Rosalía. *page 182*

WHALE-
WATCHING

SAN IGNACIO Viajes Kuyima (4-00-70) and Oscar y Dagoberto Fisher (4-03-13, fax 4-00-13) guide tours to Laguna San Ignacio during the winter months to view the gray whales that congregate there.

LORETO Blue whales and minke whales are frequently sighted in the vicinity of Isla del Carmen during the winter months. Whale-watching trips can be arranged through **Alfredo's Sportfishing** (Boulevard Mateos at Calle Juárez; 5-01-65) or **Arturo's Fishing Fleet** (Calle Juárez at Callejón 2; 5-04-09).

BAHÍA MAGDALENA Whalewatching *pangas* depart from San Carlos and Playa El Faro near Puerto Lopez Mateos during the winter months.

TENNIS

LORETO Located at the Loreto Inn Hotel, the **John McEnroe Tennis Center**'s nine hard-surfaced courts, with lights for night play, are open to nonguests for a fee. ~ 5-04-08.

GOLF

LORETO The only golf course in the region is **Campo de Golf Loreto**, located at the south end of the Nopoló resort area. The luxuriously landscaped 18-hole desert course rambles over dune-like hills close to the sea. Club rentals are available. ~ 5-07-88.

BIKING

MULEGÉ The **Hotel Hacienda** rents mountain bikes by the hour, day or longer. The unpaved road from Mulegé to Santa Clara branches into two rugged jeep roads ideal for biking, leading to canyons that form the headwaters of the Río Mulegé. ~ 3-00-21.

LORETO The road to San Javier and Comondú makes for a first-rate mountain-biking adventure. Loreto has no bike rentals.

CAVE
TOURS

SAN IGNACIO Burro trips to see the great cave murals of the Sierra de San Francisco can be arranged in San Ignacio at La Posada San Ignacio. ~ 4-03-13. You can also arrange a trip to Cueva Palmarito at Rancho Santa Marta, or one to Gardner Cave at San Francisco de la Sierra. There are numerous other painted caves in the San Francisco de la Sierra area, and most residents of this tiny village work for archaeological expeditions that study them, so visitors with plenty of time will find limitless possibilities for exploration. All of the painted caves in the area are under government protection, and it is against the law to visit them without a guide.

MULEGÉ Guided tours from Mulegé to see the rock art at Cañon La Trinidad or Gruta San Borjitas can be arranged at **Hotel Las Casitas** ~ 3-00-19 or **Hotel Vista Hermosa** ~ 3-02-22.

HIKING

All distances listed for hiking trails are one way unless otherwise noted.

Gray Whales' Endangered Lagoon

Remote, barren and pristine, Laguna San Ignacio is the unlikely site of one of Mexico's biggest environmental controversies. One of only three gray-whale calving areas on the Pacific coast, the lagoon's inaccessibility protected it from human development, providing a primeval wintering area for thousands of whales.

In 1995, Exportadora de Sal, the company that runs the world's largest salt-producing operation near Guerrero Negro, unveiled plans to open an even larger project along the northern and eastern shores of Laguna San Ignacio. Environmentalists obtained an injunction blocking the project on the grounds that its 465-page environmental-impact statement dismissed potential effects on wildlife with a single paragraph. Activists from around the world—among them prominent figures such as lawyer Robert F. Kennedy, Jr., filmmaker Jean-Michel Cousteau, and movie stars Glenn Close and Pierce Brosnan—have rallied to save the whales' lagoon.

The salt company points out that in the 30 years since their Guerrero Negro operation began, the whale population in Scammon's Lagoon has multiplied to its highest level in history. The recovery there has been so successful, in fact, that gray whales have been removed from the endangered-species list. Environmentalists counter that at Scammon's Lagoon, the salt is shipped from an offshore island; the plan at Laguna San Ignacio calls for a shipping route through the heart of the whales' territory. They also contend that the project threatens the habitat of many other species, including the endangered black sea turtle and desert pronghorn antelope.

Cynics may be justified in expecting that Exportadora de Sal will win in the end by virtue of the fact that Mitsubishi Corporation recently turned over 51 percent ownership of the salt company to the Mexican government. Meanwhile, litigation through the agonizingly slow Mexican court system is expected to protect the lagoon for at least several more years.

SAN IGNACIO   The best hike in the area is from Rancho Santa Marta to **Cueva Palmarito** (2.5 miles), an outstanding example of prehistoric rock art. A guide is required for the trip down a palm-lined canyon to the site. Guides from San Francisco de la Sierra can lead treks to other spectacular palm canyons in the high sierra.

SANTA ROSALÍA   The **Volcanes Tres Vírgenes**, the towering volcanos north of Santa Rosalía, have become favorite climbers' challenges in recent years. There is no clear trail to any of the summits, though a rugged four-wheel-drive road leads from kilometer 41 on the Baja Highway north into the volcano field. From there, it's a four-mile hike to the summit of the southernmost and tallest peak, which has a large crater that still fumes with noxious vapors now and then. It's a strenuous trip, and hikers usually spend the night at the summit and descend the next day.

LORETO   The old four-mile **burro trail** from the abandoned salt pier to the crater of the 1600-foot volcano in the center of Isla del Carmen is one of the most spectacular hikes imaginable. Backpackers can often catch a one-way trip to the island with a sportfishing boat and arrange to be picked up the next day.

▼▼▼▼▼▼▼▼▼▼▼
Transportation

AIR

Loreto has the only commercial airport in the area covered by this chapter. **Aero California** offers daily flights between Loreto and Los Angeles, La Paz, and the Mexican mainland city of Ciudad Obregón. ~ 800-237-6225.

BUS   **Autotransportes Aguila** and **Tres Estrellas de Oro** operate daily buses north to Ensenada, Tijuana and Mexicali and south as far as La Paz, with station stops at Santa Rosalía, Loreto, and Ciudad Constitución. The buses will pick up passengers at the San Ignacio highway junction, in Mulegé and along Bahía Concepción, though arrival times can be erratic and there are no bus stations —you just climb aboard and pay the driver.

BOAT   Santa Rosalía is one of the peninsula's two main ferry ports (the other being La Paz). **SEMATUR de California, S.A.** operates car ferries from the mainland Mexican seaport of Guaymas to Santa Rosalía on Tuesday and Friday, returning on Wednesday and Sunday. The ferries make the crossing in daylight, departing at 8 a.m. and arriving in midafternoon. *Salón*-class reclining seats can be booked on the day of departure; *turista*-class shared bunk rooms should be reserved a day in advance. Passenger fares for either class are inexpensive, making the ferry such a sea-cruise bargain that you could ride to Guaymas and back just for fun. Motor vehicles cost much more: one-way fares start at well over US$100 for a passenger car and reach more than $400 for a motor home. ~ 91-800-6-96-96.

All the main towns—San Ignacio, Santa Rosalía, Mulegé, Loreto, Ciudad Insurgentes and Ciudad Constitución—lie along **Route 1**, and all have large Pemex stations; Loreto and Ciudad Constitución have two apiece. Each town is about an hour's drive from the last, except Loreto, which is about two hours south of Mulegé.

Laguna San Ignacio is 68 kilometers southwest of the town of San Ignacio on an unpaved, unnumbered road. Bahía Magdalena can be reached by two paved routes—the unnumbered road from Ciudad Insurgentes to Puerto López Mateos (37 kilometers) or Route 22 from Ciudad Constitución to San Carlos (58 kilometers).

CAR

Even though Loreto has an international airport, there is no car rental agency. The last one went out of business in 1993. The nearest rentals are in La Paz.

CAR RENTALS

Mulegé and Loreto have numerous independent taxi cabs during tourist season. You can't telephone for one. Look for them around the larger hotels and in the center of town.

TAXIS

▼▼▼▼▼▼▼▼▼▼▼▼▼▼▼▼▼▼▼▼▼▼
Addresses & Phone Numbers

Hospital General de Santa Rosalía: 2-07-89

Cruz Rojo (Red Cross), Mulegé: 3-02-80; after hours 3-01-39

Cruz Rojo (Red Cross), Loreto: 5-11-11

Fondo Mixto de Loreto (municipal tourist information): Apdo. Postal 5, Loreto, BCS; 5-04-11; fax 5-08-22

Oficina de Migración y Aduana (immigration and customs), Loreto: 5-04-54

Información Turística de San Carlos: 6-02-53

EIGHT

La Paz
and Los Cabos

Stand on Lover's Beach looking out past El Arco, the trademark rock formation of Cabo San Lucas, and you may feel as if you have stepped into a travel poster. Gulls and pelicans wheel overhead. A cruise ship lies at anchor in the outer harbor. The Pacific Ocean rolls on and on. If you sailed due south from this, the southernmost point on the Baja Peninsula, the next land you'd see would be the coast of Antarctica.

The Cabo de Baja California, the peninsula's wide, tropical tip, extends 90 miles from La Paz to Land's End at Cabo San Lucas. Motorists who make the 300-kilometer loop around the cape discover remarkable contrasts. There's La Paz, the state capital, a fair-sized city with a dramatic history and a lovely promenade along a picture-perfect bay. A sea kayak excursion could take you to Isla Espiritu Santo, perhaps the most beautiful of all the desert islands off the Baja coast.

Heading south along the coast, you'll catch quick glimpses of the Sea of Cortez at two points near Bahía de Palmas, with its spectacular 25-mile beach, before reaching San José del Cabo. San José, the eastern half of the Los Cabos resort area, is a gentrified, historic town dating from the Spanish colonial era. With its galleries, restaurants and romantic ambience, it could be Santa Fe, New Mexico, or San Miguel de Allende but for the smell and sound of the surf breaking on the beach in front of the luxury hotel zone south of town. A half-hour's drive along a four-lane highway, the other half of Los Cabos, Cabo San Lucas, is the tourist industry epitomized, with little in the way of history or culture to interfere with the spending of money; but even here, there are hidden treasures—amazing undersea snorkeling and scuba experiences and long, secluded, almost empty beaches far removed from the big resorts.

Surfers head directly for West Cape and the spectacular Pacific waves around the expatriate artists' town of Todos Santos, which has so far escaped the explosive growth of the Los Cabos area. And then there's the cape's hidden heart, the Sierra de la Laguna. Adventurous souls willing to take a multi-day backpacking trip into the sierra discover a misty highland containing one of the most diverse ecosystems in North America.

La Paz is the capital of Baja California Sur and, with a population of 180,000, its largest city. Many Baja travelers are pleasantly surprised by this clean, modern, friendly community where tourism is welcome but does not dominate the economy. The urban waterfront, skirting a picturesque bay full of sailboats and yachts, is a joy for strolling or jogging, and the downtown area has the relaxed ambience of mainland Mexico's colonial cities. With good hotels and restaurants at prices much lower than the resorts of Los Cabos, La Paz makes a great home base for exploring the deserted islands and hidden beaches nearby.

▼▼▼▼▼▼▼▼▼▼

La Paz

La Paz has a tumultuous history that belies its name—Spanish for "the peace." More than two centuries before the city was founded, the name was bestowed on Bahía de la Paz by explorer Sebastián Vizcaíno, who was impressed by the friendliness and hospitality of the Pericú Indians he encountered during his visit to the sheltered bay.

Such was not the experience of other Spanish conquistadores. La Paz is located on the spot where the first Spaniards set foot on the Baja Peninsula in 1533—and were immediately slaughtered by Indians. Two years later, Hernán Cortés, governor of New Spain, founded a colony near the site of present-day La Paz and struck a tentative understanding with the Indians of the area. Cortés' colony soon failed due to food and water shortages, but his negotiations with the Indians laid the foundation for Vizcaíno's peaceful visit 61 years later.

For nearly 200 years, every Spanish attempt to establish a settlement at Bahía de la Paz failed. Throughout the 17th century, English and Dutch pirates lurked in the bay's hidden rock coves, plundering the wealth of the Spanish empire from the Manila treasure galleons, which put in at San José los Cabos to replenish water supplies after crossing the Pacific, but the pirates never settled on shore. In 1720, Jesuit missionaries from Loreto tried to establish a mission in La Paz, but the mission failed after only a few years, and no trace of it remains today.

It was not until 1829, when Loreto was destroyed by a hurricane, that La Paz became a real town: the newly independent Mexican government relocated the capital of Baja California to the sheltered shoreline of Bahía de la Paz. Turmoil plagued the settlement almost from the first. During the Mexican War (1846–48), the United States Army captured La Paz and occupied it for more than two years. Five years after the war ended and La Paz was returned to Mexican control, it was again seized by gringos—this time soldiers of fortune under the leadership of General William

Walker, who hoped to start his own republic in Baja and then annex it into the United States as the first pro-slavery state in the far west. Only after the Mexican army charged to the rescue did La Paz achieve the peace that its name promised.

In the 1870s, the invention of the diving suit made large-scale harvesting of the Bahía de la Paz oyster beds possible, and La Paz was the world's largest supplier of pearls for decades. Between 1936 and 1941, however, a mysterious disease killed all the oysters, devastating the town's economy. In response, the Mexican government granted La Paz the duty-free status that all of Baja enjoys to this day, transforming it into a busy port for goods from the United States and the Pacific Rim and stimulating tourism from the Mexican mainland.

Two books by John Steinbeck—his novel *The Pearl* and his nonfiction account *The Log from the Sea of Cortez*—focused the attention of American travelers on La Paz, and by the 1950s it was a popular sportfishing destination. But the tourist boom dwindled in the 1970s as industrial fishing brought marlin, swordfish and sailfish to the brink of extinction in the Sea of Cortez and the resort development of Cabo San Lucas eclipsed La Paz as a tourist destination. Since then, gringo visitors to the city have been mostly long-term "snowbird" retirees attracted by low prices and readily available health care. Today, the game fish population is resurgent and the waters around La Paz are being discovered by growing numbers of yachters, scuba divers and sea kayakers.

SIGHTS   Much of La Paz is a gridwork of traffic-clogged streets. Residential districts sprawl across the landscape with a sameness that makes getting lost easy for those who venture far from the main route into the city center. For pleasure travelers, however, all the in-town points of interest are situated within walking distance of one another.

The Baja Highway enters suburban La Paz as Calle Rangel. Motorists who are just passing through, following the "Mex 1" signs south toward Los Cabos, turn south through a westside neighborhood, past the **Universidad Autonimo de Baja California Sur**, and back out of town without ever seeing the city center. Sightseers, however, will want to keep going straight to where Calle Rangel reaches the waterfront and merges into Paseo Alvaro Obregón, the main street that follows the water's edge through downtown and around the bay to the Pichilingue Peninsula.

The place to start a sightseeing tour of La Paz is the **malecón**, a wide walkway shaded by laurels and coconut palms that runs along the waterfront for 16 blocks. Along the way, it passes several fishing and excursion boat piers and stretches of white sand beach, as well as the **Plaza Malecón**, where a gazebo-style band-

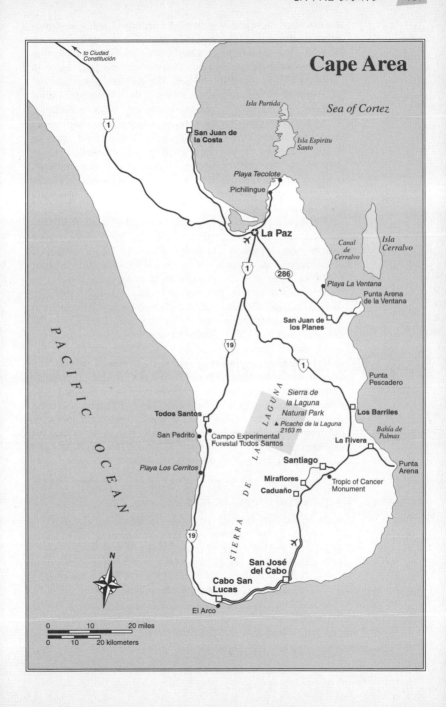

stand is often the scene of municipal concerts. The friendly tourist information office is located there, too. The *malecón* is used by impressive numbers of joggers in the early morning but becomes practically deserted during the midday heat. Activity picks up in the late afternoon, and by the time the sun sets in a prolonged blaze of color that turns the bay crimson, the promenade is filled with people strolling, socializing and savoring La Paz's finest hour.

La Paz's plaza, the **Jardín Velasco**, is four blocks south of the waterfront between Avenida Independencia and Calle Cinco de Mayo. Shaded by fig laurels, it provides a comfortable place to soak up the Mexican atmosphere. The plaza is the community's social center, and if you linger there you will inevitably find yourself drawn into conversation with local folks—even if you don't speak the same language.

On the southeast side of the plaza stands **La Catedral de Nuestra Señora de La Paz**, a rather austere brick-and-stone edifice with twin bell towers. It was built in 1860 as a "modern" revival of the architecture of the previous century's mission churches, but today the sharp edges and angles seem like a failed attempt to capture the architectural grace of the original missions. Although there is little supporting historical evidence, it is widely believed that the church stands on the spot where a short-lived Jesuit mission was built in 1720. ~ Avenida Independencia.

On the northwest side of the plaza, opposite the church, the former territorial government palace houses the **Biblioteca de Historia de las Californias**, a historical library containing thousands of source documents and the largest existing collection of books (in Spanish and English) about the Baja Peninsula, past and present. Sightseers may want to stop in if only for a look at the art exhibits, which include paintings of early-day missions and reproductions of Indian cave murals. Closed on weekends. ~ Calle Madero at Calle Cinco de Mayo; 2-26-40.

▲▲

✔ CHECK THESE OUT—UNIQUE SIGHTS

- Browse through the largest collection anywhere of books about Baja in the **Biblioteca de Historia de las Californias** in La Paz. *page 188*
- Take an evening stroll along **Boulevard Mijares**, San José's gentrified main street, window-shopping among the galleries and boutiques. *page 198*
- Bask on the sugar-soft sand of **Playa del Amante** (Lover's Beach), secluded at the southernmost tip of the Baja Peninsula near Cabo San Lucas. *page 211*
- Learn about the unique, often fantastic plants of the Baja desert at the **Campo Experimental Forestal Todos Santos**. *page 212*

The **Museo de Antropología e Historia** is inconspicuously situated next to a school, eight long blocks south of downtown. Its exhibits, captioned in Spanish, provide a close look at the nomadic people who occupied Baja before the arrival of missionaries, measles and smallpox. While most of the dioramas and artifacts are about the Indians, there are also displays about missionaries, mining, U.S. invasions and the Mexican Revolution. ~ Avenida 5 de Mayo at Calle Altamirano; 5-64-24.

Driving east from downtown on Paseo Alvaro Obregón, you soon leave the traffic congestion behind and find yourself traversing barren, rocky hillsides on the two-lane blacktop coast road to **Pichilingue**, the terminal where the huge SEMATUR ferries from Topolobampo and Mazatlán dock. Along the way, the road passes a series of secluded coves. Some, enhanced with wide beaches of imported white sand, have been transformed into mini-resorts with palapa bars and snorkel gear rental shops. Other coves remain in their natural state—narrow strands of hard brownish beach bounded by rock cliffs and stands of tamarisk, as lonely today as three centuries ago when they served as pirate hideouts.

◄ HIDDEN

Seven miles due north of the Pichilingue Peninsula, **Isla Espiritu Santo** is one of the most fascinating islands off the Baja shore. Most of the island's coast is vertical cliffs in bright hues of red, black, white and yellow. About a dozen long, narrow coves cut into the western shore; most of them have lovely, sheltered natural beaches, making this island a favorite for sea kayaking and camping adventures. Protected (along with six other large islands) as the Islas de Golfo de California Biosphere Reserve, Isla Espiritu Santo is home to a remarkable abundance of wildlife. Visitors can expect to see ospreys, snowy egrets, great blue herons, red-tailed hawks, and possibly a nocturnal great horned owl, as well as numerous species of rodents, reptiles, amphibians and elusive ring-tailed cats. A coral reef offshore attracts scuba divers.

LODGING

Built in 1940 at the dawn of La Paz's tourism boom, the **Hotel Perla** was one of the first resort hotels on the waterfront. Its location, across the street from the *malecón* and downtown beach, is in the center of the action, close to many restaurants and shops. All of the 102 American motor inn–style rooms have air conditioning and phones, and half have views of the bay. Street noise can be a problem. There's a disco on the premises, as well as an interior courtyard with a swimming pool. ~ Paseo Obregón 1570; 2-07-77, fax 5-53-63. BUDGET TO MODERATE.

Farther west along the waterfront, **Hotel Los Arcos** and the adjacent **Cabañas de los Arcos** offer some of the city's nicest accommodations. The three-story, colonial-style hotel has 180 luxurious rooms, all with air conditioning, balconies, in-room phones and cable TV. Some have bay views; others overlook the gardens and fountains of the central courtyard. The cabaña complex has 30 small individual casitas and a 22-room inn, all in a tropical garden setting, at rates slightly lower than those of the main hotel. Both the hotel and the cabañas have heated swimming pools. ~ Paseo Obregón 498; 2-27-44, fax 5-43-13. MODERATE.

Room rates plummet as soon as you get away from the waterfront. The **Hotel Lorimar**, a favorite of the international backpack set, is two blocks up the hill from the *malecón*, behind Hotel Los Arcos. It has 20 clean, plain, air-conditioned rooms with private baths, and an upstairs café with an over-the-rooftops view of the bay. ~ Calle Bravo 110; 5-38-22, fax 5-63-87. BUDGET.

An even lower-priced backpackers' hangout in a deteriorating 18th-century convent four blocks from the waterfront, the **Pensión California** has 25 smallish blue-and-white rooms with ceiling fans. The only furnishings are mattresses on concrete platforms, and the bathrooms are aging and cramped but functional. Guests gather at picnic tables around the TV in the courtyard's eccentrically decorated tropical garden. A communal kitchen and laundry room are available for guests' use. ~ Calle Degollado 209; 2-28-96. BUDGET.

Just a block from the plaza, the 20-unit **Hotel Yeneka** has larger, better-furnished rooms than most other low-budget options, though like the others its beds are mattresses on concrete platforms. It is distinguished by its crazy courtyard decor, consisting largely of painted automotive parts, including a complete though nonfunctional Model T Ford, artfully nestled in the tropical vegetation. ~ Calle Madero 1520; 5-46-88. BUDGET.

All these rock-bottom budget alternatives are more appealing than the official youth hostel, the **Villa Juvinil**. Its location, in the southwest part of the city at the Universidad Autonomía de Baja California Sur sports complex, is convenient for visiting soccer teams but inconvenient for pleasure travelers. There are 72 beds, four-to-a-room in men's and women's dormitory wings, with a laundromat and grocery store nearby. ~ Calle 5 de Febrero at Route 1; 2-46-15. BUDGET.

Two miles southwest of downtown, on Playa Sur, **La Posada de Englebert** is an atmospheric beachfront complex named for pop singer Englebert Humperdink, who opened it around 1990. Each of the 26 suites and four casitas has a ceiling fan, a brick fireplace, a front porch with a rocking chair, and a soft patina of age. There's a swimming pool. ~ Avenida Reforma at Playa Sur; 2-40-11, fax 2-06-63. BUDGET TO MODERATE.

The **Club El Moro**, across the highway from the waterfront two miles northeast of downtown, has 18 large, attractive suites with full kitchens, private patios or balconies, and cable TV but no in-room phones. Terracotta tile floors and arched windows with wrought-iron gratings create a romantic Spanish-Moorish motif. The lush tropical landscaping conceals a heated pool and the only hotel hot tub in town. Kayaks are for rent on the premises. ~ Km. 2, Carretera a Pichilingue; 2-40-84, fax 5-28-28. BUDGET TO MODERATE.

A little farther from town and a little pricier, the pink five-story **Hotel Marina**'s 70 rooms and 23 suites are light, spacious and contemporary; their sliding glass doors open onto balconies overlooking Marina Palmira, a world-class yachting haven. Facilities include a swimming pool, a jacuzzi and one tennis court. ~ Km. 2.5, Carretera a Pichilingue; 1-62-54, fax 1-61-77. MODERATE TO DELUXE.

Still farther northeast, **La Concha Beach Resort** is a self-contained resort built by the now-defunct El Presidente chain. Its 109 rooms feature Mexican tile floors, floral-print bedspreads and balconies overlooking a palm-lined white sand beach that curves gracefully along the bay. There are tennis courts and a heated swimming pool with poolside bar. A water sports center rents gear, and a free shuttle runs guests back and forth from downtown. ~ Km. 5, Carretera a Pichilingue; 1-63-44, fax 1-62-18, or 800-999-2252 in the U.S. MODERATE TO DELUXE.

Blending European and Mexican architectural touches, **Hotel Mediterrane** is a small lodging just a short walk away from the *malecón*. Six spacious rooms have private baths and air conditioning. The owners can provide helpful information on La Paz. Gay-friendly. ~ Calle Allende 36; phone/fax 5-11-95. MODERATE

Casa La Paceña, a three-room bed and breakfast one block inland from the *malecón*, caters to a mixed clientele of lesbians, gay men and sophisticated straights. The Moorish-style house is air-conditioned, and all guest rooms have views of the bay. ~ Calle Bravo 106; 5-27-48. MODERATE.

DINING

Restaurante Bermejo, at the Hotel Los Arcos, is regarded as one of the city's finest restaurants. Steak and pasta are the specialties. Overstuffed, candlelit booths and obsequious waiters set the ambience, which seems intended to make couples feel like newlyweds. ~ Paseo Obregón 498; 2-27-44. DELUXE.

La Paz Lapa de Carlos 'n' Charlie's is a branch of the chain that owns rowdy restaurant/nightclubs in just about every Mexican beach resort town. This place seems more sedate than most of its cousins, probably because La Paz attracts a more mature crowd than Puerto Vallarta or Cancún. Still, if you want to feel like you're on a real beach vacation, stop in for steak, margaritas and a fantastic view of the sunset on Bahía de la Paz. ~ Paseo Obregón; 2-92-90. MODERATE.

La Terraza, Hotel Perla's sidewalk café across from the *malecón*, is an ideal spot to while away the hours with a sailboat-studded bay view at any time from the breakfast hour late into the evening. The menu is divided half-and-half between American and Mexican dishes and features catch-of-the-day seafood specials. ~ Paseo Obregón 1570; 2-07-77. MODERATE.

Also located on the waterfront, **El Taste** serves a predictable menu of Mexican food, steaks and seafood, along with a great view. It's a perennially popular hangout for English-speaking expatriates and snowbirds. ~ Paseo Obregón at Calle Juárez; 2-81-21. MODERATE.

Rancho Baja, one of the more affordably priced restaurants along the *malecón*, serves shrimp prepared nearly a dozen ways, tantalizing stuffed crabs and catch-of-the-day fish fillets. ~ Paseo Obregón at Calle Bravo; 2-90-11. BUDGET TO MODERATE.

> On weekends in La Paz, Calle Madero and Avenida Independencia around the plaza are closed to traffic so that more than 100 vendors can set up shop in a busy flea market.

La Paz has a small Chinatown between the *malecón* and the plaza. The top restaurant in that quarter, **Restaurant Dragón** serves creative versions of familiar dishes such as *chao men* and *pollo kun pau* with a special flair derived from Mexican chiles and fresh vegetables. ~ Calle 16 de Septiembre at Calle Esquerro; 2-13-72. BUDGET.

La Pazta, a casually Italian restaurant where fresh pasta is made to order, features Mediterranean-style creations—linguini with squid marinated in wine sauce, spaghetti in white clam sauce—as well as fondues and other traditional Swiss dishes. The atmosphere, too, is modern European, with polished black-and-white decor and waiters wearing crisp white jackets and an air of high dignity. ~ Calle Allende 36-B; 5-11-95. MODERATE.

El Quinto Sol, La Paz's natural food market, has a cafeteria that offers vegetable and fruit salads, yogurt smoothies, soy chorizo and a vegetarian *comida corrida*. ~ Calle Dominguez at Calle Héroes de la Independencia; 2-16-92. MODERATE.

Restaurante Bismark II, a longtime local favorite for its seafood dishes and eclectic Mexican fare, is seven blocks inland and four blocks southeast of the plaza. The best way to find it is by taxi, and menu options such as *chiles rellenos con langosta* (poblano chiles stuffed with lobster) and *cochinita pibil* (Yucatán-style barbecued pork) are well worth the trip. Seating is at long wooden tables in a casual, smoky atmosphere. ~ Calle Degollado at Calle Altamirano; 2-48-54. MODERATE.

The **Yeneka Restaurant**, next to the backpackers' hotel of the same name, has fish and Mexican dishes at low-budget prices. The simple restaurant is accented with artwork by three generations of the owners' family. ~ Calle Madero 1520; 5-46-88. BUDGET.

Northeast of town on the road to Pichilingue, **Restaurant/Bar El Moro** is an indoor, air-conditioned place with dim lighting, tablecloths and uniformed waiters who are ultra-polite, though in no hurry. The menu features lobster and mainland Mexican cuisine, including an excellent *pollo en mole*. ~ Km. 2, Carretera a Pichilingue; 2-70-10. MODERATE.

A favorite of both locals and tourists, the **Restaurante Grill Campestre** prepares Mexican and American food in a warm, inviting setting. Specialties include spare ribs with homemade barbecue sauce, hamburgers and excellent salads. ~ Km. 5.5, Carretera a Pichilingue; 4-04-54. MODERATE TO DELUXE.

GROCERIES

La Paz's public food market, **Mercado Municipal Francisco Madero,** is four blocks inland and three blocks southeast of the plaza. Freshly caught fish and other seafood are displayed on beds of ice, and farmers from the Llano de Magdalena agricultural zone bring in truckloads of vegetables daily. Prices are posted and, although haggling is less prevalent than it once was, bargain prices can still be negotiated. ~ Calle Revolución at Calle Degollado.

SHOPPING

People come from all over Baja California Sur to do their major shopping in La Paz. The leading department stores are **Perla de La Paz** (Calle Arreola at Calle Mutualismo) and **Dorian's** (Calle 16 de Septiembre at Calle Esquerro).

For fine-quality Mexican arts and crafts, visit **La Antigua California,** where you'll find everything from majolica ceramics and delicately wrought Taxco jewelry to wooden dance masks from Michoacán and lacquer boxes from Nayarit. ~ Paseo Alvaro Obregón 220; 5-52-30.

NIGHTLIFE

The **Teatro de la Ciudad,** two miles south of the city center, presents performances by local and visiting theater and dance troupes, as well as film festivals. Call or stop by for a schedule of events. ~ Calle Legaspi at Calle Héroes de Independencia; 5-19-17.

La Paz Lapa de Carlos 'n' Charlie's attracts an exuberant crowd, especially on weekends, when live rock bands play. Weekend cover. ~ Paseo Obregón; 2-92-90. A popular disco is **Laser Disco.** Cover. ~ Paseo Obregón at Calle Degollado; 2-31-33. Or try **Xtasis.** ~ Calle Arreola at Calle Zaragoza. **La Cabaña** has a mellower lounge feel. ~ Hotel Perla, Paseo Obregón; 2-07-77.

The gay scene in La Paz is decidedly low-key. There's some cruising around Plaza Malecón in the evening, but nothing you could call a "scene" so much as a possibility of an encounter. The same can be said of the few mixed gay-and-straight clubs, such as **Aja Toro** (Avenida Revolución near Calle 16 de Septiembre).

BEACHES & PARKS

PLAYA TECOLOTE This one-and-a-half-mile-long beach on the northern end of the Pichilingue Peninsula is wide, white and backed by high dunes. There are two palapa restaurants and boat and jet ski rentals. Playa Tecolote is the departure point for sea kayak excursions to Isla Espiritu Santo, which lies a few miles to the north and can be seen clearly from the hillside behind the beach. ~ Follow the main road five miles past the Pichilingue ferry terminal. The pavement ends at the beach.

▲ Informal RV and tent camping is permitted behind the dune area. No water or hookups. There is no fee.

PLAYA LA VENTANA 🏃 ⛵ 🐟 🚤 This remote beach stretches for ten miles along the Canal de Cerralvo. It's a favorite destination of windsurfers and adventurous surf fishermen. The wreck of the *Cedro*, a modern freighter, juts out of the water just offshore near Punta Arena de la Ventana at the west end of the beach. ~ Follow Route 286 south from La Paz toward San Juan de los Planes. A gravel road forks off to the left after 40 kilometers and leads to the east end of the beach. The main paved road continues for another 21 kilometers; shortly before it reaches the coast, another unpaved road turns off to the left and goes to the lighthouse at Punta Arena de la Ventana, on the west end of the beach.

▲ La Ventana Campground, at the small fishing village of La Ventana on the east end of the beach, has shaded tent and RV campsites with restrooms but no hookups. Punta Arena, at the west end of the beach, is great for tent camping but has no facilities. There are no fees at either campground.

▼▼▼▼▼▼▼▼▼▼▼▼▼▼▼
Cabo del Este and Sierra de la Laguna

Cabo del Este, or East Cape, refers to the area along the shore of Bahía de Palmas, extending 20 miles from Punta Pescadero on the north to Punta Arena (not to be confused with Punta Arena de la Ventana, above) on the south and including the fair-sized fishing villages of Los Barriles and La Rivera. Fishing resorts, built by and for gringo pilots, began to spring up along the bay in the 1950s, long before the highway was paved, when the area was one of the most remote spots in Baja. The major tourism development of the Los Cabos area has not reached the East Cape; this remains a quiet, friendly, angler-oriented hideaway with a handful of small American-owned resorts and no telephone service.

Inland from the bay, the ranching center of Santiago is a starting point for backpacking expeditions into the Sierra de la Laguna —"hidden" interior of the cape area and one of the most unique ecosystems in North America.

SIGHTS   **Santiago** was the site of Misión Santiago el Apóstol Aiñiní, originally established by Jesuits in 1724. The bloodiest revolt of the missionary era began here ten years later, when Guayacara and Pericú Indians killed the mission's *padre*. The revolt quickly spread to all the missions in the cape area, and several years of warfare

Islands in the Sky

The Sierra de la Laguna receives more rainfall than any other part of the Baja Peninsula; in fact, their 35 inches of precipitation annually are slightly more than the amount that falls on soggy Seattle, Washington! Most of the rain falls during the monsoon season, from July to November, though Pacific fog can shroud the sierra at any time of year.

The moisture creates a microclimate that preserves a "relic environment"—an isolated area in which rare plants have survived from a time millennia ago, before Baja became a desert. Here, amid jagged granite peaks, at least 400 tropical, desert and mountain plant species grow side by side, giving the high sierra's "islands in the sky" a biological diversity found nowhere else in North America. Palms and madrone trees, oaks and wild roses, cactuses and yucca, strawberries and wild grapes, marigolds and Spanish moss are among the lush profusion of vegetation.

The high wilderness is home to coyotes, deer, mountain lions and many smaller creatures, including a species of tree frog that is extinct except in this remote area. The higher slopes of the mountains feature areas that have been termed "hummingbird flower forests" because of the dozens of kinds of hummingbirds that winter there in large numbers.

Environmentalists are campaigning to persuade the Mexican government to declare Sierra de la Laguna a national park. Although some people fear that this would greatly increase the number of hikers and put stress on the unique and fragile ecosystem, many believe that such a declaration is necessary to block the proposed diversion of water from the sierra to Los Cabos. Any hike into the relic environments of the high sierra is a demanding multi-day trek; details are in the "Outdoor Adventures" section of this chapter. Mule trips can also be arranged in Santiago.

followed before the Spanish regained control of the missions. No trace of Misión Santiago remains today.

The main sight in Santiago is **Parque Zoológico Santiago**, a small zoo containing mammals, birds and reptiles native to the Baja Peninsula as well as a lion, a tiger and a few other exotic beasts. Conditions of confinement in this zoo are less humane than they might be, with cramped cages, but this is the only zoo in Baja, and kids come from far and wide to marvel at the monkeys and big cats. Admission. ~ Santiago; no phone.

Just south of Santiago, motorists officially cross into the tropics. The **Tropic of Cancer Monument**, a simple concrete sphere beside the highway, marks the spot.

HIDDEN ▶ Hikers can reach the three major canyons of the **Sierra de la Laguna**, the roadless wilderness in the center of Baja's cape region, from the small towns of Santiago, Miraflores and Caduaño, which lie between 142 and 145 kilometers south of La Paz on the way to San José del Cabo. Each of the three trails continues all the way across the cape to the vicinity of Todos Santos, and can be hiked in either direction, though the climb into the highlands is much steeper from the west side. For more information on Sierra de la Laguna, see "Islands in the Sky" in this chapter.

LODGING There are several fishing resorts along the Cabo del Este coast. The oldest one, **Rancho Buena Vista Hotel**, was built in the early 1960s with its own air strip to cater to fly-in sportsmen. After the original American owner died in a private-plane crash in the nearby mountains, subsequent owners remodeled the hotel and expanded it to its present 50 rooms. The feel is rustic, with heavy handmade furniture; some rooms are air-conditioned, and the

---

✔ CHECK THESE OUT—UNIQUE LODGING

- *Budget:* Rest up at one of Cabo San Lucas' low-priced hotels, such as the **Hotel Marina Cabo San Lucas**, perfect for budget-minded travelers. *page 207*

- *Budget to moderate:* Hide away on the beach in La Paz at **La Posada de Englebert**, a laid-back vacation complex owned by '60s pop singer Englebert Humperdink. *page 190*

- *Ultra-deluxe:* Relax in San José del Cabo at the **Huerta Verde**, a small colonial-style bed-and-breakfast inn with a secluded hillside location and a pastoral view. *page 200*

- *Ultra-deluxe:* Experience nonpariel luxury in trendy Los Cabos at the fabulous **Meliá Cabo Real Beach & Golf Resort**, one of Baja's largest and most lavish resorts. *page 201*

Budget: under $35   Moderate: $35–$70   Deluxe: $70–$105   Ultra-deluxe: over $105

others are cooled by ceiling fans. There are no phones or TVs here, but the hotel has a swimming pool, tennis courts and its own sport fishing fleet. Meals in the dining room, included in the room rate, feature fresh-caught fish as well as meat and vegetables from the hotel's working ranch. Closed in August and September. ~ Bahía de Palmas; reservations: P.O. Box 1408, Santa Maria, CA 93456; 805-928-1719, 800-258-8200. DELUXE.

A quarter-mile south of Rancho Buena Vista, **Hotel Buena Vista Beach Resort** occupies the former vacation home of Agustín Olachea Aviles, a famous Mexican general. Accommodations in the 60-room hotel are comparable to those at Rancho Buena Vista and other resorts along this stretch of coast, and besides tennis courts and a swimming pool there is a whirlpool spa heated by mineral hot springs. Guests can rent horses at the resort's riding stables, and snorkel gear, scuba tanks or kayaks at the water sports center. Lodging is available on either the American plan (all meals included) or the European plan (meals cost extra). ~ Bahía de Palmas; 1-00-33, fax 1-01-33, or 100 West 35th Street, National City, CA 91950; 619-425-1551, 800-752-3555, fax 619-425-1832 in the U.S. MODERATE TO DELUXE.

Farther south along the coast, the **Rancho Leonero Resort** accommodates anglers and scuba divers. The 27 large guest units have rock walls, palapa roofs, private patios and sea views. Rates are on the American plan (all meals included). ~ Camino Rancho Leonero, La Rivera; reservations: 22603 La Palma Avenue, Suite 307, Yorba Linda, CA; 714-692-6965, 800-334-2252, fax 714-692-6976. ULTRA-DELUXE.

Budget lodging options are few and far between in the East Cape area. Hikers bound for Sierra de la Laguna can find low-priced, no-frills rooms with private baths in Santiago at the 20-room **Hotel Palomar**. ~ Santiago; 1-28. BUDGET.

DINING

Most East Cape resorts operate on the American plan, with all meals included as part of the lodging rate, and few independent restaurants have sprung up in the area. Several years ago, the **Rancho Leonero Resort** opened its dining room to nonguests, and since then it has acquired a reputation as one of the best restaurants on the peninsula. People often drive an hour from Los Cabos just to eat here. The bill of fare, which changes daily, normally features seafood entrées. ~ Camino Rancho Leonero, La Rivera. DELUXE.

In Santiago, the **Hotel Palomar**'s restaurant specializes in seafood, offering grilled lobster, thick fish steaks and giant steamed clams at some of the best prices in Baja. ~ Santiago; 1-28. BUDGET.

BEACHES & PARKS

PLAYA DE LAS PALMAS 🏃 🐎 🦞 🦅 🏊 🎣 🚤 ⚓ This beautiful palm-lined beach extends in an unbroken arc for 25 miles along the shore of Bahía de Palmas, widening toward the south end, where an abundance of seashells makes for fun beach-combing. ~ The northern end of the beach starts two miles north of Los Barriles. A sandy unpaved road runs from there to the south end of the bay, Treacherous four-wheel-drive roads turn off toward the water's edge, but many motorists leave their vehicles near the main road and hike the quarter-mile or so. The unpaved coast road continues all the way to San José los Cabos, but the southern section of it was washed out during the mudslides of 1993; bring a high-clearance vehicle and plenty of nerve.

▲ There are four RV parks around Los Barriles. **Playa de Oro RV Park** has restrooms with hot showers and eight RV sites with full hookups; $12 per night. **Juanito's RV Park** also has restrooms with hot showers and 26 RV sites, all with full hookups; $10 per night. **Martin Verdugo's RV Park** has restrooms with hot showers, a swimming pool, 67 RV sites with full hookups ($12 per night) and 25 beachfront tent sites ($10 per night). **La Capilla RV Park** has palapas, restrooms with hot showers, and 10 tent and RV sites with full hookups for $8 per night.

▼▼▼▼▼▼▼▼▼▼▼▼▼
San José del Cabo

One of two communities that make up the Los Cabos resort area, San José del Cabo is the site of the international airport and the area's banking, business and local government center. Though lacking the world-class marina facilities of its twin town, Cabo San Lucas, San José more than compensates with the gentrified colonial charm of its streets lined with galleries and cafés. The permanent population is around 25,000, and this figure doubles in winter with the influx of seasonal residents.

San José lies beside a freshwater estuary that was used by Spanish sea captains in the 1600s to replenish their water supplies after the long Pacific crossing from the Philippines. A Jesuit mission was established there in 1730, but was closed down by an Indian rebellion. Several years later, after the rebellion was put down, the town began to grow as a military garrison designed to control the problem of pirates preying on the Manila galleons.

SIGHTS

San José del Cabo's main street is Boulevard Mijares. It starts at the north end of town, a block from the **zócalo** (which has been split in two by the long, narrow state tourism office in its center). The plaza boasts a gazebo bandstand and shaded wrought-iron benches.

On the west side of the plaza is the **Iglesia San José**. Step inside this simple church to see a painting that memorializes the massacre of the clergy at San José's original mission church during the Indian revolt of 1734. ~ Calle Morelos.

Boulevard Mijares continues south, an attractive avenue of sidewalk cafés, art galleries and boutiques, passing the Los Cabos

Club de Golf on its way to the beachfront hotel zone. This highly gringo-fied street is named after a Mexican army lieutenant who died leading a heroic last stand against invading U.S. Marines during the Mexican War.

Centrally located a block south of the plaza, in the heart of the Boulevard Mijares shopping and restaurant zone, the new three-story **Tropicana Inn** is built around a walled pool area and courtyard. The Tropicana Restaurant isolates the hotel from the street and provides a feeling of seclusion. The 40 guest rooms overlook the courtyard and have all the amenities of a typical U.S. motor inn—two double beds apiece, satellite TV with English-language channels, and air conditioning. It's San José's best in-town hotel, though a long way from the beach. ~ Boulevard Mijares 30; 2-15-80, fax 2-15-90. MODERATE.

LODGING

Practically a youth hostel, with some of the lowest rates in town, the **Hotel San José Inn** has 20 fair-sized, pink-walled rooms cooled by ceiling fans. The floors and mattress platforms are concrete, and the decor is drab, but the location—on a dirt back street three blocks from the plaza—is fine, and the price is right. ~ Calle Obregón 2; 2-14-91, fax 2-14-28. BUDGET.

Another good low-budget bet, the **Posada Señor Mañana** has jungle lodge–style thatch-roofed rooms, some with private baths, as well as open-air palapas for hammock camping. Guests are welcome to use the communal kitchen and dining room and to pick tropical fruit from the trees in the overgrown courtyard. Although this funky backpackers' haven seems a world apart from sleekly touristy Los Cabos, its downtown location is just a block from the plaza. ~ Calle Obregón 1; 2-04-62. BUDGET.

Four blocks from the plaza and the Boulevard Mijares shopping and restaurant zone, the **Posada Terranova** is a small, modern European-style hotel. The 20 guest rooms are bright and clean; each has two double beds, color TV, modern plumbing and air conditioning. The Italian-Mexican management is friendly and personable, and the café-style tables on the front patio are ideal for lounging and getting to know other guests. ~ Calle Degollado; 2-04-34, fax 2-09-02. BUDGET TO MODERATE.

The **Howard Johnson Plaza Suite Hotel** is located midway between downtown San José and the beach, across the road from the nine-hole Los Cabos golf course and tennis club. (Guests at the hotel get discounted rates.) The exterior architecture, a striking departure from the familiar orange-and-blue HoJos in the United States, incorporates Spanish-Moorish and Mexican colonial features. The 172 spacious, bright guest rooms and suites have an all-American feel, with air conditioning, cable TV and in-room phones. All rooms open off exterior walkways surrounding a courtyard swimming pool. The four-story hotel has no elevator, so the top-floor rooms—the ones with the best view—are best for guests with strong legs and light luggage. ~ Paseo Finisterra 1; 2-09-99, fax 2-08-06. DELUXE.

In contrast to the huge resort complexes that dominate Los Cabos, the **Huerta Verde** has just eight air-conditioned guest suites surrounding a swimming pool and walled patio nestled amid palms, vines and colorful flowering bushes that attract humming birds and cardinals. Situated on a terraced hillside with a pastoral view, the inn is an architectural fantasy of tropical palapas, Spanish colonial domes and arches, rustic viga-and-latilla ceilings and contemporary touches. Rooms are individually decorated with queen- and king-size beds, *equipal* furniture and primitive art. Although the inn is three miles inland, you can still hear and smell the sea. A full breakfast is included in the room rate. ~ Camino Las Animas Altas; 6-85-11, or 303-431-5162, fax 303-431-4455 in the U.S. ULTRA-DELUXE.

The **Presidente Los Cabos Forum Resort** has survived several changes of ownership and management since it opened in the 1970s as the first resort in San José's beachfront hotel zone. Location and ambience have helped it to maintain its status as the best on the beach as other resorts have sprung up to the west. The hotel's three-story, adobe-look buildings sprawl between the uncrowded end of Playa de California, the entrance to Los Cabos Club de Golf, and a natural freshwater estuary teeming with bird life. The 250 guest rooms are large and luxurious, with king-size beds, oversized bathtubs and shaded balconies overlooking Bahía de San José. Recreational facilities include the largest swimming pool in the hotel zone, plus tennis courts, rental horses and sportfishing charter boats. ~ Boulevard Mijares at Paseo San José; 2-02-11, fax 2-02-32. ULTRA-DELUXE.

One of a cluster of international chain hotels in the center of San José's beachfront hotel zone, the **Posada Real Los Cabos** is the most modestly priced beach resort in San José's hotel zone. The 150-room hotel offers air-conditioned rooms with two double beds, cable TV, showers and the rest of the motor inn amenities you'd expect of a Best Western establishment; most (though not all) rooms have views of the beach and sea. There's a swimming pool and jacuzzi, bicycle rentals and fishing charters. ~ Paseo San José; 2-01-55, fax 2-04-60. MODERATE.

The rental condos at **La Jolla de Los Cabos** are some of the homiest-feeling accommodations in the hotel zone. Three- to six-story sandstone-colored buildings contain 55 studio, one-bedroom and two-bedroom suites with simple pastel furnishings. All have phones, cable TV, refrigerators and coffeemakers, and many have full kitchens. Guests have the use of four swimming pools, two lighted tennis courts, exercise rooms, saunas, steam rooms and jacuzzis. Shuttles run guests into downtown San José, five kilometers away. ~ Km. 29, Carretera Transpeninsular; 2-30-00, fax 2-05-46. DELUXE.

The **Meliá Cabo Real Beach & Golf Resort** represents the state of the art in glamour tourism. It's a long way from town, almost midway between San José Los Cabos and Cabo San Lucas, but the elaborate landscaping—water surging from fountains, spilling over waterfalls, shimmering in ponds, in dramatic contrast to desert gardens of native and exotic cactuses—is designed to distract guests from any thought of leaving the hotel grounds. Boutiques, restaurants and night clubs add to the gravitational pull. Countless truckloads of white sand were imported to enhance the beach, and a stone jetty creates a sheltered area for snorkeling. One of Los Cabos' largest resorts, the Meliá has 309 air-conditioned rooms with Mayan-style bas-reliefs sculpted into the stucco walls and sliding doors that open onto private garden terraces. Guests have privileges at the adjacent 18-hole Cabo Real golf course, and there are a swimming pool, one tennis court, a health club and sauna, and a dive shop that rents scuba and snorkel gear. ~ Km. 19.5, Carretera Transpeninsular; 4-00-00, fax 4-01-01. ULTRA-DELUXE.

Built in 1956 by the son of Mexican president Abelardo Luis Rodriguez, the **Hotel Palmilla** was the first luxury resort in the Los Cabos area. Constantly expanding and updating its resort facilities to keep ahead of the competition, it continues to reign as the premier hotel in the area. The 115 spacious guest rooms, suites and villas are individually decorated with hand-carved furniture and fine folk art, and all have balconies or terraces with ocean views. Service is extraordinarily attentive; hotel employees outnumber guests by three to one. In addition to a large swimming pool and tennis courts, the hotel has a croquet court, riding stables and its own sportfishing fleet, as well as a complete health spa and a 27-hole golf course designed by Jack Nicklaus. ~ Km. 7.5, Carretera Transpeninsular; 4-50-00, fax 4-51-00, or 800-637-2226 in the U.S. ULTRA-DELUXE.

DINING

Locals and long-term snowbirds know that **Cafetería Rosy** serves the best shrimp tacos in Los Cabos, plus great *comidas corridas* (lunch specials). Located at the only stoplight in town, this hole-in-the-wall eatery often ties up traffic with its enthusiastically double-parked carry-out customers. Closed Sunday. ~ Calle Zaragoza at Calle Alfonso Green. BUDGET.

Damiana, a steak and seafood restaurant in an extensively renovated 18th-century hacienda on the east side of the plaza, has outdoor seating on a romantic patio shaded by pines and shrouded in bougainvillea. It offers the finest candlelight dining in San José del Cabo, including such house specialties as charcoal-broiled lobster in achiote sauce and grilled abalone in *salsa ajillo* (garlic and chile *guajillo* sauce). ~ Boulevard Mijares; 2-04-99. DELUXE.

Vegetarians head for **El Café Fiesta**, located at the north end of Boulevard Mijares across from the plaza and the Palacio Municipal. The sidewalk cafe features low-fat and low-cholesterol fare such as "Mother's Earth soup"—containing lentils, garbanzo beans, split peas and eight kinds of fresh vegetables—and a veggie club sandwich made with onions, avocado, cucumber, tomato and mushrooms. There are also a few cheese-heavy Mexican appetizers such as *queso fundido* (fondue) made with soy chorizo sausage, and, for carnivores, lean-beef cheeseburgers with french fries. ~ Boulevard Mijares; 2-28-08. MODERATE.

The restaurant with the best view of the plaza is the second-floor **Dos Gorditos**, across the street from the Palacio Municipal. Open for dinner only, the establishment specializes in "Mexican-Cajun" seafood dishes such as shrimp sizzled with chipotle (smoked jalapeño) peppers and chile-spiced gumbo. ~ Boulevard Mijares; 2-37-33. MODERATE.

Homesick? A good place to get your bearings is **Sandrick's Bar and Grill**, the upstairs eatery next to the Tropicana Inn. This traveler-friendly establishment serves burgers and fajitas, along with one of the town's best selections of cold imported beers. ~ Boulevard Mijares 28; 2-12-70. BUDGET.

Asian stir-fry dishes and Mediterranean pastas are prepared at the **Tequila Restaurante**. Guests can dine in a lush courtyard garden with attentive service and strolling musicians. Closed Wednesday. ~ Calle Doblado between Boulevard Mijares and Calle Hidalgo; 2-11-55. DELUXE.

For a truly Mexican eating experience—a rarity in the Los Cabos area—stop in at **Restaurante Vista al Mar**, on the west side

---

✔ CHECK THESE OUT—UNIQUE DINING

- *Budget:* Expect simple Mexican fare and seafood in an arty atmosphere at La Paz's **Yeneka Restaurant**, a favorite backpackers' hangout. *page 192*
- *Moderate:* Enjoy the freshest seafood in Los Cabos at the **Pescadería Sea Food Market** in San José del Cabo—or bring in your own catch and let them cook it for you. *page 203*
- *Moderate to deluxe:* Savor gourmet Italian cuisine and fresh organic vegetables in a renovated historic hacienda at **Café Santa Fe** in Todos Santos. *page 213*
- *Deluxe:* Though its East Cape location is off the beaten path, the **Rancho Leonero Resort**'s dining room has earned a reputation as one of the best restaurants in Baja. *page 197*

Budget: under $5   Moderate: $5–$10   Deluxe: $10–$18   Ultra-deluxe: over $18

of town near the Los Cabos hospital. Spicy cheese enchiladas and fried chicken are served with stacks or tortillas and heaps of beans and rice in the front area of the cook's home. ~ Calle Castro at Calle Doblado; 2-06-32. BUDGET.

Operated by the same vegetarian owners as El Café Fiesta, **Pizza Fiesta** features whole-wheat crusts and a choice of 26 toppings, half of them vegetarian, as well as a selection of modified Mexican specialties including the "Fiesta Grande"—a soy chorizo tostada, a whole-wheat quesadilla with mushrooms, a veggie tamal, guacamole, black beans and salsa. Beer, wine and fresh-squeezed juices round out the menu at this cheerful terrace restaurant. ~ Calle Coronado at Calle Degollado; 2-18-16. MODERATE.

The **Mercado Municipal,** located toward the west end of town, has an eating area where eight *comedores* serve inexpensive meals ranging from fish tacos to roast chicken, plus soft drinks, fresh fruit juices and *licuados* (fruit smoothies). ~ Between Calles Castro and Coronado. BUDGET.

Just off Route 1 on the road into town, **Pescadería Sea Food Market** has just seven tables in a dining area beside the smoke-house. It offers one of the widest choices of seafood *antojitos* and entrées in Los Cabos, from marinated raw oysters to smoked marlin steaks. They will also cook and serve fish you've caught yourself, or smoke them so you can take them home. ~ Calle Castro at Carretera Transpeninsular; 2-32-66. MODERATE.

A standout among the resort restaurants in San José's beach-front hotel zone, **Hugos at La Jolla** presents a gourmet menu of steak and seafood dishes in a dignified atmosphere. Whole roast quail is a specialty. The restaurant also has a breakfast buffet. ~ Km. 29, Carretera Transpeninsular; 2-30-00. DELUXE.

Zipper's Bar & Grill on Playa Costa Azul is a big beachfront palapa long known as a surfers' hangout. In simpler times it was a basic hamburger joint, but as the surrounding resort area has grown, it has added mesquite-grilled steaks and barbecued ribs to the menu. The restaurant uses only imported U.S. beef, which is more tender and juicy than the free-range Mexican beef served in many Baja steakhouses. ~ Km. 28.5, Carretera Transpeninsular. MODERATE.

San José's **Mercado Municipal** is located near the intersection of Boulevard Mijares and Calle Gonzales. While locals still come to this market to buy produce, much of it is given over to arts and crafts.

SHOPPING

Copal has a selection of folk art from the Mexican mainland, including dance masks, furniture and ceramics. ~ Calle Zaragoza 20; 2-30-70. For Mexican clothing, stop into **La Casa Vieja.** ~ Boulevard Mijares at Calle Doblado; 2-02-70.

One of the most interesting folk art galleries in town is **Huichol Collection Galeria Museo**, one of a nationwide chain of shops that sell the intricate beadwork, embroidery and decorated lacquer trays and boxes made by the deeply traditional Huichol Indians of Nayarit. ~ Boulevard Mijares at Calle Zaragoza.

NIGHTLIFE   San José lacks the rowdy night life scene of neighboring Cabo San Lucas. This is a town for romantic moonlight strolling. If you just gotta dance, head for **Eclipse** (Boulevard Mijares at Calle Coronado; 2-16-94) or **Bones Disco** (Presidente Los Cabos Forum Resort; 2-00-38). There's live rock-and-roll most weekends at the **Iguana Bar**. ~ Boulevard Mijares; 2-02-66.

BEACHES & PARKS   **PLAYA COSTA AZUL** Sections of this long, straight beach in front of the San José hotel zone are sometimes known by various names, including Playa de California and Playa del Nuevo Sol, but it's all one wide, straight beach. Sometimes it's idyllic. At other times, waves crash against it with the force of dynamite blasts. ~ Southeast of San José del Cabo.

▲ Sharing the beach with resort hotels, **Brisa del Mar Trailer Park** has 112 tent and RV sites, all with water and electricity and most with sewer hookups. Facilities include restrooms with hot showers, a swimming pool, a laundry room, a volleyball court, and a game room with pool and ping-pong tables. Sites cost $10 to $18 per night.

Cabo San Lucas

Welcome to the least "hidden" place in Baja. As recently as 1970, Cabo San Lucas was a tiny fishing village of 500 people, both smaller and more remote than such hidden destinations as Bahía de los Angeles or Bahía Tortugas. All that changed when the Mexican government, flush with newfound wealth from skyrocketing crude-oil prices in the mid-seventies, set plans in motion to create a series of beachfront mega-resorts: Cancún, Zihuatanejo, Puerto Vallarta—and Cabo San Lucas. Building a marina and installing an ambitious infrastructure of public utilities and paved roads, the government soon enticed a number of major resort chains to build hotels, and the flood of development began as sport fishermen, scuba divers and sun worshippers from the United States and Canada poured into the little village.

Today, any semblance of the sleepy hideaway of years past has been obliterated by what old-timers perceive as construction run amok. For many, the symbol of excessive growth was the construction of the five-story Plaza Las Glorias shopping mall and condominium development, which created a solid four-block-long wall between the marina and the main street, blocking not only the view but also the sea breezes that used to cool the town.

Cabo San Lucas is self-explanatory. The center of the action is **SIGHTS**
Marina Cabo San Lucas, a 338-slip facility that can accommodate
yachts up to 150 feet in length. The marina fills the inner harbor,
which has been dredged and carved into a perfect square. Highrise shopping malls, hotels, restaurants and condominiums box
the marina on three sides, isolating it from the rest of the town.

The small, rocky cape of land that gives the town its name
extends southward, forming the west shore of the outer harbor.
These days, it is often called Land's End to distinguish it from the
town. No road reaches the tip of the cape, so you have to take a
water taxi or hike to get there. **El Arco,** the distinctive natural rock
arch at the tip of the cape, is perhaps Baja's most familiar landmark and the southernmost point of land on the peninsula. Beyond El Arco, two rock pillars known as **Los Frailes** rise from the
sea and are frequented by seals and sea lions.

The main street of Cabo San Lucas, **Calle Lázaro Cárdenas**
is lined with bars, galleries and shops. The town plaza, at Calles
Lázaro Cárdenas and Zaragoza, has recently been refurbished
with picturesque wrought-iron benches and lampposts, and the
buildings surrounding it are undergoing beautification and gen-
trification. To the north of the main street, the town's residential
district comprises small houses and unpaved streets that form a
stark contrast with the luxury resorts south of the marina.

Travelers heading west along the corridor from San José to Cabo **LODGING**
San Lucas pass one resort complex after another. Probably the
most striking, though far from the largest, is the **Twin Dolphin
Hotel,** a small luxury hotel on a private beach. . . . Well, legally
speaking it's public like all Baja beaches, but gawkers have to walk
through the hotel under the scrutiny of the staff to get there. The
resort enjoys a reputation as a celebrity hideout and takes care to
protect guests' privacy, but sightseers often wander in for a look
at the replicas of ancient Indian cave murals that decorate the
lobby walls. Recreation facilities include a riding stable, a putting
green, a swimming pool and a charter fishing fleet. ~ Km. 11.5,
Carretera Transpeninsular; 3-02-56, fax 3-04-96, or 800-421-
8925 in the U.S. ULTRA-DELUXE.

Cabo San Lucas' biggest resorts are located along Playa El
Medano, the sheltered swimming beach east of town. The reign-
ing queen of the beach is the **Meliá San Lucas.** All of its 188 spacious, air-conditioned rooms and suites, decorated in cool blue
hues and furnished in wicker, share a perfect view of El Arco
across the water. Palm trees shade a free-form swimming pool
and outdoor hot tub. Watersports equipment rentals and fishing
charters are available. ~ Playa El Medano; 3-44-44, fax 3-04-20,
or 800-524-5104 in the U.S. ULTRA-DELUXE.

Located on the point between the east side of the marina and Playa El Medano, the **Hotel Hacienda** is an elegant manifestation of Spanish colonial charm—replete with fountains, aqueducts, bell towers and pseudo-ancient statuary accented by bright tropical flowering vines. Its 112 rooms, suites and casitas looking out on the sea are simply furnished and accented with Mexican folk art. There's a putting green, a swimming pool, tennis courts and a beachfront water sports center that rents everything from snorkels to Waverunners. ~ Calle Gomez Farias; 3-01-22, fax 3-06-66, or 800-733-2266 in the U.S. DELUXE TO ULTRA-DELUXE.

In striking contrast to the big resort hotels that line much of Playa El Medano, friendly little **Casa Rafael's** has just 12 rooms. This pink boutique hotel, originally a single-family home, was converted in 1994. One block from the beach and a short walk from town, it is fully air-conditioned and has a swimming pool, sun decks and jacuzzi amid lush tropical gardens, as well as a small gym, a pool table, a ping-pong table and a library. The guest rooms are individually decorated, and some have private jacuzzis. Rates, which vary widely depending on the view, include a full gourmet breakfast; other meals are also served. ~ Calle Medano at Camino de Pescadores; 3-07-39, fax 3-16-79. DELUXE TO ULTRA-DELUXE.

If you want to be in the center of the action, consider the **Marina Fiesta Resort Hotel**—that seven-story wall of balconies and sliding glass doors along the east side of the marina. Rooms have the upscale severity often associated with time-share condos. All of the 122 air-conditioned rooms and suites have microwaves and refrigerators, and half of them have full kitchens. There's a swimming pool, and taxis shuttle guests to the beaches. ~ Marina 37; 3-28-57, fax 3-26-88, or 800-338-2252 in the U.S. ULTRA-DELUXE.

The **Hotel Finisterra**, the old-timer among Cabo resorts, stands on a hilltop; a steep driveway winds up from Boulevard Marina. The original hotel was built in the 1950s of sandstone blocks quarried nearby, and it blended perfectly into the natural surroundings until a recent expansion multiplied the number of rooms to

FUN, SUN 'N' SEWAGE

Cabo San Lucas' year-round population has grown to more than 5000, virtually all of whom are employed in the construction, hotel and restaurant industries, and swells to 30,000 residents during the winter months. The rapid growth has outstripped public utilities and sanitation facilities, and Cabo San Lucas has become the only place in Baja where tap water is not safe to drink.

197 by adding two eight-story towers that overshadow the old lodge. Rooms in the new section are brighter and more spacious, with one king-size or two queen-size beds and balconies overlooking the water. Prices are slightly higher for rooms facing the ocean than those facing the bay, because they provide the best vantage in the area for whalewatching right from your room, especially on the higher floors. The resort has three swimming pools, charter fishing boats, and a dive shop that rents snorkeling and scuba gear. ~ Boulevard Marina; 3-33-33, fax 3-06-06, or 800-733-2226 in the U.S. DELUXE.

The **Hotel Solmar Suites**, a white, modern, two-story complex located on the far side of the sandstone ridge south of the marina, stands alone on Playa Solmar. The wide beach is dangerous for swimming, and the waves swelling in from the open ocean often strike shore with explosive crashes, drowning out the noise from town. There are 125 suites decorated in Southwestern adobe style, each with a separate sitting area, a king-size bed or two double beds, and a patio or balcony with a view of the Pacific. The hotel grounds have three heated swimming pools, tennis courts and a dive shop, but the biggest draw is its sportfishing charter fleet. ~ Avenida Solmar; 3-35-35, fax 3-04-10. ULTRA-DELUXE.

Cabo San Lucas has few mid-range accommodations. Lodging rates drop astonishingly as you get away from the water. **Hotel Marina Cabo San Lucas**, centrally located on a busy shopping street just a block from the marina, has 30 clean, modest, air-conditioned rooms around a courtyard swimming pool and hot tub. The decor consists of flowers handpainted on otherwise bare white walls. Avoid the rooms on the street side of the hotel: they can be noisy. ~ Calle Madero at Boulevard Marina; 3-00-30, fax 3-24-84. BUDGET.

In a similar price range, the **Hotel Dos Mares** is on a side street a block and a half from the marina and an equal distance from the town plaza. It has 18 basic rooms with one double or two single beds and color TV. Some rooms have kitchenettes and air conditioning. Others, with only ceiling fans, cost a few dollars less. ~ Calle Zapata; 3-03-30. BUDGET.

The **Siesta Suites Hotel** is on the same block as the Dos Mares. Built in 1994, this three-story hotel has 15 plain but spacious efficiency units, each with a kitchen. Some have cable TV and air conditioning, and others have only ceiling fans. The friendly folks who run the hotel have quickly built up a steady, year-after-year clientele, so reservations are essential in the winter months. ~ Calle Zapata; phone/fax 3-27-72, or 909-945-5940 in the U.S. BUDGET.

A longtime fishermen's favorite, the **Hotel Mar de Cortés** is located along lively Calle Lázaro Cárdenas a block from the marina. All 82 air-conditioned rooms and suites surround a garden courtyard with a swimming pool and a palapa bar with a fireplace. The older section of the hotel has small, dim rooms with twin beds or one double bed, and plenty of historic character. Those in the newer part are larger, though more ordinary, with two double beds. Some units have kitchens. ~ Calle Lázaro Cárdenas at Calle Madero; 3-00-32, fax 3-02-32, or 800-347-8821 in the U.S. BUDGET TO MODERATE.

The **Casa Blanca**, in a dusty, mainly residential neighborhood four blocks north of the marina, is one of the lowest-priced places in town, and the rooms look it—painted cinderblock walls, concrete floors, and concrete bed platforms with firm mattresses. The 22 rooms are shady, dimly lit and cooled by ceiling fans. They have private baths with plumbing that usually works. Staying here is cheaper than camping on the beach, but probably less appealing. ~ Calle Revolución at Calle Madero; 3-02-60. BUDGET.

Villas Turismo Juvenil, the large, lively youth hostel in Cabo San Lucas, is located across Calle Lázaro Cárdenas from the north end of the marina—a location that sounds convenient but isn't. Because of the circuitous streets, it's a long walk (or a short taxi trip) to either the nearest beach or the shopping, restaurant and nightclub zone along Boulevard Marina. Still, you can rent a dormitory bed or a cramped and spartan private room for about what a cup of coffee costs in any of the big resort hotels. Boasting 176 beds and no curfew, this place parties around the clock during spring break but is usually so empty it echoes the rest of the time. ~ Avenida de la Juventud; 3-01-48. BUDGET.

DINING   Cabo San Lucas has more than 100 restaurants, nearly all of them clustered around the marina, on Calle Lázaro Cárdenas or along Playa El Medano. Some have signs so familiar you may feel as if you're back home—KFC, Domino's Pizza, Subway, Dairy Queen. . . .

You can pretend you're anywhere on earth as you scarf down a cheeseburger and fries or barbecued chicken at the windowless **Hard Rock Café**, with a view of Tom Petty's old guitar. ~ Plaza Bonita Mall; 3-38-06. MODERATE.

Or you can pretend you're dining with the stars as you savor a crisp salad and a low-fat turkey burger at the windowless **Planet Hollywood**, with a view of Whoopi Goldberg's handprint. ~ Plaza Bonita Mall; 3-39-19. MODERATE.

At least you get a view of the marina with your fajitas at **Salsitas**, one of the largest and most touristy restaurants in this totally tourist-oriented town. Mexican food is prepared with *muy poco chile* in deference to gringo tastes. Musicians in full mariachi garb make their way among close-packed tables. Service is speedy. ~ Plaza Bonita Mall; 3-17-40. MODERATE.

For a splurge meal that you'll remember as wonderful instead of just overpriced, dine at **El Galeón**, the hillside restaurant at the turnoff to the Hotel Solmar Suites. Make reservations for seating on the terrace after dark for a dazzling view of the marina's lights under a starry sky. The international menu features everything from pasta to lobster. Thick, tender steaks, roast beef, veal scallopini and Caesar salad are specialties. ~ Boulevard Marina; 3-04-43. DELUXE.

If you thought you knew what Mexican food was all about, a fine dinner at **Mi Casa Restaurante** may be an eye-opener. Fresh, high-quality ingredients are used in making regional specialties from the Mexican mainland. Dorado comes smothered in a tangy green tomatillo salsa, and tuna is prepared in a Yucatecan achiote marinade and served with warm homemade tortillas. The *pollo en mole* shows why the Aztecs considered this chocolate-and-chile delicacy the food of the gods. Most seating is on a romantic, secluded patio behind the restaurant. The able service uses handmade Mexican ceramics, glassware and silverware and bright handwoven tablecloths and napkins. ~ Avenida Cabo San Lucas; 3-19-33. DELUXE.

There are also plenty of local hideaways where the clientele doesn't look as if it just stepped off a cruise ship. The **Broken Surfboard**, a sidewalk eatery also known as the Taquería San Lucas, has long catered to the backpacker set with delicious fish tacos with all the fixings. It opens at dawn and serves outstanding *huevos rancheros* for breakfast. ~ Calles Hidalgo and Zapata; 3-04-54. BUDGET.

Pancho's Restaurant prepares traditional Mexican food on a big mesquite grill and serves it in a traditional Mexican atmosphere, complete with local musicians six nights a week. While the food is exceptional, Pancho's is better known for having the most extensive stock of tequilas in Los Cabos—more than 200 varieties at four pesos (less than 50 cents) a shot. Bet you can't sample them all. . . . ~ Calle Hidalgo at Calle Zapata; 3-09-73. BUDGET TO MODERATE.

Mariscos Mocambo, another longtime local favorite, specializes in huge seafood cocktails and ceviche. Whole fried *huachinango* (red snapper) are sold by weight. Other specialties include *congrejo al mojo de ajo* (crab in garlic sauce) and grilled lobster. ~ Calles Morelos and 20 de Noviembre; 3-21-22. BUDGET TO MODERATE.

The **Fish Company**, a hole-in-the-wall place that serves a mostly local crowd, offers huge portions of grilled fish and lobster with beans, tortillas and a choice of Mexican rice or baked potato on the side. Fishermen can bring in their catch and have it cooked and served in garlic sauce with all the trimmings. ~ Calles Guerrero and Zapata; 3-14-05. MODERATE.

Pazzo's Pizzería Cabo has great Italian food with service that's just as good. The house specialty is excellent pizza with a wide range of fresh toppings. There's also lasagna and assorted pasta dishes, including several with seafood sauces. Red checkered tablecloths and friendly service set the tone. ~ Calles Morelos and Niños Héroes; 3-43-13. MODERATE.

Despite its unpromising name and out-of-the-way location, the **Trailer Park Restaurant** has been serving some of the best barbecued meats and seafood in town for more than 20 years. Guests at Cabo's most exclusive resorts find their way through the unpaved back streets to the Faro Viejo Trailer Park for dinner and margaritas in the patio garden with its wrought-iron benches and dragon lampposts. The menu, which changes often, lists more than 100 entrées, and there is an extensive wine list. Dinner reservations are essential. ~ Calle Mijares between Calles Matamoros and Abasolo; 3-42-11. DELUXE.

The mesquite-grilled steaks and lobsters at **Edith's Café** are great, and the exotic drinks and elaborate desserts are even better. There's music nightly—sometimes salsa, other times mellow jazz or jump-up calypso. But the best thing about this restaurant is its hillside location with a spectacular view of El Arco. Dinner only. ~ Playa El Medano at Paseo del Pescador; 3-08-01. MODERATE TO DELUXE.

GROCERIES Stock up for a beach picnic with imported meats and cheeses, organic produce and homemade salads from **Cabo Gourmet**. They also make great submarine sandwiches and box lunches. ~ Calle Lázaro Cárdenas at Calle Matamoros; 3-45-55.

SHOPPING Most Cabo San Lucas shopping is located around the Marina in two big shopping malls, **Plaza Las Glorias** and **Plaza Bonita**. The shops, which sell sportswear, silver jewelry and upscale Mexican folk art, change constantly and seem designed for cruise ship passengers ashore for a few hours with nothing to do but shop. **Libros/Books** in Plaza Bonito has one of the most extensive selections of English-language books in Baja.

For work by local artists, check out **Galería El Dorado**. ~ Boulevard Marina; 3-08-17. One of the best arrays of folk art from mainland Mexico is found at **Faces of Mexico**. ~ Calle Hidalgo at Calle Zapata. Amazing handicrafts from the Huichol Indians of Nayarit are exhibited at **Huichol Collection Galería Museo**. ~ Boulevard Marina; 3-40-55.

NIGHTLIFE Calle Lázaro Cárdenas is party central. Among the liveliest saloons are **Squid Roe** (Calle Lázaro Cárdenas; 3-06-55), the pricier **Giggling Marlin** (Calle Lázaro Cárdenas; 3-11-82) and the **Río Grill**. None of these places has a cover charge, and revelers stumble up and down the street from one to the next. The one club that does charge a cover—and often a stiff one—is **Cabo Wabo**, owned by Van Halen veteran Sammy Hagar, which presents big-name rock bands on many weekends. ~ Calle Guerrero; 3-11-88. If your preference is for someplace mellow, cool out at the piano bar in **El Galeón**. ~ Boulevard Marina; 3-04-43.

PLAYA DEL AMANTE "Lover's Beach" lies just north of the famous, photogenic rock arch at the tip of the promontory southeast of town, with good swimming and great snorkeling and scuba diving. Despite the fact that no road goes near it, it's by far the most popular and crowded beach around. Flotillas of water taxis and glass-bottom boats run back and forth from the marina constantly, carrying visitors to and from this beach. It is also possible to reach it by a 15-minute hike over the ridge from the end of Playa Solmar. Bring your own beverages; there are no snack bars or refreshment vendors.

BEACHES & PARKS

PLAYA SOLMAR This beach on the Pacific side of Land's End is unprotected from the crashing waves; it's dangerous to swim there. For this reason, resort development along the beach has been minimal, and it's a great place for solitary hiking. ~ Take the road that leads from Boulevard Marina to the Hotel Solmar Streets and hike down to the beach from there.

PLAYA EL MEDANO Also known as Playa Las Palmas, this is Cabo's resort beach, lined with big hotels and palapa restaurants. Nearly every day, you'll find thousands of people sunbathing and swimming here. All kinds of water sports equipment, including snorkels, kayaks and jet skis, are for rent along the beach. ~ Take Paseo El Pescador south from Calle Lázaro Cárdenas to Paseo El Medano.

Sixty-seven kilometers north of Cabo San Lucas on Route 19, Todos Santos is the Shangri-La of the Baja cape. This small town is devoid of the kind of resort development that has transformed Los Cabos into a tourist industry icon. Like San José del Cabo, Todos Santos is protected as a national historic district. Unlike San José, no one has yet poured millions of dollars into gentrifying it. The unpredictable weather along the Pacific coast has discouraged large-scale investment. Precisely for this reason, hundreds of expatriate artists from the United States have chosen to make their homes in Todos Santos.

Todos Santos

This town of 6000 dates back to 1724. One of the longest-lived Jesuit missions, it hosted survivors from several other southern Baja missions that had been abandoned because of catastrophic epidemics. Misión Santa Rosa de Todos Santos lasted until 1840, and as soon as the missionaries left, plantation owners put the local people to work in cane fields that produced much of the West Coast's sugar during the 19th century.

SIGHTS

The **Campo Experimental Forestal Todos Santos**, a botanical garden containing virtually all native cactuses, trees and shrubs of the Baja peninsula along with examples of other tropical desert vegetation from around the world, is seven kilometers south of town.

LODGING

The inspiration for the classic 1970s song by the Eagles, Todos Santos' Spanish colonial–style **Hotel California** was built long before the first paved road reached the west side of the cape. This historic hotel has been renovated to meet the expectations of today's travelers, with handmade furniture, modern private bathrooms and ceiling fans, but its pre-tourism personality is still reflected in its crooked hallways and massively thick, not-quite-perpendicular walls. The 16 guest rooms surround a courtyard swimming pool, and those on the upper floor share a long, shady balcony. ~ Calle Benito Juárez; 5-00-02. BUDGET.

Across the street and down the block, the **Motel Guluarte** has eight clean, very plain rooms cooled by table fans. There's a small swimming pool and a shaded second-floor balcony. Room rates are less than half those at Hotel California. ~ Calle Benito Juárez. BUDGET.

Also very low-priced is the 12-room **Hotel Miramar**, located on the southwest edge of town. Rooms here are larger than at the Motel Guluarte and have central cooling. The name is a little misleading—the only semblance of a sea view is the glimpse you can catch from the upstairs balcony—but there is a swimming pool, and you'll find a laundromat and an inexpensive *taquería* nearby. ~ Calle Mutualismo; 5-03-41. BUDGET.

A recent addition to the local lodging scene is the elegant, colonial-style **Todos Santos Inn**. Four guest rooms, individually furnished in dark wood, open onto a classic courtyard garden complete with a fountain. ~ Calle Legaspi 33; phone/fax 5-00-40. DELUXE.

DINING

The central gringo hangout in town is the **Caffe Todos Santos**, where you can sip an espresso, cappuccino or latté in the 19th-century hacienda courtyard or indoors surrounded by local artists' paintings. The menu includes Mexican dishes, French pastries, sandwiches of imported deli meats and cheeses on home-baked multigrain bread, and all-organic fresh fruit plates. ~ Between Calles Centario and Legaspi. MODERATE.

For authentic Mexican fare at low prices, try one of the little open-air eateries across from the park near the bus station. Typical among them is **Loncheria Karla**, where a plate of three tacos or tamales costs just 20 pesos. ~ Colegio Militar. BUDGET.

The premier restaurant in Todos Santos, **Café Santa Fe** attracts diners all the way from Los Cabos with its sensational Italian cuisine. The interior of this historic hacienda has been beautifully renovated, and there is additional seating on the garden patio. Salads are made with locally grown organic vegetables. House specialties include a unique version of lasagna, gourmet pizza, and shrimp-and-lobster ravioli. There's tiramisu for dessert. ~ Calle Centenario; 5-03-40. MODERATE TO DELUXE.

GROCERIES

There are three small grocery stores in town, located at the corner of Calles Juárez and Marquez de León, Calles Juárez and Zaragoza, and Calles Morelos and Colegio Militar.

SHOPPING

Several galleries exhibit both the works of local artists and imported folk art from mainland Mexico. Among them are **Mano a Mano** (Calle Juárez at Calle Morelos; 5-01-51), **Charles Stewart's Gallery** (Calle Centenario at Calle Obregón; 5-02-65), **Gallery Santa Fe** (Calle Centenario at the Plaza; 5-03-40) and **Galeria de Todos Santos** (Calle Legaspi at Calle Topete).

One of only two English-language bookstores on the Baja Peninsula, **El Tecolote** also carries a good selection of American magazines and newspapers. ~ Calle Juárez at Calle Morelos; 5-03-72.

BEACHES & PARKS

PLAYA SAN PEDRO 🏖️ 🏄 This small beach bordered by palm trees is a surfer's dream and a motor-home driver's nightmare. ~ Seven kilometers south of Todos Santos and two kilometers west of the highway.

▲ Tent camping is permitted on the beach. No fee or facilities.

PLAYA PESCADERO 🏖️ 🏄 Another surfers' favorite, this beach is covered with round boulders at the north end but becomes smooth and wide as it sweeps southward for about four miles. ~ Eight kilometers south of Todos Santos.

▲ San Pedrito RV Park has restrooms with hot showers, a swimming pool, a laundry room and a restaurant with TV. There are 72 RV sites with full hookups ($13 per night), plus about a dozen beachfront tent sites with shade palapas ($4 per night).

PLAYA LOS CERRITOS 🏃 🏖️ 🏄 The most spectacular of the beaches around Todos Santos, this broad, white sand beach curves gracefully over an expanse of six miles. Surfers and beachcombers love it. ~ Twelve kilometers south of Todos Santos and three kilometers west of the highway.

▲ There was once a large *ejido* campground at the north end of this beach, but it was destroyed by a storm and abandoned.

Today, RV travelers can camp without hookups or restrooms in the forlorn ruins, and tenters can camp on the beach beyond. Somebody from the *ejido* may or may not come around to collect a token fee.

Outdoor Adventures

FISHING

LA PAZ Isla Cerralvo, southeast of the Pichilingue Peninsula, is renowned for its 70- to 80-pound amberjack and grouper and for *pargo*, a giant red snapper that has been called the strongest and most difficult of all fighting fish. Fishing trips to Cerralvo are operated by **Fisherman's Fleet** (5-28-28) at the Club El Moro. Other fishing charter services operating out of La Paz marinas include the **Dorado Velez Fleet** (Los Arcos Hotel; 2-27-44, ext. 608) and **La Paz Fishing** (Marina La Paz; 2-13-13).

LOS CABOS The waters off Los Cabos are famous worldwide for marlin, sailfish and swordfish. Sport fishermen catch some 10,000 of them each year. Other game fish common to the area are wahoo, dorado and yellowfin tuna.

Keenly aware of the decline of big-game fisheries farther north in the Sea of Cortez, and the economic devastation that would follow if the same thing happened around Los Cabos, all fishing fleets promote catch-and-release sport fishing, and a growing number insist on it. A fishing trip can be arranged through any resort hotel. Reputable companies include **Palmilla Sportfishing Fleet** (Hotel Palmilla, San José Los Cabos; 2-05-82, or 800-637-2226 in the U.S.), **Pisces Sportfishing Fleet** (Marina Cabo San Lucas; 3-12-88, or 800-946-5599 in the U.S.) and **Minerva's** (Marina Cabo San Lucas; 3-12-82).

SURFING & WIND-SURFING

LA PAZ Windsurfers head for Playa La Ventana in the winter, when strong winds blow on the channel between the beach and Isla Cerralvo.

CABO DEL ESTE Bahía de Palmas is gaining a reputation for great windsurfing, and Los Barriles is the site of the annual Vela-O'Neill Baja Championships sailboard races. Sailboards are available for rent at several East Cape hotels. At the south end of the bay, Punta Arena has a point break that makes for good board surfing during the August-to-October *chubasco* winds. It is virtually the only place on the Sea of Cortez that attracts surfers.

LOS CABOS The best surfing spot in the area is a small cove known locally as **The Monuments**, reached via the Mirador del Medano turnoff five kilometers east of Cabo San Lucas. This cove is perfectly situated to catch the swells deflected from Land's End. Boards can be rented at **Killer Hook Surf Shop** (Avenida Hidalgo, San José del Cabo; 2-24-30) or **Pisces Water Sports Center** (Marina Cabo San Lucas; 3-12-88).

TODOS SANTOS   The Pacific side of the cape is considered one of Baja's best surfing areas during the winter months, with many and varied point and beach breaks. Great surfer beaches include Playa El Pescadero, Playa los Cerritos, Punta Gasparino and Playa Migriño. Bring your own board or rent one in Los Cabos.

LA PAZ   Popular dive destinations from La Paz include the wreck of the ferry *Salvatierra* and the white coral reef off the coast of **Isla Espiritu Santo**. The ultimate dive in Baja, however, lies nine miles north of the island. **El Bajo** (also called the Marisla Seamount) is a group of three underwater mountain peaks, the tallest of which reaches to within 60 feet of the surface. The seamount attracts large fish, including 16- to 20-foot manta rays and hammerhead sharks. Though guides insist that both are harmless, this is not a dive for the faint of heart. You might even encounter a whale shark, the largest fish on earth. Trips can be arranged at **Scuba Baja Joe** (Malecón at Calle Ocampo; 2-40-06, fax 2-40-00); **Baja Expeditions** (Sonora 586; 5-38-28); **Sea & Scuba** (Malecón; 3-52-33); or **Scuba Aguilar** (Independencia 107; 2-18-26, fax 2-86-44).

LOS CABOS   The best spot for snorkeling is the vicinity of **Playa del Amante**. The cliffs that isolate the beach on both sides drop about ten feet below the water's surface to a sandy bottom with coral and colorful fish.

Cabo San Lucas' famous dive zone is between the inner harbor and Land's End, where several underwater canyons descend into an enormous gorge, 3000 feet deep, that lies off Playa del Amante. "Rivers" of sand flow down the bottoms of these canyons and spill over cliffs in spectacular sandfalls.

Expert divers head for **Banco Gorda Primero**, which lies at a depth of 110 feet. On this bank of rare black coral, divers are often rewarded by a close encounter with a large billfish, a whale shark or even a gray whale. Los Cabos dive shops include **Killer**

◆◆

✔ CHECK THESE OUT—OUTDOOR ADVENTURES

- Rent a sailboard at one of the East Cape resorts and experience the world-class windsurfing on Bahía de Palmas. *page 214*
- Go scuba diving off Land's End at Cabo San Lucas for a look at unique "sandfalls" in spectacular underwater canyons. *page 215*
- Take a sea-kayaking day trip or camping excursion to Isla Espiritu Santo, a picturesque island with colorful cliffs, coral reefs, hidden beaches and abundant bird life. *page 216*
- Backpack into the little-known wilderness of the Sierra de la Laguna to discover the last remnant of the lush subtropical forest that once covered the Baja Peninsula. *page 216*

Hook Surf Shop (Avenida Hidalgo, San José del Cabo; 2-24-30), Palmilla Divers (Hotel Palmilla, San José Los Cabos; 2-05-82) and Amigos del Mar (Cabo San Lucas Marina; 3-05-05).

KAYAKING   **LA PAZ**   Isla Espiritu Santo has recently begun to rival Bahía Concepción as Baja's most popular sea-kayaking destination. Multiday guided trips along the island's west coast, with its sea canyons, hidden beaches and resident sea lions, can be arranged through Fenton's Outfitters. ~ Club El Moro, Km. 2, Carretera Pichilingue; phone/fax 2-40-84. Casa La Paz offers customized kayaking tours for four or more people. ~ 5-27-48, or 707-869-2374 in the U.S.

WHALE-   **LA PAZ**   Fenton's Outfitters offers whalewatching excursions in
WATCHING   winter. ~ Km. 2, Carretera Pichilingue; phone/fax 2-40-84. Two-hour sunset cruises on the Bahía de la Paz are offered by the Hotel Marina. ~ Km. 2.5, Carretera Pichilingue; 1-62-54.

LOS CABOS   Dos Mares Tour Boats operates whalewatching trips from Marina Cabo San Lucas during the winter months. ~ Marina Cabo San Lucas; 3-32-66. Another, though not necessarily a less expensive, option is to spot passing whales from the Whalewatchers' Bar in the Hotel Finisterra.

TENNIS   **LOS CABOS**   Eight lighted, hard-surfaced tennis courts are open to the public for a fee at Los Cabos Club de Golf. ~ 2-09-05. While this is the only public tennis complex in Los Cabos, several beach resort hotels have courts for guests' use.

GOLF   Although La Paz, the state capital and largest city in Baja California Sur, does not have a single golf course, Los Cabos has no fewer than four, with more in the planning stages. The public Los Cabos Club de Golf (2-09-05), located between the town and hotel zone in San José, has nine holes. Jack Nicklaus designed both the 27-hole course at the Palmilla Golf Club (2-07-08) and the 18-hole course at Cabo del Sol (2-17-01), while Robert Trent Jones designed the 36-hole Cabo Real Golf Club (2-90-00, ext. 9205) at the Meliá Cabo Real. All courses are open to the public.

RIDING   If your idea of a good time encompasses the popular Mexican
STABLES   sport of riding a horse in the crashing surf, head for Marcos' Horse Rentals. The stable also offers four-hour, very scenic guided rides to Faro Viejo. ~ Hacienda Beach Resort, Playa El Medano, Cabo San Lucas; 3-01-23.

HIKING   The Sierra de la Laguna is probably the most fascinating destination in Baja for trekkers, and one of the most difficult. Dense vegetation and extremely rugged terrain make north–south travel virtually impossible in the sierra, but three major east–west trails provide access to the high country. All three trails were often used by local residents to travel across the cape in the days before the coastal highway was built. Then they faded into obscurity and were confused by animal trails, but with increased use by hikers in the 1990s, they are becoming clearly defined again. None of the sierra's most interesting areas can be reached on a day hike. Trekkers should be prepared for near-freezing nights in the high country in winter, and fog or rain at other times of year.

The most spectacular and popular of the sierra trails is **Cañon San Dionisio**. It runs 18 miles between Rancho San Dionisio on the east end (19 kilometers up an unpaved road from Santiago) to La Burrera on the west end (18 kilometers up another unpaved road from the highway, a few kilometers south of Todos Santos). The eastern half of the trail runs through the canyon, with pools and waterfalls, before climbing through a boulder field to La Laguna, the heart of the sierra. La Laguna was a mountain lake more than a mile across until about 1870, when erosion ruptured it and sent its water pouring down Cañon San Dionisio. Today it is a broad meadow about 5500 feet above sea level, flanked on the north and south by the sierra's two tallest mountains— Picacho La Laguna (6507 feet) and Cerro Las Casitas (6855 feet). Allow three or four days to hike to La Laguna and back from the east, two or three days from the west, or three to five days to go from one end of the trail to the other. Guides and pack animals are often available at Rancho San Dionisio.

The other two trails go through canyons on the north and south sides of 6002-foot Cerro Blanco, a steep granite peak that lies ten impassable miles south of La Laguna. Both are easier than the San Dionisio route, reaching maximum elevations of less than 4000 feet, but the climb is more demanding from these trails up the mountainsides to the hummingbird flower forests on the high slopes. The 14-mile **Cañon San Bernardo** trail goes between the tiny villages of Boca de la Sierra on the east (8 kilometers on an unpaved road from Miraflores) and Santo Domingo on the west (15 kilometers along a maze of dirt roads that branches off the road from Todos Santos to San Juan del Asseradero). Watch for signs and, when in doubt, ask locals for directions to Santo Domingo. The ten-mile **Cañon San Pablo** trail goes from Rancho El Salto on the east (6.5 kilometers on an unpaved road from Caduaño) to the village of El Guerigo on the west (35 kilometers on a tricky maze of unpaved roads from El Pescadero off Route 19).

In La Paz, **Aeropuerto General Manuel Márquez de León** has daily flights to and from Tijuana and Loreto on Aero California, as well as Aeroméxico flights from Los Angeles, Tucson and Mexico City.

▼▼▼▼▼▼▼▼▼▼
Transportation

AIR

Los Cabos International Airport, north of San José del Cabo, serves both San José and Cabo San Lucas, landing more than two dozen flights daily from the United States. Aero California flies in from Los Angeles, Phoenix and Denver. Mexicana also has flights from Denver, as well as San Francisco, Los Angeles, San Diego, Tokyo and many Mexican cities. Strangely enough, one of the leading carriers to Los Cabos is Alaska Airlines, with service from San Diego, Los Angeles, Portland, Seattle, Victoria and Anchorage.

BOAT

Servicios Maritimos y Turisticos de California, S.A. (SEMATUR) operates ferries between the Pichilingue ferry terminal east of La Paz and the mainland cities of Topolobampo (8 hours) and Mazatlán (18 hours) daily except Sundays. Fares are very reasonable for foot passengers, but expensive for vehicles—over US$100 for a car and several hundred dollars for a motor home.

Cabo San Lucas is a port of call for cruise ships operated by **Royal Caribbean** (800-327-0271), **Carnival** (800-327-9501) and **Princess** (800-421-0522). All three lines offer seven-day cruises from Los Angeles to the "Mexican Riviera"—meaning Cabo San Lucas, Puerto Vallarta, and either Mazatlán or Acapulco. Passengers' day in Cabo is a cursory visit, almost incidental to the cruise experience itself, with its shipboard casino, dancing, lounge entertainment, nonstop organized activities and food, food, food!

BUS

Autotransportes Aguila runs 13 buses a day from the U.S. border to Los Cabos. All of them stop in La Paz en route. From there, seven of them travel clockwise around the cape, by way of Santiago, and six go counterclockwise by way of Todos Santos.

CAR

Route 19 branches off from Route 1, 26 kilometers south of La Paz. The two highways meet again in Cabo San Lucas, forming a 299-kilometer loop around the cape and linking all the towns mentioned in this chapter.

CAR RENTALS

In La Paz, **Hertz** (2-09-19) and **Avis** (2-26-51) have offices at the international airport.

In Los Cabos, the many car rental agencies that have airport desks include **Avis** (2-06-80), **Budget** (3-02-41), **Dollar** (2-06071), **National** (3-60-00) and **Thrifty** (2-16-71).

PUBLIC TRANSIT

Taxis are the only mode of public ground transportation serving both the La Paz and Los Cabos airports. In La Paz, the cab fares set by the government for the short trip into the city are so expensive that you might as well rent a car.

In Los Cabos, where the taxis are government-owned, fares depend on the number of passengers. They are fairly reasonable to San José del Cabo, more expensive to the Los Cabos Corridor resorts and Cabo San Lucas. Many Los Cabos resorts have free airport shuttles.

La Paz has an extensive local bus system. Most buses run to and from the Mercado Municipal at Calles Revolución and Degollado, where passengers transfer to reach other parts of the city.

Fares are very low. Los Cabos has no local buses, but ten **Autotransportes Aguila** intercity buses stop in San José every day, on their way between Cabo San Lucas and La Paz.

Water taxis are a key mode of public transportation in Cabo San Lucas, where a major visitor destination, Playa del Amante, cannot be reached by road.

▼▼▼▼▼▼▼▼▼▼▼▼▼▼▼▼▼▼▼▼▼▼

Addresses & Phone Numbers

Tourist Information Center, La Paz: 2-59-39
Tourist Office, San José del Cabo: 2-04-46
Migración (Immigration), Cabo San Lucas: 3-01-35
American Consulate, Cabo San Lucas: 3-35-66
Cruz Roja (Red Cross), La Paz: 2-11-11
Cruz Roja, Cabo San Lucas: 3-33-00
Cruz Roja, San José del Cabo: 2-03-16
Clínica La Paz (English-speaking doctors on staff): 2-06-85
Centro Mujeres, La Paz (health clinic with an English-speaking staff): 2-35-70
General Hospital, San José del Cabo: 2-37-13
Policia, La Paz: 2-66-10
Policia, Cabo San Lucas: 3-39-77
Policia, San José del Cabo: 2-03-61
Patrulla de Caminos (Highway Patrol): 2-24-50
Los Cabos International Airport: 2-04-41

CUISINE

almejas—clams

atún—tuna

birria—goat

cabrilla—sea bass

calamar—squid

callos—scallops

camarones—shrimp

cangrejo—crab

carne asada—barbecued beef strips marinated in a red-chile sauce

ceviche—uncooked seafood marinated in lime juice, vinegar, oil, cilantro and spices

chilaquiles—tortilla strips, chicken and cheese scrambled together

chiles rellenos—stuffed chile peppers

cochinita pibil—pork barbecued in an orange marinade

cokteles—cocktails

comedor—an open-air, fast-food eatery

comida corrida—daily special

dorado—mahimahi

elotes—corn on the cob served with chili powder, lime and cream

gambas—prawns

huachinango—snapper

jurel—yellowtail

langosta—lobster

lenguado—halibut

pescado—fish

pez espada—swordfish

pollo en mole—chicken in a chile-and-chocolate sauce

pulpo—octopus

sabalo—tarpon

sierra—mackerel

tiburón—shark

MÁS PALABRAS (MORE WORDS)

abarrotes—groceries

abierto—open

aciete—motor oil

acumulador—vehicle battery

agua—water

angeles verdes—Green Angels

bahía—bay

ballena—whale

banda de ventilador—fan belt

baño—bath; restroom

bolsa de dormir—sleeping bag

calambre—sunburn
camino—road
campar—to camp
caña de pescar—fishing rod
carretera—highway
casita de campaña—tent
cerrado—closed
cuota—toll
chubasco—tropical storm
delfin—dolphin
ejército—army
ejido—agricultural commune
equipo de bucear—diving gear
estacionar—to park
farmacia—pharmacy
foco de mano—flashlight
gemelos—binoculars
gringo—person from the United States or Canada
gruta—cave
guía—guide
isla—island
licencia de manejar—driver's license
llanta—tire
magna sin—unleaded gasoline
malecón—waterfront promenade
maquiladora—border factory
mecánico—mechanic
mochila—backpack
pájaro—bird
palapa—thatch-roofed shelter
panadería—bakery
panga—open wooden fishing boat
peligroso—dangerous
Pemex—gas station
picacho—peak
pinturas rupestres—rock art
playa—beach
punta—point
refaccionería—auto-parts store
seguros—insurance
sierra—mountain range; mackerel
supermercado—supermarket
tienda—store
velocidad maxima—speed limit
zopilote—vulture

Index

Lodging Index

Dining Index

HIDDEN GUIDES
Adventure travel or a relaxing vacation?—"Hidden" guidebooks are the only travel books in the business to provide detailed information on both. Aimed at environmentally aware travelers, our motto is "Adventure Travel Plus." These books combine details on unique hotels, restaurants and sightseeing with information on camping, sports and hiking for the outdoor enthusiast.

THE NEW KEY GUIDES
Based on the concept of ecotourism, The New Key Guides are dedicated to the preservation of Central America's rare and endangered species, architecture and archaeology. Filled with helpful tips, they give travelers everything they need to know about these exotic destinations.

ULTIMATE FAMILY GUIDES
These innovative guides present the best and most unique features of a family destination. Quality is the keynote. In addition to thoroughly covering each destination, they feature short articles and one-line "teasers" that are both fun and informative.

Ulysses Press books are available at bookstores everywhere. If any of the following titles are unavailable at your local bookstore, ask the bookseller to order them.

You can also order books directly from Ulysses Press
P.O. Box 3440, Berkeley, CA 94703
800-377-2542 or 510-601-8301
fax: 510-601-8307
e-mail: ulysses@ulyssespress.com

Order Form

HIDDEN GUIDEBOOKS

____ Hidden Arizona, $13.95
____ Hidden Bahamas, $12.95
____ Hidden Baja, $14.95
____ Hidden Boston and Cape Cod, $11.95
____ Hidden Carolinas, $16.95
____ Hidden Coast of California, $16.95
____ Hidden Colorado, $13.95
____ Hidden Florida, $16.95
____ Hidden Florida Keys & Everglades, $11.95
____ Hidden Hawaii, $16.95
____ Hidden Idaho, $13.95
____ Hidden Maui, $12.95
____ Hidden Montana, $13.95

____ Hidden New England, $17.95
____ Hidden New Mexico, $13.95
____ Hidden Oahu, $12.95
____ Hidden Oregon, $13.95
____ Hidden Pacific Northwest, $17.95
____ Hidden Rockies, $16.95
____ Hidden San Francisco and Northern California, $17.95
____ Hidden Southern California, $17.95
____ Hidden Southwest, $17.95
____ Hidden Tahiti, $16.95
____ Hidden Tennessee, $15.95
____ Hidden Utah, $13.95
____ Hidden Wyoming, $13.95

THE NEW KEY GUIDEBOOKS

____ The New Key to Belize, $14.95
____ The New Key to Cancún and the Yucatán, $14.95
____ The New Key to Costa Rica, $16.95

____ The New Key to Ecuador and the Galápagos, $16.95
____ The New Key to Guatemala, $14.95

ULTIMATE FAMILY GUIDEBOOKS

____ Disneyland and Beyond, $12.95

____ Disney World and Beyond, $13.95

Mark the book(s) you're ordering and enter the total cost here ⇨

California residents add 8% sales tax here ⇨

Shipping, check box for your preferred method and enter cost here ⇨

❏ BOOK RATE   **FREE! FREE! FREE!**

❏ PRIORITY MAIL $3.00 First book, $1.00/each additional book

❏ UPS 2-DAY AIR $7.00 First book, $1.00/each additional book

Billing, enter total amount due here and check method of payment ⇨

❏ CHECK   ❏ MONEY ORDER

❏ VISA/MASTERCARD_____EXP. DATE _____

NAME _____PHONE _____

ADDRESS_____

_____

CITY_____ STATE _____ ZIP_____

MONEY-BACK GUARANTEE ON DIRECT ORDERS PLACED THROUGH ULYSSES PRESS.

ABOUT THE AUTHOR

RICHARD HARRIS has written or co-written eight other guidebooks including Ulysses' *Hidden Cancún and the Yucatán* and the bestselling *Hidden Southwest*. He has also served as contributing editor on guides to Mexico, New Mexico and other ports of call for John Muir Publications, Fodor's, Birnbaum and Access guides. He is a director of PENCenter USAWest and president of PEN New Mexico. When not traveling, Richard writes and lives in Santa Fe, New Mexico.

ABOUT THE ILLUSTRATOR

DOUG MCCARTHY has illustrated a number of Ulysses Press guides, including *Hidden Wyoming*, *Hidden Tennessee*, *Hidden Bahamas* and *The New Key to Ecuador and the Galápagos*. A native New Yorker, he lives in the San Francisco Bay area with his family.